New Directions in the Sociology of Chronic
and Disabling Conditions

Also by Graham Scambler

THE EXPERIENCE OF ILLNESS (*co-authored*)
SOCIOLOGICAL THEORY AND MEDICAL SOCIOLOGY (*edited*)
EPILEPSY
MENSTRUAL DISORDERS (*co-authored*)
RETHINKING PROSTITUTION: Purchasing Sex in Britain in the 1990s (*co-edited*)
MODERNITY, MEDICINE AND HEALTH (*co-edited*)
HABERMAS, CRITICAL THEORY AND HEALTH (*edited*)
HEALTH AND SOCIAL CHANGE: A Critical Theory
MEDICAL SOCIOLOGY (*edited*)
SPORT AND SOCIETY: History, Power and Culture
SOCIOLOGY AS APPLIED TO MEDICINE (*edited*)

Also by Sasha Scambler
THE SOCIAL WORLD OF OLDER PEOPLE (*co-authored*)

New Directions in the Sociology of Chronic and Disabling Conditions

Assaults on the Lifeworld

Edited by

Graham Scambler
University College London Medical School, UK

and

Sasha Scambler
Kings College London Dental Institute, UK

First published 2010 by
PALGRAVE MACMILLAN

Palgrave Macmillan in the UK is an imprint of Macmillan Publishers Limited,
registered in England, company number 785998, of Houndmills, Basingstoke,
Hampshire RG21 6XS.

Palgrave Macmillan in the US is a division of St Martin's Press LLC,
175 Fifth Avenue, New York, NY 10010.

Palgrave Macmillan is the global academic imprint of the above companies
and has companies and representatives throughout the world.

Palgrave® and Macmillan® are registered trademarks in the United States,
the United Kingdom, Europe and other countries.

ISBN: 978-0-230-22270-0 hardback

This book is printed on paper suitable for recycling and made from fully
managed and sustained forest sources. Logging, pulping and manufacturing
processes are expected to conform to the environmental regulations of the
country of origin.

A catalogue record for this book is available from the British Library.

Library of Congress Cataloging-in-Publication Data

New directions in the sociology of chronic and disabling conditions :
assaults on the lifeworld / edited by Graham Scambler, Sasha Scambler.
    p. cm.
    Summary: "This book charts the new directions in theory and research in
disability studies, giving purpose and shape to the emerging confluence of
ideas between traditionally opposed groups" – Provided by publisher.
    Includes bibliographical references and index.
    ISBN 978-0-230-22270-0 (hardback)
    1. People with disabilities. 2. Disabilities. I. Scambler, Graham.
II. Scambler, Sasha Jane.
HV1568.N49 2010   200904853.
305.9'08—dc22

10 9 8 7 6 5 4 3 2 1
19 18 17 16 15 14 13 12 11 10

Printed and bound in Great Britain by
CPI Antony Rowe, Chippenham and Eastbourne

Dedicated to the memory of David Kelleher

Contents

List of Tables   ix

Notes on Contributors   x

1   Introduction: The Sociology of Chronic and Disabling
    Conditions; Assaults on the Lifeworld   1
    Graham Scambler and Sasha Scambler

2   Studying the Experience of Chronic Illness
    through Grounded Theory   8
    Kathy Charmaz

3   Medical Sociology and Disability Theory   37
    Carol Thomas

4   Beyond Models: Understanding the Complexity
    of Disabled People's Lives   57
    Tom Shakespeare and Nick Watson

5   'Where the Biological Predominates': Habitus,
    Reflexivity and Capital Accrual within the Field of
    Batten Disease   77
    Sasha Scambler and Paul Newton

6   Discerning Biological, Psychological and Social
    Mechanisms in the Impact of Epilepsy on the Individual:
    A Framework and Exploration   106
    Graham Scambler, Panagiota Afentouli and Caroline Selai

7   Retheorizing the Clinical Encounter: Normalization
    Processes and the Corporate Ecologies of Care   129
    Carl May

8   'Chronicity', Proto-Stories and the Doctor-Patient
    Relationship   146
    Alan Radley

9   Chronic Illness, Self-management and the Rhetoric of
    Empowerment   161
    Mike Bury

10   Understanding Incapacity   180
     Gareth H. Williams

11   The Biopolitics of Chronic Illness: Biology,
     Power and Personhood   205
     Simon J. Williams

Index   225

Tables

4.1	Disability as an interaction	66
4.2	Schema of interventions for the example of spinal cord injury	66
6.1A	Appendix: Study participants' characteristics	126
10.1	Incapacity claimant rate, top 20 GB districts, August 2006	184
10.2	Comparison of the proportion of adults aged 45 to 64 with long-standing illness in different regions	186

Contributors

Panagiota Afentouli recently completed the MSc in Clinical Neuroscience at UCL Institute of Neurology and is now undertaking further training in psychology.

Mike Bury is Emeritus Professor of Sociology at the University of London. He was appointed to a personal chair in Sociology in the University of London in 1991. From 1996–2002, Mike was the Head of the Department of Social and Political Science at Royal Holloway. His main research interests have been in social dimensions of health and illness, especially chronic illness, disability and ageing, and on wider aspects of culture and medicine. He was co-editor of the journal *Sociology of Health and Illness* 1995–2001. In 2001, Mike completed a four-year term on two boards of the Medical Research Council. In 2001, he received an honorary doctorate from the University of Linköping, Sweden. Mike is a member of the Public Health Interventions Advisory Committee at the National Institute for Health and Clinical Excellence. His most recent book is *Health and Illness,* published by Polity Press in 2005.

Kathy Charmaz is Professor of Sociology and Director of the Faculty Writing Program at Sonoma State University, USA in which she helps faculty with their research and scholarly writing. She has written, co-authored, or co-edited eight books including *Developing Grounded Theory: The Second Generation* (with Janice Morse, Phyllis Stern, Juliet Corbin, Barbara Bowers and Adele Clarke), the *Handbook of Grounded Theory* (with Antony Bryant) and *Health, Illness, and Healing: Society, Social Context and Self* (with Debora Paterniti) as well as two award-winning books, *Constructing Grounded Theory: A Practical Guide through Qualitative Analysis,* and *Good Days, Bad Days: The Self in Chronic Illness and Time.* She writes numerous chapters and articles on grounded theory methods and qualitative inquiry and also publishes in the areas of social psychology and writing for publication.

Carl May is Professor of Medical Sociology at Newcastle University, UK. He has also held honorary appointments in Melbourne, Kansas, and Victoria, British Columbia, and at the Mayo Clinic. Carl May's methodological interests are in discourse analysis and ethnography, and he has researched and published widely on professional-patient interaction in the management of chronic illness and chronic pain, and on the ways that these interactions are shaped by new technologies and patterns of knowledge production. An ESRC research fellowship between 2004 and 2008 allowed him to develop a set of interests in the dynamics of trials and complex health-care interventions. This work led to the development of Normalization Process Theory. In Newcastle, he leads a multi-disciplinary research group on Health Technologies and Human Relations Research. With Tracy Finch, he is the co-author of *Normalizing Health Technologies*, to be published by Palgrave Macmillan in 2010.

Paul Newton is a researcher at Kings College London Dental Institute. As an undergraduate, he studied Social Policy, followed by an MSc in International Health Policy. He has recently completed his doctoral thesis in Sociology as Applied to Healthcare which explored the application of sociological approaches to the self-care experiences of people with Type 2 Diabetes. He has also researched and published on policy and sociological issues in relation to self-care in Type 2 Diabetes, Dentistry and Oral Health as well as Patient and Public Involvement in the health and welfare arenas.

Alan Radley is Professor of Social Psychology in the Department of Social Sciences at Loughborough University, UK. He is the founding editor of the journal *Health: An Interdisciplinary Journal for the Social Study of Health, Illness and Medicine*. His research interests include the experience of chronic illness and its treatment, homelessness and the use of visual methods in the study of social life. Recently, he has completed a study of the making and use of artworks in relation to life-threatening disease, published as *Works of Illness: Narrative, Picturing and the Social Response to Serious Disease*.

Graham Scambler is Professor of Medical Sociology and Director of the 'Centre for Sociological Theory and Research on Health' at University College London. His interests include social and critical theory, health-related stigma, chronic illness and disability, health inequalities, sex work and sport. He has published widely in these areas. He is editor of the textbook *Sociology as Applied to Medicine*, the sixth edition of which was published in 2008. He is also a founding editor of the international journal *Social Theory and Health*, which was established in 2003. In 1998, he was Visiting Professor at Emory University in the USA.

Sasha Scambler is a Lecturer in Sociology at Kings College London Dental Institute. She studied Sociology at the University of Bristol before specializing in the Sociology of Health at University College London. Sasha has carried our extensive research into the experiences and support needs of families with Batten disease and was a founder member and Trustee of the Batten Disease Family Association Charity. She has also researched and published on the application of Disability Theory to Chronic Disabling Conditions; the application of sociology to Special Care Dentistry and loneliness and social isolation in later life. Sasha is co-editor of the newly released journal *Social Science and Dentistry* and with Christina Victor and John Bond, she is co-author of *The Social World of Older People*, published by Open University Press in 2009.

Caroline Selai is Senior Lecturer in Clinical Neuroscience at University College London and a Chartered Psychologist with a research interest in Outcome Measures. In recent years, she has worked on the development of disease-specific measures of Health-Related Quality of Life (HR-QoL) for patients and the carers of patients with neurological conditions including epilepsy, dementia, movement disorders and Gilles de la Tourette syndrome.

Tom Shakespeare trained in sociology at Cambridge, and has researched and taught at the Universities of Sunderland, Leeds and Newcastle. He has conducted research on disability and childhood, disability and sexuality, bioethics, science engagement, and quality of life in restricted growth. His books include *Disability Rights and Wrongs*. He is currently consulting with the World Health Organization on disability and rehabilitation. He has been involved with the disabled people's movement since 1986.

Carol Thomas is a Professor of Sociology at Lancaster University, based in the School of Health and Medicine. She is best known for her publications in Disability Studies – including her books *Female Forms: Experiencing and Understanding Disability* and *Sociologies of Disability and Illness: Contested Ideas in Disability Studies and Medical Sociology*. She has also researched and published widely on 'patients' and 'carers' experiences of living with cancer – and has recently completed a project funded by the ESRC on illness narratives in cancer contexts (ESRC project: RES-000–22-2031).

Nick Watson is Professor of Disability Research and Director of the Strathclyde Centre for Disability Research, Department of Sociology, Anthropology and Applied Social Science at the University of Glasgow. He has written widely on a range of disability issues including disability theory, disability and identity, disability and social policy, the history of the wheelchair and disability and childhood. His most recent work has focused on disabled people's access to the outdoors and on changes to anti-discrimination legislation in the UK. He is the editor of a four-volume series *Disability: Major Themes in Health and Social Welfare* published by Routledge in 2007. He is an active member of the disabled people's movement.

Gareth H. Williams has worked in the School of Social Sciences at Cardiff University since 1999, where he teaches medical sociology, and is currently a Professor of Sociology. He is Director of the Wales Health Impact Assessment Support Unit, Co-Director of the Regeneration Institute (jointly with colleagues in the School of City and Regional Planning), and Associate Director of the Cardiff Institute of Society, Health and Ethics. Gareth has written and published widely in journals and books on the themes of chronic illness and disability, health policy, health inequalities and lay knowledge. He has undertaken research on and with local communities dealing with the consequences of health inequalities (see *Community Health and Well Being: Action Research on Health Inequalities*), and the particular health impacts of housing renewal and open-cast coalmining.

Simon J. Williams is a Professor of Sociology at the University of Warwick, UK. He has published widely on the body, health, medicine, science and society, including a recent co-edited international volume (with J. Gabe and P. Davis) on *Pharmaceuticals and Society*, and a forthcoming single-authored book on *The Politics of Sleep: Governing (Un) Consciousness in the Twenty-First Century*. He is currently also researching the social shaping and social implications of neuroscience, neurotechnology and neurocultures, with particular reference to the problems, promises and prospects of cognitive enhancement across the life course.

1
Introduction: The Sociology of Chronic and Disabling Conditions; Assaults on the Lifeworld

Graham Scambler and Sasha Scambler

Contributions to the sociology of chronic and disabling conditions might be considered to have entered a transitional phase. It is generally accepted that Western modernity has been characterized by a considerably extended human lifespan accompanied by a growing prevalence of chronic, degenerative disorders; a 'compression of morbidity' in the fourth age (Fries, 1983); and a norm of slow as opposed to quick dying. Chronic and disabling conditions, in other words, have become highly significant objects of investigation, attracting increasing politico-economic as well as social, psychological and, of course, biological attention. Their salience has precipitated divisions of orientation, most conspicuously, but not only, between medical sociologists and disability theorists. The fact that these divisions are currently under debate justifies our reference to a 'transitional phase'. It also underpins the rationale for this book.

This book brings together leading figures from both medical sociology and disability theory, in the process further facilitating exchanges and the emergence of new options. It is also theoretically driven, with most contributors explicitly challenging past orthodoxies. This does not mean that the arguments are ventured without reference to research, far from it: all chapters have a strong empirical grounding, while the theses of some arise directly from studies in the field. One theme that unites their otherwise diverse standpoints is the notion of chronic illnesses and disabilities as 'assaults on the lifeworld'. This broad focus allows for a range of different theorizations and interpretations of the interrelations of the biological, psychological and social. The result, we believe, is a sharp and lively collection at the cutting edge of enquiry.

1

Although not the first to theorize the related roles of patient and doctor in US society and health care, Parsons (1951) gave crucial impetus to the mainstream sociological study of medical encounters. His delineation of the sick role, however, allowing for a legitimate if conditional space in which to recover from 'illness as deviance', seemed to leave chronic illness out in the cold. While it is possible to interpret Parsons' notions of the sick and practitioner roles as inclusive rather than exclusive of chronic illness, the charge of failing to adequately deal with chronic illness largely stuck.

Twenty years later Freidson's (1970) critique of Parsons' structural-functionalist analysis of medicine in society prepared the ground for what was to become, not least in the UK, a wave of qualitative studies of how people adapt to living with specific chronic disorders (Bury, 2005). Freidson insisted that people as patients are often 'active' rather than 'passive' when face-to-face with medical expertise; that their concepts of 'illness' may overlap with but are rarely identical to medical concepts of 'disease'; and that their experiential expertise affords a basis for rational action sometimes at odds with putatively functional role expectations. There exists a 'voice of the lifeworld' as well as a 'voice of medicine' (Mishler, 1984). Freidson's critique also drew on labelling theorists of deviance like Lemert, Erikson and Becker to address the social construction of illness and disease: doctors not only decide who has what disease but also what counts as disease. His analysis also reached out to the predictable aftermath of medical labelling: to be diagnosed with multiple sclerosis, diabetes, breast cancer or epilepsy by an authoritative, state-licensed practitioner is to undergo a significant identity change for self and for others, often with lasting consequences.

In this vein followed numerous subtle and detailed investigations of the 'personal tragedy' of becoming and being chronically ill or disabled, almost all of them cast within the 'deviance paradigm'. The 'hows' as well as the 'whys' of the intrusion of chronic and disabling conditions into individuals' lifeworlds, either dramatically via a tonic-clonic seizure in a crowded public arena, or insidiously via an early touch of angina, were examined in intimate detail. Some of the resultant conceptual innovations have survived the test of time. Bury (1982) focused on the 'biographical disruption' occasioned by chronic illness, initially in relation to rheumatoid arthritis. Charmaz (1983) identified a 'loss of self' as compromised individuals put on the back foot sought to reinvent themselves. Gareth Williams' (1984) notion of 'narrative reconstruction' was of a piece with these pressures on the chronically ill and disabled to devise ways of putting themselves back together in the face of unanticipated and persisting biological assault. In their study of epilepsy, Scambler and Hopkins (1986) introduced the terms 'enacted' and 'felt stigma' to acknowledge that individual biographies can be as disrupted as much by fears of stigmatization as by concrete experience of exclusion.

Even as such studies saw the light of day, new and different perspectives were being developed from outside medical sociology demanding interrogation of the largely unexamined premises of the personal tragedy orientation. In part these required medical sociologists to revisit issues they had come to neglect. Harking back to Freidson and his mentors, why study only the labelled and not the labellers? While studying the labelled invites an individualistic mindset, studying the labellers suggests a more genuinely social, or sociological, commitment. But arguments within disability studies went further than this. The social model of disability pioneered in the UK by writers such as Oliver (1990) championed the academic *and political* displacement of a deviance by an 'oppression paradigm'. Systems of categorization and labelling rooted in deeply problematic norms of normality and normalization were contested. The sometimes intemperate debates between medical sociologists and disability theorists around this time have been well documented. They still resonate two decades later, but a new dialogue has now been joined and possible resolutions of differences are being ventured.

One pivotal issue, or family of issues, concerns the theorization of (psycho-)pathology in all its guises. The social model of disability was posited in unequivocal opposition to ubiquitous WHO definitions of 'impairment', 'disability' and 'handicap'. The WHO labellers were exposed as unwitting or non-reflexive agents of oppression. More recently there have been a number of compelling attempts on the part of disability theorists to move beyond the social model, not least to reconceptualize impairment. Sociologists for their part have shown a belated awareness of discourses emanating from disability theory/studies. One product of these transitional developments is an exciting set of embryonic projects to explore interfaces between the biological, psychological and social. It seems clear that in some chronic degenerative conditions, impairment effects can be such as to render psychosocial factors more or less redundant. But it is no less certain that in instances of misdiagnosis a considerable psychosocial price can be paid in the absence of any underlying (psycho-)pathology: a label can in and of itself prove decisive for quality of life.

In the meantime a raft of macro-level, in many respects global, social changes have impacted on system and lifeworld alike. In relation to health and health care, many governments have come to promote neoliberal or post-welfare statist, individualized consumer choice, *and responsibility*, over the more collectivist citizen entitlement characteristic of the post-war Keynesian welfare state, few with more consistency and vigour than Britain's 'New Labour' regime. These changes have multiple ramifications for people with chronic and disabling conditions. A renewed emphasis on personal responsibility, for example, might be accompanied by state 'help' to re-enter gainful employment, the sanction for irresponsible resistance being the termination of publicly funded support. In sociological terms, the threat of blame can be added to the threat of shame (Scambler, 2009). Empowering rhetorics of 'self-management' have a strong *prima facie* appeal, but can also provide ideological cover for politically motivated policies designed to cut service demand, most specifically on hospital-based specialist treatment and care. Self-management may appear to epitomize the liberal aspirations to autonomy and empowerment while in fact being motivated by *neo*liberalist agendas.

The new managerialism in health-care systems like the British National Health Service (NHS) is another product of macro change. Inevitably it has led to shifts in doctor-patient relations. The institutionalized charisma of the medical practitioner has been subjected to third-party constraint, whether from local NHS Trust executives or the edicts of bodies like the National Institute for Clinical Excellence (NICE). The rights and wrongs and benefits and costs of health service reform continue to be debated, but reform has certainly had as yet under-examined effects on the nature and substance of encounters between physicians and patients with chronic and disabling conditions.

Not all of the issues raised overtly or by implication in this brief introduction are examined in this volume. We think it is fair, however, to describe it as a series of significant commentaries on a sociology, or on sociologies, of chronic illness and disability at a time of flux or transition.

The book begins with a comprehensive, 'insider' review of sociological studies of chronic illness by Kathy Charmaz. Many of the studies she cites deploy a version of grounded theory, and Kathy gives an account, at once engaged and critical, of the past success and future potential of this flexible methodology. She argues for a coming together of micro- and macro-perspectives on chronic illness, and concludes by foreseeing and commending a move 'from studying assaults on the lifeworld to studying lifeworlds that assault those who are mired in them'. This is followed by an analysis by Carol Thomas on medical sociology's social deviance versus disability theory's social oppression paradigms of chronic illness and disability. She tells the story of their separation and opposition but also discusses recent examples of 'boundary crossing'. She closes her chapter by recommending that medical sociologists forgo their traditional 'sociology of chronic illness and disability' in favour of a 'sociology of disablism and impairment effects'.

Tom Shakespeare and Nick Watson offer a chapter in which they remain committed to going beyond extant models to arrive at an 'adequate conceptualization of disability'. Disabled people, they contend, 'need good science, not only inspiring ideology'. This involves combining the passion of writers from materialist disability studies with the scholarship and empirical thrust of the chronic illness perspective. What is required, in a sentence, is an engaged sociology of disability. Sasha Scambler and Paul Newton focus on a rare degenerative condition involving multiple disabilities, Batten disease. They stress that such conditions represent a largely irresistible and overwhelming assault on the lifeworlds of those affected and their carers: it is a situation – too often neglected by medical sociology and disability theory alike – in which the biological 'predominates'. They draw on the work of Pierre Bourdieu to suggest ways in which experiences like this might be theorized. Graham Scambler, Panagiota Afentouli and Caroline Selai adopt a critical realist framework to show how simultaneously active biological, psychological and social mechanisms can combine in different ways to shape quality of life in people with epilepsy. They concentrate on the various ways in which social mechanisms can be salient, and conclude by suggesting that the presence or absence of an 'epilepsy habitus' is pivotal for quality of life.

Carl May utilizes his own body of work on the clinical encounter to formulate and illustrate an innovative theoretical approach. This theory is articulated by means of a dozen specific hypotheses about the forms, constraints and investments through which 'sickness work' is accomplished. Sickness work is not specifically attributed to patients or doctors. It is 'distributed horizontally and vertically through networks that extend a long way from the doctor's office'. Alan Radley's contribution concerns regimes of signification – embodied, spoken, material, spatial – in doctor-patient communication. He distinguishes between 'medico-scientific' and 'medico-presentational' ways of signifying; the first involves transforming information via measurement, while the second involves preserving information through re-shaping it – acting it, picturing it and 're-storying' it. These two ways of making sense of illness are not reducible to doctors' or patients' styles of communication, and may operate 'in tandem' in the same consultation. This chapter is based on an earlier paper by Radley and Colleagues (Radley, Mayberry and Pearce, 2008).

Mike Bury sets his discussion against the background of past contributions of medical sociology and disability theory to the understanding of chronic illness and disability. He gives a critical account of demographic and epidemiological transitions and changing policy towards the long-term management of chronic illness, focusing in particular on the recent emphasis on self-management. He explains why enthusiasm might have outrun realism in relation to self-management and offers a penetrating analysis of prevailing rhetorics: 'where once the "new age" rhetoric of personal growth, autonomy, empowerment and the like were used by social movements to challenge state controlled bureaucratic structures and systems, today they have become part and parcel of state activity itself'.

In explicating the notion of incapacity, Gareth Williams raises issues to do with chronic illness and disability hitherto under-investigated in medical sociology. He argues that incapacity and its distribution bear eloquent testimony to 'the functional relationships between chronic illness and disability, labour markets, and the impact of "economic progress" and "public policy" (or "order-building") on people and their ways of life in post-industrial regions'. Gareth provides an exemplar for a much needed research programme linking macro- and micro-perspectives to better grasp the distribution and impact of chronic illness and disability in changing times.

Finally, Simon Williams addresses what has come to be called the biopolitics of illness. He picks up on Rose's (2007) contention that the 'clinical gaze' is being supplemented by a new 'gaze' which sees life at the molecular level of DNA. The task he sets himself is to consider the possibilities and problems associated with this development. The issues he raises are crucial for anyone committed to a sociology of chronic illness and disability with credibility in the twenty-first century.

This book is dedicated to the memory of David Kelleher, whom many contributors knew as a friend as well as a colleague. David died unexpectedly in 2008 at the age of 71, leaving behind him a strong and scholarly input into themes recurring through the chapters in this collection. While the Habermasian distinction between system and lifeworld deployed by David and some of his collaborators here may not have an across-the-board appeal, the idea of chronic and disabling disorders constituting 'assaults on the lifeworld' has more resonance. He made a distinctive mark on our understanding of lifeworld adaptation to conditions like diabetes and of lifeworld resistance via an embryonic 'culture of challenge', as well as in other areas, for example, on ethnicity and health. More than this, David left his personal mark on the community of medical sociologists in Britain and further afield. His presence at seminars and conferences well beyond formal retirement is missed, as are those shrewd interrogations of speakers fooled by his calm and gentle manner. The editors and authors of the chapters that follow dedicate this volume to David's memory.

References

Bury, M. (1982) Chronic Illness as Biographical Disruption. *Sociology of Health and Illness*, 4: 167–82.

Bury, M. (2005) *Health and Illness*. Cambridge: Polity Press.

Charmaz, K. (1983) Loss of Self: A Fundamental Form of Suffering in the Chronically Ill. *Sociology of Health and Illness*, 5: 168–95.

Freidson, E. (1970) *Profession of Medicine*. New York: Dodds, Mead & Co.

Fries, R. (1983) The Compression of Morbidity. *Milbank Quarterly*, 397–419.

Mishler, E. (1984) *The Discourse of Medicine: Dialectics of Medical Interviews*. Norwood, NJ: Ablex.

Oliver, M. (1990) *The Politics of Disablement*. London: Macmillan.

Parsons, T. (1951) *The Social System*. London: Routledge and Kegan Paul.

Radley, A., Mayberry, J. and Pearce, M. (2008) Time, Space and Opportunity in the Outpatient Consultation. *Social Science and Medicine*, 66: 1484–96.

Rose, N. (2007) Molecular Biopolitics, Somatic Ethics and the Spirit of Biocapital. *Social Theory and Health*, 5: 3–29.

Scambler, G. (2009) Review Article: Health-Related Stigma. *Sociology of Health and Illness*, 31: 441–55.

Scambler, G. and Hopkins, A. (1986) Being Epileptic: Coming to Terms with Stigma. *Sociology of Health and Illness*, 8: 26–43.

Williams, G. (1984) The Genesis of Chronic Illness: Narrative Reconstruction. *Sociology of Health and Illness*, 6: 175–200.

2
Studying the Experience of Chronic Illness through Grounded Theory

Kathy Charmaz

To address how, when, and to what extent experiencing chronic illness assaults people's lifeworlds, social scientists need to consider class and context as well as the relative intrusiveness of illness and effects on identity. Certainly the notion of assaults on the lifeworld suggests loss, suffering and a diminished quality of life. Assaults on the lifeworld through experiencing chronic illness in Western middle- and upper-class cultures mean loss of one's taken-for-granted world (Berger and Luckmann, 1966; Schutz, 1970). The known world has become deeply problematic and unpredictable. In this case, assaults on the lifeworld become assaults on self and identity (Ciambrone, 2007). Assaults on the lifeworld among impoverished people can mean a relentless barrage of calamity and misfortune that chronic illness exacerbates (see, for example, Abraham, 1993; Pierret, 2007; Scheper-Hughes, 1992). A stable taken-for-granted world was never theirs to enjoy. Assaults on the lifeworld have permeated their existence. Thus, the vicissitudes of chronic illness may be blurred by overwhelming hardships of everyday life.

My task here entails representing and reviewing the grounded theory tradition for studying chronic illness with an eye towards envisioning its future. To foresee grounded theory studies of illness in the future, we need to know about the method and its contributions in the past. Like other forms of enquiry, grounded theory studies reflect the conditions of their production. Social, cultural and historical conditions of the discipline have shaped the development of the method and the substantive studies it spawned. Grounded theorists have attended to specific empirical problems that take individual experience as the primary focus of analysis. They seldom explicated the contexts of research participants' lives or the conditions of enquiry.

Although much empirical work remains to be done, grounded theory studies have contributed to understanding how, when and to what extent working- and middle-class people with chronic illness experience an assault on their life worlds. To date, grounded theory studies have focused more on losing a taken-for-granted world than adding the travails of chronic illness to lives already devastated by constant, uncontrollable crises (see, for example, Caldwell et al., 2007; Corbin and Strauss, 1988; Foote-Ardah, 2003; Kenen, Ardern-Jones and Eeles, 2007; Lonardi 2007; Nack, 2008; Sandstrom, 1990).[1]

Yet how grounded theory methods have been used in the past does not preclude researchers from repositioning their studies or from pursuing new foci in the future. The very process of conducting grounded theory opens possibilities for studying how differential effects of assaults on the lifeworld can wreak devastation on people's lives – and how experiencing chronic illness may lead some individuals to change in ways in which they value. Similarly, the grounded theory method has always contained possibilities for researchers to analyse the conditions that shaped their studies, as Adele Clarke (2005, 2006) has argued. The pragmatist underpinnings of grounded theory not only foster understanding the multiplicity of perspectives (Mead, 1934) taken in the empirical world, but also those that researchers hold as their research unfolds (Charmaz, 2005, 2006, 2009; Clarke, 2005, 2006). Perhaps ironically, grounded theorists have not yet fully taken up how attending to these multiple perspectives, standpoints and starting points can advance the research process and reshape the research product.

Instead, grounded theorists have emphasized two interrelated themes that subsume multiple concerns in the sociology of the experience of illness: (1) how people with chronic illness manage their lives and (2) its effects on self and identity. Grounded theorists who studied managing life looked for how people constructed their daily regimens and routines. These grounded theorists often brought interests in policy and practice to their studies. Other grounded theorists who studied the effects of chronic illness on self and identity brought explicit sociological questions to their research and viewed chronic illness as a magnifying mirror through which problems of the human condition could be seen. Nonetheless, their work also illuminates how people manage daily life and suggests policy implications. Similarly, an explicit focus on managing life with chronic illness includes implicit emphases on quality of life, self and identity, suffering and loss of autonomy.

Rather than believing that quality of life assumes some universal meaning and shared criteria, grounded theorists have sought to discover what it means in their research participants' experience. Thus, the extent to which chronic illness constitutes an assault on subjective life worlds depends on the degree to which people view it as intruding on their lives and whether it stays in the foreground or recedes into the background of daily life (Charmaz, 1991).

As I review the method, I outline the analytic foci of various studies in relation to how, when, why and to what extent these studies reveal assaults on the self. This task becomes complicated for four reasons: (1) numerous researchers use grounded theory methods to legitimize conducting qualitative research, not to engage grounded theory strategies; (2) methods sections of published works emphasize data collection rather than analytic strategies; (3) many researchers do not understand basic grounded theory strategies; and (4) grounded theory is an evolving and contested method (Charmaz, 2008b, 2009). Any review of grounded theory studies of chronic illness is partial and limited because the wide adoption of the method precludes covering the range of publications in the health professions and other social sciences.[2] Through emphasizing managing illness and reconstruction of self and identity, I also bring in considerations of loss, difference, embodiment, temporality – and transformation – that pervade North American, British, Australian and European studies and note the theoretical implications of the authors' ideas. I occasionally situate grounded theory studies in relation to other types of enquiry and mention early studies of disability because the divide between studies of illness and disability had not yet occurred.

Ambiguities in classifying and using grounded theory

Growing academic and professional interests in the lives of people with chronic illness in the 1970s converged with researchers' increasing use of grounded theory methods. This convergence not only strengthened explicit recognition of the experience of illness as a sub-field of medical sociology and a focus of nursing research,[3] but also brought attention to grounded theory as a distinctive qualitative method. Links between theory and method, however, were unclear in many grounded theory studies. Aspiring qualitative researchers welcomed Barney G. Glaser and Anselm L. Strauss's *The Discovery of Grounded Theory* (1967) because their arguments justified inductive qualitative studies during a time of quantitative hegemony. Did these researchers use grounded theory guidelines? Probably not in ways that Glaser taught.[4] The *Discovery* book provided more explicit analytic strategies than its predecessors, but how to use them remained opaque. Glaser's (1978) later methodological

treatise developed grounded theory strategies but also made his positivistic assumptions more apparent.

Between quests to legitimize qualitative enquiry and misinterpret-
ations of the method, what stood as a *bona fide* grounded theory study
became ambiguous. Strauss and Corbin's (1990, 1998) publication of
Basics of Qualitative Research changed the method, although except for
Glaser (1992) few researchers noticed (but see Atkinson, Coffey and
Delamont, 2003; Bryant and Charmaz, 2007, forthcoming; Charmaz,
2000a, 2006). By now, grounded theory strategies of coding data and
writing memos have become standard practices in qualitative research[5]
and three versions of grounded theory have developed: constructivist
(Bryant and Charmaz, 2007; Charmaz, 2006; Clarke, 2005), postposi-
tivist (Corbin and Strauss, 2007) and objectivist (Glaser, 1998, 2001).

Given the ambiguities and multiple versions of the method, what
distinguishes a grounded theory study from other types of qualitative
research? Presumably, grounded theory studies aim to construct theory
and this purpose makes them distinctive. Many grounded theorists talk
about theory construction but produce description. Do these studies
fall under the rubric of grounded theory? I contend that telling distinctions resides in researchers' actions. Hence, grounded theorists:

1. Conduct data collection and analysis simultaneously in an iterative
   process
2. Analyse actions and processes rather than themes and structure
3. Use comparative methods
4. Draw on data (for example, narratives and descriptions) in service of
   developing new conceptual categories
5. Develop inductive categories through systematic data analysis
6. Emphasize theory construction rather than description or application of current theories
7. Engage in theoretical sampling
8. Search for variation in the studied categories or process
9. Pursue developing a category rather than covering a specific empirical topic

Most researchers who claim grounded theory, or are placed under its
umbrella, do 1–5, but do not make the remaining actions evident.[6] To
detail how grounded theorists engage in these actions exceeds the scope
of this chapter but descriptions appear in recent works (Charmaz, 2006,
2007, 2008a, 2008b; Corbin and Strauss, 2007). Grounded theory has
become a general method whose strategies have permeated qualitative

research. Thus, researchers adopt its strategies to fit their purposes and may not mention – or realize – how grounded theory has influenced them. I advocate that researchers use grounded theory strategies to fit their purposes, which may not be theory construction, but to be aware of what they do (Charmaz, 2006).

A few authors (Kenen, Ardern-Jones and Eeles, 2007; Wilson and Luker, 2006) indicate that they use some grounded theory strategies but not all. Similarly, some authors combine grounded theory with other approaches such as phenomenology (Schoenberg et al., 2003), narrative analysis (Hansen, Walters and Baker, 2007; Mathieson and Stam, 1995; Salander, 2002) and thematic analysis (Somerville et al., 2008). Still others say that they use grounded theory methods although their categories remain descriptive or thematic (Bowes, Tamlyn and Butler, 2002). Occasionally an analysis looks like a grounded theory but the author does not indicate having used it.[7] If researchers engage in actions 1–5, their analyses will take a different form than that in other qualitative studies. In keeping with grounded theory objectives, their conceptual categories take precedence over stories and descriptions. By engaging in the remaining actions, however, researchers will move their analyses into theory construction.

Current debates about interview methods pertain to grounded theory studies of chronic illness because most grounded theorists in this area choose interviewing, and it is the logical choice when studying problems that cut across a range of illnesses. Interview methods elicit trenchant criticisms from inside and outside the grounded theory method. Glaser (2003) asserts that interview guides force the data because the questions reflect the interviewer's preconceived interests. Other qualitative researchers argue that interview questions elicit accounts, rather than obtain direct experience (for example, Silverman, 2007). Accounts are performances constructed in specific situations for a particular audience. What people say differs from what they do. Like other qualitative researchers, grounded theorists may assume that their participants' stories are true. Yet an embellished account matters much more when researchers have skimpy rather than abundant data. The latter affords the comparative material to place an embellished account into perspective. Even so, the logic of grounded theory does not impose a quest for absolute accuracy.

Herein lies a key difference between grounded theory and other qualitative approaches. Certainly any careful researcher tries to represent research participants' views and actions fairly and to remain faithful to the studied world. As grounded theorists, however, we look for recurrent patterns in our data and we treat these data as *theoretically plausible,* rather than as requiring empirical verification.[8] Instead of assuring accuracy, we aim to create robust categories that offer useful interpretations of the data. Grounded theorists check categories rather than belabouring the veracity of interview accounts.

The Chicago School roots of grounded theory studies of chronic illness

Grounded theory research on chronic illness emerged in sociology from its Chicago School heritage of pragmatist philosophy and naturalistic enquiry. Chicago traditions included field research in natural settings and symbolic interactionist social psychology, although not every Chicago School sociologist adopted both. The Chicago School links between grounded theory studies and its predecessors using naturalistic enquiry are evident in Julius Roth's (1963) classic portrayal of patients and practitioners' contrasting and often conflicting views of treatment and recovery in a tuberculosis hospital in *Timetables*. Links to symbolic interactionism are apparent in numerous early Chicago School classic works of the Second Chicago School (Fine, 1995) such as Erving Goffman's *Asylums* (1961) and *Stigma* (1963); Fred Davis's *Passage through Crisis* (1963), and Barney G. Glaser and Anselm L. Strauss's *Awareness of Dying* (1965) and then later, *Time for Dying* (1968). These studies all raised sociological questions about health and illness and thus created the foundation for a sociology of the illness experience.

Glaser and Strauss (1967) developed grounded theory through explicating the methods they used in their empirical studies of death and dying. Strauss's publication of *Chronic Illness and the Quality of Life* (1975) established the experience of chronic illness as a new area of sociological and grounded theory enquiry. Interest in studying this experience spread across disciplines and professions and later became a focus for phenomenological, narrative and discourse analyses (see, for example, Ezzy, 2000; Frank, 1991, 1995; Gerhardt and Brieskorn-Zinke, 1986; Radley, 1989; Riessman, 1990; Williams, 1984). In *Chronic Illness and the Quality of Life* (1975), Strauss (1975) and his students (Fagerhaugh, 1975; Reif, 1975; Suczek, 1975; Wiener, 1975) directed attention to how people with a chronic illness handled daily problems. Other sociological and nursing researchers saw that grounded theory methods could help them learn how people with chronic illnesses managed their situations, particularly at home.

In conjunction with other Chicago School works on illness and disability, early grounded theory studies of illness challenged the theoretical

hegemony of Talcott Parsons' (1953) concept of the 'sick role.' This concept did not fit the lives of people with chronic illness (see also, Charmaz,
1999a; Gallagher, 1976; Twaddle, 1969) nor did it address assaults on the
self or the lifeworld. Instead, Parsons treated illness as deviance and
addressed institutionalized mechanisms of controlling it. He assumed
a model of acute illness and theorized that the patient (1) entered the
role involuntarily; (2) remained a passive, acquiescent, although emo-
tionally vulnerable, recipient of medical intervention; (3) concentrated
on recovery from illness; and (4) received temporary exemption from
adult roles. Being a patient affected the individual's entire existence –
for a short period. Parsons' concept of the sick role outlined an abstract
hypothetical construct; he did not base it on empirical research. His
concept assumes that illness is self-evident to the trained professional
whose expert judgement legitimizes the patient's entry into this role.
What stands as illness, however, and who has it is much murkier, particularly in contested chronic illnesses (see, for example, Barker, 2006;
Clarke and James, 2003; Dumit, 2006; Kroll-Smith, 1997; Mishler, 1981;
Nettleton et al., 2004).

   In obvious contrast to the concept of the sick role, people with chronic
illnesses do not recover. They must live with their illnesses and spend
relatively little time in the patient role (Conrad, 1987). They often try to
manage their symptoms; participate in their care; and carry on ordinary lives, to the extent possible. From the early days to the present,
both sociologists and health professionals have used grounded theory to investigate how people live with illness and manage their lives.
Taken together, the early grounded theory studies demonstrated that
Parsons' concept of the sick role did not capture the experience of living
with chronic illness. Because early grounded theorists (Benoliel, 1975;
Fagerhaugh, 1975; Reif, 1975; Strauss, 1975; Wiener, 1975) emphasized
empirical studies of how people managed their illnesses, grounded
theorists became known as offering an 'insider's' view of chronic illness, as opposed to Parson's distanced hypothetical view. Although not
devoid of political and epistemological issues, taking an insider's view
has shaped studies of chronic illness throughout medical sociology and
beyond.

Grounded theory contributions to studying
the experience of illness

Studying the experience chronic illness raises interrelated themes that
shape managing illness and the effects of illness on self and identity

(Charmaz, 2000b). Themes concerning awareness and uncertainty that dominate Glaser and Strauss's (1965, 1968) studies of dying have informed grounded theory studies of chronic illness, which turned its gaze to the *patient's* experience and meanings rather than the staff's. This turn brought questions about self and identity into view although the early studies primarily focused on managing illness. Concrete problems in managing illness and care often force reconstruction of self and identity, as grounded theorists have noted. In the following section, I discuss these themes and emphasize how managing illness and its effects on self and identity are intertwined. I bring in notions of embodiment, the significance of interaction, and the social context of illness although grounded theory contributions in these areas far exceed my coverage here.

Awareness, uncertainty and meanings of illness

Learning that one has a serious chronic illness commonly becomes a pivotal point in a person's life, symbolizing an assault on the self. This point in time may stand out forever in memory, as a woman in my study (Charmaz, 2008c) recalled, 'My husband was diagnosed with inoperable lung cancer on the same day I was diagnosed with chronic fatigue syndrome and fibromyalgia and he died a few weeks later' (Charmaz, 2008c: 7). This woman had led an autonomous life and accrued skills that served her well in managing chronic illness and resultant poverty. For her, chronic illness meant a 'biographical disruption' (Bury, 1982), albeit one that lasted. For already marginalized people who have had multiple assaults on their lifeworlds, serious chronic illness may mean 'biographical reinforcement' (Carricaburu and Pierret, 1995) rather than a disruption (Charmaz and Rosenfeld, forthcoming). Janine Pierret (2007) found that receiving the diagnosis of HIV infection destabilized people who already had chaotic, unanchored lives, fostered their passivity and withdrawal, and 'plunged them into a void without resources for coping' (1602). Their fortunes changed somewhat because French social policy designated them as 'patients' and thus conferred respectability and gave them a more stable social status because patients were eligible for life-sustaining welfare benefits. Structural policies altered their meanings of illness and, subsequently, of self. Pierret's observations make the kind of significant link between structural conditions and subjective meanings that grounded theorists can build on in the future.

A diagnosis may initiate or confirm biographical disruption or spawn beliefs that life is temporarily interrupted requiring a timeout, rather than permanently changed (Charmaz, 1991). Temporality matters.

Some people learn that they have an illness long before they receive a diagnosis and others long after. Diagnoses may be ambiguous, contested or delayed – whether by default or intent. Somerville et al. (2008) note that small differences in patients' performance of the pain narrative led to whether or not they were diagnosed with angina and that physicians' narrow canon resulted in disattending to patients' descriptions of pain that did not quite fit this canon. Similarly, Schoenberg et al. (2003) report that women receive delayed diagnoses of heart disease because their symptoms do not fit the standard based on men. Schoenberg et al. also find that women delay or give up seeking help because of (1) facing structural barriers such as lack of health insurance and transportation (2) being demeaned or humiliated by health-care providers and (3) giving higher priority to competing family obligations than to seeking care.

When physicians either form a disheartening prognosis or hold a disparaging view of a patient implying that 'it's all in your head', they may invoke obfuscating or delaying tactics with patients. Their patients' dawning awareness of trouble while in the midst of seeming diagnostic uncertainty hearkens back to Glaser and Strauss's (1965) and Quint's (1965) studies of how organizational practices of controlling bad news affected patients' relative awareness of their impending demise. Such problems of awareness and uncertainty also recall Davis's (1963, 1972/1956) and Roth's (1963) observations of how professionals manufacture uncertainty and thus decrease patients and families' awareness of the patient's plight. Wilson and Luker (2006) interviewed several cancer patients who learned of their diagnosis after being sent to the cancer hospital, which in one patient's words could 'only mean one thing' (1620).

Problems concerning awareness of illness and uncertainty about it pervade the stories of people with esoteric and contested illnesses. Rather than fighting against having a disease, they struggle to obtain a diagnosis (Charmaz, 1991, 2008c; Clarke and James, 2003; Dumit, 2006; Kroll-Smith, 1997; Lillrank, 2003) – and with it a legitimate moral status. Andrea Stockl (2007) found that people with systemic lupus erythematosus (SLE) experienced existential uncertainty due to a lengthy ambivalent diagnostic process. Stockl describes a woman's account that reflected the 'typical SLE trajectory' (1552) one in which individuals had suffered from symptoms for years but despite a lengthy diagnostic search, remained undiagnosed. This woman's account stated:

In fact, all were classic symptoms of the autoimmune disease lupus, which is notoriously hard to diagnose. But two months after my son's birth, I started a crusade to get a diagnosis. All along doctors had told me that my problems were due to stress and viruses, but I knew this couldn't be true. I was sure something was seriously wrong. (1553)

Experiencing defined, but not validated, physical symptoms often leads to a heightened bodily awareness when people pursue a diagnostic quest (Corbin and Strauss, 1988). Such individuals focus on minute physical sensations and changes while pursuing their diagnostic quest for some kind of certainty. When people suffer from undiagnosed symptoms for long periods, they may welcome a devastating diagnosis. The woman above seems resolute in her belief that her symptoms were consequential. Other people question whether their symptoms are real or imagined, particularly when health professionals, family members and friends have doubted their validity. Experiencing symptoms without validation produces invalidated selves (Charmaz, 1991, 2000b; Stockl, 2007).

In this case, doubt and uncertainty work in reciprocal ways. Professionals doubt the validity of their patients' symptoms and thus question their perceptions and prolong their uncertainty. What may stand as prolonged uncertainty for patients simultaneously hardens into professionals' attributions of emotional causes and, thus, justifies ignoring their patients' symptoms. Physicians may also develop interactional tactics for dealing with these patients' claims of having legitimate physical symptoms. Asbring and Närvänen (2003) state that physicians of patients with chronic fatigue syndrome and fibromyalgia use tactics such as looking for other causes than biomedical, making the patient responsible for managing the illness, distancing themselves from the patient, or trying to persuade the patient to accept the situation. Moral judgements of the patients often shape their tactics. Subsequently, their patients' suffering and loss of autonomy likely increase as they experience self-doubt, loss of dignity and dwindling treatment possibilities (Charmaz, 1991, 2002; Lillrank, 2003; Swahnberg, Thapar-Björkert and Berterö, 2007).

Expertise trumps patients' awareness but paradoxically Stockl (2007) found patients' doubts increased about their physicians' expertise (see also Charmaz, 2002). Receiving a diagnosis also does not end ambiguity for people who do not have symptoms yet, or for those whose symptoms do not quite match clinical descriptions of the diagnosed condition. These people may not view themselves as ill and may doubt their diagnoses (Charmaz 1991, 2002; Schoenberg et al., 2003).

Stockl sees her analysis as consistent with Nettleton's (2006) argument that this 'embodied doubt' (1558) reflects late modernity and that people who have unexplained symptoms make apparent the kind of doubt and uncertainty everyone faces in late modernity. In this way, Stockl links micro processes to macro conditions and thus increases the theoretical reach of her analysis.

The biographical timing of illness influences the extent of its defined disruptiveness. Young adults often find that serious chronic illness disrupts, if not destroys, their life path and plans. It constitutes an assault on the self that threatens their lifeworld. If so, reconstruction of self means identity redirection. Young and middle-aged adults often make major identity changes after having attempted to enact their past identity goals but find that they cannot realize their preferred identities and, thus, move down their implicit identity hierarchy (Charmaz, 1987). Older adults may construct biographical continuity after illness as Hinojosa et al. (2008) found in lower- and middle-class stroke survivors who drew upon discourses of age expectations and religious beliefs. Sanders, Donovan and Dieppe (2002) found coexisting yet somewhat contradictory meanings among their older, mostly working-class interviewees who viewed their discomfort from osteoarthritis as a normal part of growing old. Simultaneously, however, these interviewees also viewed their symptoms as disrupting daily life. Sanders et al. argue that their interviewees wanted to present themselves as ageing well, which would diminish emphasis on disruption. Similarly, Pound, Patrick and Ebrahim (1998) interviewed older working-class people who had strokes but wanted to be seen as stoic and self-sufficient.

These studies all situate individual meanings in societal structures. Both Sanders et al. and Pound et al. argue that their research sheds light on why some older people may not seek treatment or services. Their reports suggest that relationships between age, class and cultural discourses influence people's meanings of illness and their actions about it. Elderly research participants' stoic silence perpetuated documented treatment inequities for older patients' joint problems in Sanders et al.'s study, and reduced their use of resources and services for which they were eligible in Pound et al.'s study.

Chronic illness changes over time; sometimes for the better, often for the worse. Lengthy plateaus may follow change, although ups and downs sometimes occur quickly. Definitions of uncertainty fade when people adapt to a plateau or have long stretches of time between exacerbations or crises. Again temporality influences people's meanings, actions and narratives of illness (see also, Roberts, 2004). As Neil Drummond (2000) observes, 'the temporary experience of severe exacerbation is located in the prevailing experience of what is perceived as "normal life"' (242). When swept into crisis, a person who had mini-mized uncertainty may wonder if the crisis will ever end, and with it, the uncertain outcome. After the crisis, however, meanings of illness as uncertain and the present as tenuous may fade into the past (Charmaz, 1991). When people have a lengthy period without tangible signs of illness, they may question whether their diagnosis is correct, despite having once had intrusive symptoms.

Meanings of illness likely shift as embodied experience changes. Increased visibility of symptoms and disability provide tangible reminders of a changed body (Charmaz and Rosenfeld, 2006). In their longitudinal study of people with diabetes, Lawton et al. (2008) show that people's experience of having a progressive chronic illness alters their meanings. Their research participant's shifted their accounts of the cause of diabetes from controllable factors remedied by individual responsibility to uncontrollable factors such as ageing and heredity. Meanings shape managing illness and care and, in turn, subsequent events and exigencies reshape meanings. The vicissitudes of experienc-ing chronic illness can make meanings fragile, not only of illness but also of self, situations and relationships.

Nonetheless, through experiencing illness and its complications and disabilities, people may learn valuable new ways of being in the world (Charmaz, 1994a; Moore, 2005; Sandstrom, 1990). Dena L. Moore (2006) writes of Shay, who had multiple sclerosis and severe disabili-ties from a car accident. Shay exemplified Moore's major category of 'Being a Part of Something Larger than Oneself', because she continu-ally reached out to other people and served as their confidante, advi-sor and kin-keeper. Despite having had harrowing times, Shay tried to see beyond her losses and treated her situation with humour. Seeing beyond loss usually requires re-evaluation of life and sustained emotion work occurring after a person has relinquished dreams of returning to life before illness.

Managing life with illness

Since the publication of *Chronic Illness and the Quality of Life*, numer-ous grounded theory studies have emphasized how people with chronic illnesses manage their lives at home (see, for example, Benoliel, 1975; Chamberlayne and King, 1997; Ciambrone, 2007; Corbin and Strauss, 1984, 1985, 1988; Fagerhaugh, 1975; Foote-Ardah, 2003; Johnson, 1991; Peyrot, McMurray and Hedges, 1987; Schneider and Conrad, 1983; Wilson, Kendall and Brooks, 2007). Perhaps ironically, the explicit links

that Strauss (1975; Strauss et al., 1984) made between illness and quality of life became subsumed by concrete problems of managing illness
and care (but see, Drummond, 2000). Yet this emphasis brings embodiment into the analytic picture (see Charmaz, 1995, 1999b; Corbin and
Strauss, 1987) and hints of the assaults on the self and the lifeworld that
chronic illness may exact.

Major themes in Strauss (1975) and his students' initial studies of the
experience of illness included re-designing lifestyle to make life manageable (Reif, 1975), managing regimens and controlling symptoms
(Benoliel, 1975; Davis, 1973; Fagerhaugh, 1975; Strauss, 1975), managing uncertainty (Strauss, 1975; Wiener, 1984), involving others in care
(Benoliel, 1975; Reif, 1975; Strauss, 1975; Wiener, 1984) and normalizing illness and care (Wiener, 1975), which I discuss in the following
section. Such actions typically involve making large and small changes
in daily life – and often in personal and social identities. What prompts
people to alter their lives to manage their illnesses?

A prognosis can be ignored, particularly when symptoms are absent
or quiescent. The situation reverses when symptoms are immediate,
unpredictable and mortifying. Immediate unpredictability combined
with potential mortification is a powerful incentive, more so than receiving a diagnosis with an uncertain prognosis. Reif (1975), for example,
shows how people with ulcerative colitis try to prevent, reduce, conceal
or correct pollution by fasting, wearing rubber pants, mapping routes
to toilets and timing their activities. The more unpredictable, embar-
rassing or mortifying symptoms people have, the more they engage in
such overt management strategies – or withdraw from social life (see
also, Schneider and Conrad, 1980; Mitteness, 1987a, 1987b; Peyrot,
McMurray and Hedges, 1987, 1988). Strategies for managing the day
also allow people to maintain some semblance of their earlier lives
such as keeping their jobs, raising their children and maintaining their
independence.

Intrusive chronic illness forces a new relationship between body and
self (Charmaz, 1991, 1995; Corbin and Strauss, 1987, 1988; Johnson,
1991). As the once taken-for-granted body intrudes on a person's actions
and consciousness, people learn to read and listen to their bodies in
new ways. The learning process is revelatory for some people because
of its implications and because they had not attended to their bodies
earlier. After their heart attacks, Joy Johnson's (1991) research participants believed, 'they needed to be in "better touch" with their bodies.'
If they defined learning from their bodies as prerequisite for maintaining or reconstructing some semblance of their former lives, they pay

close attention to them. Similarly, Geralyn A. Meyer (2002) found that women who needed to function but had unpredictable severe migraine headaches exercised vigilance by developing what she calls 'the art of watching out'. Their vigilance helped them ward off episodes and maintain biographical continuity.

Managing illness is work. What is done, who does it, how much time and effort it takes shapes the lifeworld of ill people and those around them. In the second edition of *Chronic Illness and the Quality of Life*, Strauss et al. (1984) devoted considerable attention to chronic illness as work, a focus that Corbin and Strauss (1984, 1985, 1988) developed and others have continued (Timmermans and Freidin, 2007; Williams, 2000, 2003). Lifeworlds are shared; the consequences of illness and disability spread throughout the family and, sometimes, the workplace. When parents of young children or spouses realize the implications of their family member's illness and/or disability, they often become deeply involved in managing symptoms and care. Clare Williams (2000, 2002) developed the notion of 'the alert assistant' (Charmaz, 1991: 69) who is in tune with the ill person's symptoms, regimen and physical capacities. She found that mothers of boys with asthma and diabetes anticipated situations their sons would face in public and acted as mediators for them in the family, often without their sons' knowledge. Williams (2000) tells of one boy's mother who said, 'I see the signs of uproar and I know when to back off and not get too heavy with him about things, whereas I don't think James [partner] does – he doesn't realize that he's not feeling too good' (264). Mothers did not, however, act in similar ways for their daughters. Williams found gendered patterns in managing illness and care, as I did (Charmaz, 1994b). Mothers were more likely to serve as alert assistants for boys in similar ways that wives helped their husbands.

Both visibility of symptoms and behavioural indicators influence family members' involvement in managing care of the chronically ill person. Timmermans and Friedin (2007) show how mothers of asthmatic children learn to read symptoms:

> Every mother explained how she learned to read the signs of pending asthma episode. For example, 'if I notice his cheeks starting getting real beet red and he's all out of breath, he could be having an asthma attack... He'll be coughing, coughing, constant coughing like a whooping cough. But it's not, it's his asthma kicking in.' (1357)

Mothers monitor and sometimes control their child's actions. Corbin and Strauss (1984, 1985, 1988) found that middle-class couples worked in concert to manage symptoms. These couples treated managing the ill person's illness and disabilities as problems to solve together. Corbin and Strauss point out that a strong sense of duty or obligation sustains the caregiver, as does discussing plans and practices of managing daily care. They found couples balancing tasks and working together to try to put life back together. How partners talk about subsequent lifestyle changes may be interpreted as caring or criticism and unwanted control. Whether a couple's conversations stress desirable identity outcomes and relational meanings affect whether the ill partner makes these changes (Goldsmith, Lindholm and Bute, 2006).

Not all couples or families work in concert. Caregiver overload with resulting conflict is common, as is anger towards the ill person for such reasons as failing to remain independent or ignoring medical advice. Conflict around trust and betrayal may result. In my 1991 study, a middle-aged lesbian felt betrayed by her girlfriend who had told her heart specialist that she had resumed smoking. Similarly, David Kelleher (1988) states that one concerned husband felt compelled to tell his wife's physician that she persisted in eating sweets but simultaneously felt that he had betrayed his wife.

Attempts to manage illness and care may fail. At this juncture, an ill person's symptoms may become evident, but to whom are they visible? Ill people themselves sometimes only discern their symptoms after they are in trouble, if they discern them at all. Peyrot et al. (1988, 2001) find that people with diabetes experienced traumatizing moments, 'One felt, "I'm going crazy," another "totally helpless", a third was really scared to think that I couldn't remember that I wasn't in control' (119). Quite commonly, people having an insulin reaction do not realize it but their spouses do, as Peyrot et al. report. They interviewed one wife who remarked, 'when he goes into insulin reactions, his personality changes – it's like Dr. Jekel and Mr. Hyde, living with different people' and another wife came home to find her husband bloodied after a rampage of smashing furniture and throwing himself against the wall (119).

Normalizing

Normalizing is a process in which the person treats a symptom, disability or accommodation to illness as routine. It is a way of managing appearances and views of self as well as a strategy for managing life with illness. Thus, its relative effectiveness typically depends on having regimens and symptoms that can be kept at least partially hidden.

Normalizing fosters adapting to an impaired body rather than struggling against it. By minimizing the effects of illness and regimens, normalizing also checks 'identity spread' (Strauss et al., 1984: 81) and when successful, it reduces the potential for stigmatizing responses from other people (Scambler, 1984; Scambler and Hopkins, 1986). The actions that constitute normalizing support continuing past identities and defining continuity of self. Hence, people whose normalizing goes unquestioned are unlikely to feel pressures to reconstruct a different self and identity.

By looking at the concept of normalizing from a structural standpoint, we can see new dimensions of it that early grounded theorists may not have noticed. The concept of normalizing assumes a shared normative world in which the presence and actions of people who are defined as different become problematic. This collective view may, moreover, inform ill individuals' views and actions and thus may heighten their feelings of difference and devaluation. In this situation, their attempts to normalize blend with passing because acting 'normal' hides their symptoms and disabilities. People perform normalizing and passing. Normalizing may be a taken-for-granted response; passing is strategic when people organize their lives to keep their symptoms hidden (Schneider and Conrad, 1980, 1983). As Carolyn Wiener (1984: 91–92) suggests, people who can 'cover up' their symptoms and disabilities and 'keep up' what they define as normal activities are able to normalize despite uncertainty. Wiener observes that people who adopt these strategies, normalize at cost of being irritable at home and of finding it hard to justify inaction.

At least two types of normalizing occur. The first consists of gradual accommodation to a situation or symptom without the person's awareness; they have normalized it without realizing its presence. Middle-aged and older people often attribute diffuse symptoms such as fatigue or joint pain to ageing. Over time, some people reduce their activities and shrink their worlds to fit their changed bodies without awareness of the extent they have changed (Charmaz, 1991). Hence, they do not develop the intensified bodily awareness that people with discernible symptoms often cultivate. Normalizing vague or unexpected symptoms extends to other major players in an ill person's life. Physicians who dismiss or diminish their patients' symptoms encourage normalizing such as when they tell a patient with chest pressure, 'You're too young to have a heart attack' or 'it's probably indigestion' (Schoenberg et al., 2003: 276). Subsequently, when people have become accustomed to their situations or dismissed symptoms, they may feel shocked to discover consequential meanings of them.

A second type of normalizing depends on the person's awareness of having experienced physical changes or chronic symptoms. Here normalizing indicates a person's acceptance of or adaptation to a changed body or altered circumstances and typically takes time. As time passes, what had been disruptive or distressing becomes taken-for-granted and thus viewed as familiar and customary in the person's present situation (Gerhardt and Brieskorn-Zinke, 1986; Schlesinger, 1996). People with diabetes may initially find the monitoring and treatment regimen to be intrusive but later as Kelleher (1988) observes, some people minimize the significance of their disease and treatment regimen, which they follow. These individuals granted relatively low salience to the effects of diabetes on their lives. Kelleher sees their response as containing elements of denial rather than indicating that they may have integrated diabetes in their lives in taken-for-granted ways. In countries such as US, the high incidence of diabetes may foster this type of normalizing.

When people with chronic and serious illnesses have relatively stable symptoms and disabilities for periods of time, normalizing may occur multiple times as a person's health wanes. Normalizing may move in the opposite direction, too, when treatment and regimens help or the person's health improves and the person adapts to his or her new situation. In either case, people come to take their bodies and/or situations for granted.

Normalizing takes different forms, depending on the person's illness and situation. People who must work as long as possible often create clever ways of covering up their symptoms and keeping up with their work, such as scheduling their most difficult tasks before their daily fatigue begins (Charmaz, 1999b; Wiener, 1984). People may normalize their illness to protect others as well as to preserve self. Parents gloss over their symptoms to keep their children unaware of the seriousness of their conditions. Spouses minimize distress and discomfort so as not to alarm their partners.

When people have a serious diagnosis but do not yet have symptoms, normalizing may occur before the disease becomes evident. Carrie Foote-Ardah (2003) states that people with HIV-positive infections tried to reconstruct normal lives and to keep their situations manageable. Routines may provide a comforting structure for those with life-threatening conditions such as cancer or AIDS who feel that they have lost control over their bodies and worlds. Pär Salander (2002) suggests that routines are comforting because they foster expectations and by extension, hope. People whose conditions may suddenly worsen often normalize their lives to the extent that they can, while they simultaneously reassess and monitor their situations (Charmaz, 1991, 1995; Foote-Ardah, 2003; Johnson, 1991).

Normalizing is not limited to the ill individual. Mothers of sick children and wives of ill husbands may assist in normalizing the ill person's condition and to assist him or her to carry on usual activities (Charmaz, 1994b; Williams, 2003). The caregivers may engage in considerable emotion work to normalize symptoms and routines and to maintain a positive emotional climate in the family. Young et al. (2002) found that mothers of children with cancer felt that they had to maintain a cheerful demeanour for their child while feeling grave concern. The pressures to keep life normal contradict dominant cultural narratives about children with cancer and the prevailing identity of 'heroism and stoicism' (1481). Under such circumstances, both mothers and children may receive silent lessons that foster reconstruction of self and identity, as they deal with the vicissitudes of illness and treatment.

Disclosing illness

Questions concerning disclosure affect almost everyone with chronic illnesses, particularly those who have invisible conditions. Moral questions and ethical decisions surround what, when, and how to disclose, for people with chronic illnesses as well as their health professionals. The act of disclosing risks, likely, highlights subsequent definitions of difference and a reduced moral status for people with serious illnesses and disabilities. After interviewing patients with diabetes, Peyrot et al. (1988) wrote:

> Many feel stigmatized and discriminated against; one said he was regarded as a 'freak.' Another patient said that he 'didn't want anybody's sympathy.' These patients feel that if they talk about their diabetes, 'sometimes people try to make a weakness out of it.' These patients avoid such displays in order to normalize their condition more completely. (369)

I found that the ethics of disclosure turned on attachment for young people and autonomy for elders (Charmaz, 1991). Young single people often felt agonized about disclosing their conditions to potential partners. Telling too early was presumptuous and risked losing a chance to nurture a relationship with the new person. Telling too late smacked of trapping the person and of betraying whatever trust had been established. Elderly individuals often concealed nagging symptoms and worrisome incidents from their adult children. Maintaining their autonomy meant being independent and living life on their terms. They sacrificed companionship and safety to maintain independence.

AIDS intensifies dilemmas of disclosure and brings them into the public arena because it is sexually transmitted and potentially lethal. Here an assault on the self can be transported to the lifeworlds of unwitting strangers. David Rier (2007) traces the moral judgements that arise in anonymous online support groups for people with HIV-AIDS. He states that posters (online participants) invoke a moral discourse about disclosure ethics. This discourse polices the boundaries of the group, contradicts the opposing position that no one expects honesty, and attempts to persuade lurkers and uncommitted members to make full disclosures. The discourse replicated professional views of disclosure and confronted posters who defended non-disclosure such as, 'Do you think there is any value in asking a total stranger his HIV status?? The response is always, "What answer gets me [sex]?" ... I'm positive, and when guys ask me "Are you healthy" or "Are you clean?" I always say yes, because I'm horny and want sex!' (10). We can extend Rier's point by adding that these moral judgements coalesce into measures for evaluating claims to moral standing. Consider the following response to a poster who had glossed over his HIV+ status by telling a sex partner that he was 'clean':

> Oops??? Ooops, I accidently said I didn't have a fatal illness when you asked me?! There is no excuse for being dishonest about that. You may have cost someone their life. Anyone who defends that kind of action is basically saying it's okay to spread AIDS. I hope for that poor guy he didn't get it, and in the future think of others suffering before your sexual gratification. (Rier, 2007: 10)

Conclusions

The analysis above has implications in three interrelated areas that point to directions for the future: (1) grounded theory studies in health and illness (2) debates about the divide between the sociology of chronic illness and disabilities studies, and (3) the development of grounded theory methods to enable moving in new directions and resolving these debates. Relationships between social structure, inter-action, self and identity reside in the background of many grounded theory works, including mine. Now it is time to bring them into the foreground. Sanders et al. (2002), Pound et al. (1998) and Schoenberg et al. (2003) offer possibilities for making links between individual views and actions and social structure visible. Similarly, Hinojosa et al. (2008) suggest how to specify connections between shared values and collective actions. Such studies show how people make sense of and enact wider values and constraints. Schoenberg et al. (2003) also show that the absence of lay perspectives in medical care perpetuates victim-blaming in cultural narratives, as well as during face-to-face interaction. In addition, these micro studies begin to take variables such as class, gender and age and analyse how they are constituted as well as delineate when and how they come into play.

In considering what constitutes the sociology of illness, grounded theory studies show that categories of chronic illness and disability blur. Some types of chronic illness cause lasting visible disabilities; other types lead to intermittent or invisible disabilities. People who have stable disabilities such as paraplegia become susceptible to certain chronic conditions in middle and late life. Thus, a clear divide between studies of illness and those of disability becomes tenuous. Our analyses need to reflect empirical realities. The sharp divide between the social model of disability and the sociology of chronic illness can be bridged. Despite some claims to the contrary, studying the experience of chronic illness includes much more than reductionist personal tragedies. As the contributions in this volume indicate, a personal tragedy *vs* a social model is simplistic, over-stated and ignores realities of human experience such as ageing and embodiment. Such a dichotomy also ignores the collective in the personal and obscures formation of collective tragedies.

Furthermore, earlier imputations that micro-sociologists who study the experience of illness only *intend* to tell personal tragedies are simply wrong. The literature is replete with tales of people who define positive changes such as becoming more appreciative of life, valuing relationships, gaining compassion and giving to others (see for example, Auerbach, Salick and Fine, 2006; Charmaz, 1994a; Hernandez, 2005; Kaiser, 2008; Moore, 2006; Sandstrom, 1990). Studies of chronic illness contain stories of loss, but they also include stories of hope, courage and transformation, and grounded theory studies can delineate the conditions of their emergence.

How grounded theorists have used the method in the past need not outline boundaries *for* the method. The contemporary revision of grounded theory (Bryant and Charmaz, 2007; Charmaz, 2006) provides tools for repositioning and reconstructing studies of the experience of illness. Grounded theory emphases on comparative methods, processual analyses and theory construction have always made the method distinctive although its potential has not been fully tapped. Grounded theorists can turn these emphases to build systematic analyses of intersections between individual experience and collective practices. At the substantive level, for example, studying biomedicalization in treating chronic illnesses fosters defining such intersections and developing nuanced analyses of them (Clarke et al., 2003).

Attending to the conditions of the research process encourages researchers to locate observed experience within larger structures. Shifting standpoints and situations shape the research process and product (Charmaz, 2006, 2008b, 2009; Clarke, 2005, 2006; Clarke and Friese, 2007), particularly when the researcher delves into the studied world. Many grounded theory studies of the past have taken a distanced view. Instead, we can move closer to the studied experience and take our varied standpoints and situations into account. As we locate the construction of our research, the situated locations of our research participants' views and actions become visible.

This methodological move may mean acknowledging the researcher's embodied experience as well as that of the researched. Observing the suffering of people with chronic illness may remind researchers of their own vulnerability. Perhaps critics of studies of experiencing illness shy away from suffering now as 1960s social scientists shied away from studying death and dying when Glaser and Strauss pioneered inquiry in this once taboo area? When researchers keep themselves separate from suffering, might not its structural differentiation remain less visible – even to those who view social structure as the salient level of analysis? Rather than juxtaposing micro empirical studies against macro theoretical perspectives, we can aim for greater integration of levels of analysis. We can use grounded theory methods to move from studying assaults on the lifeworld to studying lifeworlds that assault those who are mired in them.

Acknowledgements

Thanks are due to Graham Scambler and Sasha Scambler for their invitation to contribute to the volume. I appreciate the comments on an earlier version of this chapter from Lianna Hart and from members of the Sonoma State University Faculty Writing Program: Christina Baker, Noel Byrne, James Dean, Diana Grant, Melinda Milligan, Tom Rosin, Richard Senghas and Gisela Wendling. I also thank Tina Balderamma, Lianna Hart and Kristine Snyder for seeking relevant articles during the early stages of writing this chapter.

Notes

1. These two forms of assaults on the lifeworld may partially converge. The effects of chronic illness may reverberate through people's lives, cause identity upheaval and result in poverty, particularly in societies that lack a safety net. Such convergence is only partial because people's prior situation and knowledge affect how they view and handle having a chronic illness and disability. Possessing organizational savvy, for example, can give well-educated patients advantages in negotiating their medical care.

2. Criteria for a qualitative dissertation or study have shifted downward over the past 40 years. As a result, many qualitative researchers have conducted tiny studies, some of which purport to use grounded theory methods. I include few of these studies in this review.

3. The nursing profession was the first auxiliary health profession to move to the doctoral level. The School of Nursing at the University of California, San Francisco took an early leading role in training doctoral level nursing educators and researchers. Anselm Strauss joined the School of Nursing and created the Graduate Program in Sociology under its auspices. Many of the early graduate students in nursing learned grounded theory methods from Glaser and/or Strauss and focused their research on people who had chronic or terminal illnesses (see, for example, Davis, 1973; Fagerhaugh, 1975; Quint, 1967; Wilson 1977). Since then, studies of the experience of chronic illness have been an important area in nursing and other health professions, as they, too, initiated doctoral programmes and research agendas.

4. Glaser developed many of the basic grounded theory strategies and was the first in establishing a way of teaching these strategies that emphasized analysing basic processes, core variables and their properties.

5. However, the ways in which researchers conduct coding and memo writing differ. For example, as the method became a general method, researchers often favoured coding and sorting for topics and themes rather searching for actions and processes (Charmaz, 2008a).

6. Not surprisingly, researchers draw the lines distinguishing grounded theory at different points. I view actions 1–5 as evidence of a grounded theory study. Jane Hood (2007) views theoretical sampling as the crucial criterion for grounded theory studies.

7. Ruth Pinder's (1988) chapter, 'Striking Balances: Living with Parkinson's Disease', looks like a grounded theory analysis. She adopts a symbolic interactionist perspective, captures a significant process, takes an insider's view and sees her research participants as active agents. Pinder makes no mention of grounded theory but does say that her concept of balancing derives from Fagerhaugh and Strauss's (1977) grounded theory study of pain management.

8. I agree with Glaser (1992) here that grounded theory is not a verification method; it is a theory construction method. Grounded theory builds explicit checks into the analysis that strengthen the researcher's claims and categories but these checks are not equivalent to verification. The extent and quality of the data in grounded theory studies, however, is a concern. Too many grounded theorists rely on too few and too thin data.

References

Abraham, Laurie Kaye (1993) *Mama Might Be Better Off Dead: The Failure of Health Care in Urban America.* Chicago, IL: University of Chicago Press.
Asbring, Pia and Närvänen, Anna-Lisa (2003) Ideal versus Reality: Physicians Perspectives on Patients with Chronic Fatigue Syndrome (CFS) and Fibromyalgia. *Social Science & Medicine,* 57(4): 711–21.
Atkinson, Paul, Coffey, Amanda and Delamont, Sara (2003) *Key Themes in Qualitative Research: Continuities and Changes.* New York: Rowan and Littlefield.
Auerbach, Carl F., Salick, Elizabeth and Fine, Jacqueline (2006) Using Grounded Theory to Develop Treatment Strategies for Multicontextual Trauma. *Professional Psychology: Research and Practice,* 37(4): 367–73.
Barker, Kristin K. (2006) *The Fibromyalgia Story: Medical Authority and Women's Worlds of Pain.* Philadelphia, PA: Temple University Press.
Benoliel, Jeanne Quint (1975) Childhood Diabetes: The Commonplace in Living Becomes Uncommon. In A. L. Strauss (ed.), *Chronic Illness and the Quality of Life* (pp. 89–98). St. Louis: Mosby.
Berger, Peter and Luckmann, Thomas (1966) *The Social Construction of Reality: A Treatise in the Sociology of Knowledge.* Garden City, NY: Anchor Books.
Bowes, Denise E., Tamlyn, Deborah and Butler, Lorna J. (2002) Women Living with Ovarian Cancer: Dealing with an Early Death. *Health Care for Women International,* 23: 135–48.
Bryant, Antony and Charmaz, Kathy (2007) Introduction. In A. Bryant and K. Charmaz (eds), *Handbook of Grounded Theory* (pp. 1–28). London: Sage.
Bryant, Antony and Charmaz, Kathy (forthcoming) Grounded Theory. In P. Vogt and M. Williams (eds), *Handbook of Methodological Innovations in the Social Sciences.* Los Angeles and London: Sage.
Bury, Michael (1982) Chronic Illness as Disruption. *Sociology of Health & Illness,* 4: 167–82.
Caldwell, Patricia Helen, Arthur, Heather, Natarajan, Madhu, and Anand, Sonia (2007) Fears and Beliefs of Patients Regarding Cardiac Catherization. *Social Science and Medicine* 65(5): 1038–48.
Carricaburu, Danièle and Pierret, Janine (1995) From Biographical Disruption to Biographical Reinforcement: The Case of HIV-Positive Men. *Sociology of Health & Illness,* 17(1): 65–88.
Chamberlayne, Prue and King, Annette (1997) The Biographical Challenge of Caring. *Sociology of Health & Illness,* 19(5): 601–21.
Charmaz, K. (1987) Struggling for a Self: Identity Levels of the Chronically Ill. In P. Conrad and J. A. Roth (eds), *Research in the Sociology of Health Care: The Experience and Management of Chronic Illness,* 6: 283–321. Greenwich, CT: JAI Press.
Charmaz, Kathy (1991) *Good Days, Bad Days: The Self in Chronic Illness and Time.* New Brunswick, NJ: Rutgers University Press.
Charmaz, K. (1994a) Discoveries of Self in Illness. In M. L. Dietz, R. Prus and W. Shaffir (eds), *Doing Everyday Life: Ethnography as Human Lived Experience* (pp. 226–42). Mississauga, Ontario: Copp Clark, Longman.
Charmaz, Kathy (1994b) Identity Dilemmas of Chronically Ill Men. *The Sociological Quarterly,* 35: 269–88.

Charmaz, Kathy (1999a) From the 'Sick Role' to Stories of Self: Understanding the Self in Illness. In Richard D. Ashmore and Richard A. Contrada (eds), *Self and Identity, Vol. 2: Interdisciplinary Explorations in Physical Health* (pp. 209–39). New York: Oxford University Press.

Charmaz, Kathy (1999b) Stories of Suffering: Subjects' Tales and Research Narratives. *Qualitative Health Research*, 9: 369–82.

Charmaz, Kathy (2000a) Grounded Theory Methodology: Objectivist and Constructivist Qualitative Methods. In Norman K. Denzin and Yvonna E. Lincoln (eds), *Handbook of Qualitative Research 2nd ed* (pp. 509–35). Thousand Oaks, CA: Sage.

Charmaz, Kathy (2000b) Experiencing Chronic Illness. In G. L. Albrect, R. Fitzpatrick and S. C. Scrimshaw (eds), *Handbook of Social Studies in Health & Medicine* (pp. 277–92). Thousand Oaks, CA: Sage.

Charmaz, Kathy (2002) The Self as Habit: The Reconstruction of Self in Chronic Illness. *The Occupational Therapy Journal of Research*, 22(Supplement 1): 31s–42s.

Charmaz, Kathy (2005) Grounded Theory in the 21st Century: Applications for Advancing Social Justice Studies. In N. K. Denzin and Y. E. Lincoln (eds), *Handbook of Qualitative Research 3rd ed.* (pp. 507–35). Thousand Oaks, CA: Sage.

Charmaz, Kathy (2006) *Constructing Grounded Theory: A Practical Guide through Qualitative Analysis.* London: Sage.

Charmaz, Kathy (2007) Constructionism and the Grounded Theory Method. In J. A. Holstein and J. F. Gubrium (eds), *Handbook of Constructionist Research* (pp. 397–412). New York: Guilford.

Charmaz, Kathy (2008a) Grounded Theory as an Emergent Method. In S. Hesse-Biber and P. Leavy (eds), *The Handbook of Emergent Methods* (pp. 155–70). New York: Guilford.

Charmaz, Kathy (2008b) Reconstructing Grounded Theory. In L. Bickman, P. Alasuutari and J. Brannen (eds), *Handbook of Social Research* (pp. 461–78). London: Sage.

Charmaz, Kathy (2008c) Views from the Margins: Voices, Silences, and Suffering. *Qualitative Research in Psychology*, 5(1): 7–18.

Charmaz, Kathy (2009) Shifting the Grounds: Constructivist Grounded Theory Methods for the Twenty-First Century. In Janice Morse, Phyllis Stern, Juliet Corbin, Barbara Bowers, Kathy Charmaz and Adele Clarke (eds), *Developing Grounded Theory: The Second Generation* (pp. 127–54). Walnut Creek, CA: Left Coast Press.

Charmaz, Kathy and Rosenfeld, Dana (2006) Reflections of the Body, Images of Self: Visibility and Invisibility in Chronic Illness and Disability. In D. D. Waskul and P. Vannini (eds), *Body/Embodiment: Symbolic Interaction and the Sociology of the Body* (pp. 35–50). London: Ashgate.

Charmaz, Kathy and Rosenfeld, Dana (forthcoming) Chronic Illness. In W. C. Cockerham (ed.), *The New Companion to Medical Sociology.* London: Blackwell.

Ciambrone, Desirée (2007) Illness and Other Assaults on Self: The Relative Impact of HIV/AIDS on Women's Lives. *Sociology of Health & Illness*, 23 (4): 517–40.

Clarke, Adele E. (2005) *Situational Analysis: Grounded Theory after the Postmodern Turn.* Thousand Oaks, CA: Sage.

Clarke, Adele E. (2006) Feminisms, Grounded Theory, and Situational Analysis. In S. Hess-Biber and D. Leckenby (eds), *Handbook of Feminist Research Methods* (pp. 345–70). Thousand Oaks, CA: Sage.

Clarke, Adele E. and Friese, Carrie (2007) Grounded Theorizing: Using Situational Analysis. In A. Bryant and K. Charmaz (eds), *The Handbook of Grounded Theory* (pp. 363–97). London: Sage.

Clarke, Adele E., Fishman, Jennifer, Fosket, Jennifer, Mamo, Laura and Shim, Janet (2003) Biomedicalization: Technoscientific Transformations of Health, Illness, and U.S. Biomedicine. *American Sociological Review*, 68(April): 161–94.

Clarke, Juanne N. and James, Susan (2003) The Radicalized Self: The Impact on the Self of the Contested Nature of the Diagnosis of Chronic Fatigue Syndrome. *Social Science & Medicine*, 57: 1387–95.

Conrad, Peter. (1987) The Experience of Illness: Recent and New Directions. In J. A. Roth and P. Conrad (eds), *Research in the Sociology of Health Care: The Experience and Management of Chronic Illness*, 6: 1–32. Greenwich, CT: JAI Press.

Corbin, Juliet M. and Anselm Strauss (1984) Collaboration: Couples Working Together to Manage Chronic Illness. *Image*, 4: 109–15.

Corbin, Juliet M. and Anselm Strauss (1985) Managing Chronic Illness at Home: Three Lines of Work. *Qualitative Sociology*, 8: 224–47.

Corbin, Juliet M. and Anselm Strauss (1987) Accompaniments of Chronic Illness: Changes in Body, Self, Biography and Biographical Time. *Research in the Sociology of Health Care: The Experience and Management of Chronic Illness*, 6: 249–81. Greenwich, CT: JAI Press.

Corbin, Juliet M. and Anselm Strauss (1988) *Unending Work and Care: Managing Chronic Illness at Home.* San Francisco, CA: Jossey-Bass.

Corbin, Juliet M. and Anselm Strauss (2007) *Basics of Qualitative Research 3rd. ed.* Los Angeles, CA: Sage.

Davis, Fred (1963) *Passage Through Crisis: Polio Victims and Their Families.* Indianapolis, IN: Bobbs-Merrill.

Davis, Fred (1972/1956) Definitions of Time and Recovery in Paralytic Polio Convalescence. In Fred Davis (ed.), *Illness, Interaction and the Self* (pp. 83–91). Belmont, CA: Wadsworth.

Davis, Marcella z. (1973) *Living with Multiple sclerosis: A Social Psychological Analysis.* Springfield, IL: Thomas.

Drummond, Neil (2000) Quality of Life with Asthma: The Existential and the Aesthetic. *Sociology of Health and Illness*, 22(2): 235–53.

Dumit, Joseph (2006) Illnesses You Have to Fight to Get: Facts as Forces in Uncertain, Emergent Illnesses. *Social Science & Medicine*, 62(3): 577–590.

Ezzy, Douglas (2000) Illness Narratives: Time, Hope and HIV. *Social Science and Medicine*, 50: 605–17.

Fagerhaugh, Shizuko (1975) Getting Around with Emphysema. In A. L. Strauss (ed.), *Chronic Illness and the Quality of Life* (pp. 99–107). St. Louis: Mosby.

Fagerhaugh, Shizuko Y. and Strauss, Anselm L. (1977) *The Politics of Pain Management.* Reading, MA: Addison-Wesley.

Fine, Gary A. (1995) *The Second Chicago School? The Development of a Postwar American Sociology.* Chicago, IL: University of Chicago Press.

Foote-Ardah, Carrie E. (2003) The Meaning of Complementary and Alternative Medicine Practices among People with HIV in the United States: Strategies for Managing Everyday Life. *Sociology of Health & Illness*, 25(5): 481–500.

Frank, Arthur W. (1991) *At the Will of the Body*. Boston, MA: Houghton Mifflin.
Frank, Arthur W. (1995) *The Wounded Story-teller*. Chicago, IL: University of Chicago Press.
Gallagher, Eugene B. (1976) Lines of Reconstruction and Extension in the Parsonian Sociology of Illness. *Social Science & Medicine,* 10: 207–18.
Gerhardt, Uta and Marianne Brieskorn-Zinke (1986) The Normalization of Hemodialysis at Home. In J. A. Roth and S. B. Ruzek (eds), *Research in the Sociology of Health Care: The Adoption and Social Consequences of Medical Technologies,* 4: 271–317. Greenwich, CT: JAI.
Glaser, Barney G. (1978) *Theoretical Sensitivity,* Mill Valley, CA: Sociology Press.
Glaser, Barney G. (1992) *Basics of Grounded Theory: Emergence vs. Forcing,* Mill Valley, CA: Sociology Press.
Glaser, Barney G. (1998) *Doing Grounded Theory: Issues and Discussions,* Mill Valley, CA: Sociology Press.
Glaser, Barney G. (2001) *The Grounded Theory Perspective: Conceptualization Contrasted with Description,* Mill Valley, CA: Sociology Press.
Glaser, Barney G. (2003) *The Grounded Theory Perspective II: Description's Remodeling of Grounded Theory Methodology.* Mill Valley, CA: Sociology Press.
Glaser, Barney G. and Strauss, Anselm L. (1965) *Awareness of Dying,* Chicago, IL: Aldine.
Glaser, Barney G. and Strauss, Anselm L. (1967) *The Discovery of Grounded Theory: Strategies for Qualitative Research,* Chicago, IL: Aldine.
Glaser, Barney G. and Strauss, Anselm L. (1968) *Time for Dying,* Chicago, IL: Aldine.
Goffman, Erving (1961) *Asylums*. Garden City, NY: Doubleday Anchor Books.
Goffman, Erving (1963) *Stigma*. Englewood Cliffs, NJ: Prentice-Hall.
Goldsmith, Daena J., Lindholm, Kristin A. and Bute, Jennifer J. (2006) Dilemmas of Talking about Lifestyle Changes among Couples Coping with a Cardiac Arrest. *Social Science & Medicine,* 63: 2079–90.
Hansen, Emily C., Walters, Julia and Baker, Richard Wood (2007) Explaining Chronic Obstructive Pulmonary Disease (COPD): Perceptions of the Role Played by Smoking. *Sociology of Health & Illness,* 29(5): 730–49.
Hernandez, Brigida (2005) A Voice in the Chorus: Perspectives of Young Men of Color on their Disabilities, Identities, and Peer-mentors. *Disability and Society*: 20(2): 117–33.
Hinojosa, Ramon, Boylstein, Craig, Rittman, Maude, Hinojosa, Melanie Sberna and Faircloth, Christopher A. (2008) Constructions of Continuity after a Stroke. *Symbolic Interaction,* 31(2): 205–24.
Hood, Jane (2007) Orthodoxy vs. Power: The Defining Traits of Grounded Theory. In A. Bryant and K. Charmaz (eds), *Handbook of Grounded Theory* (pp. 1–28). London: Sage.
Johnson, Joy L. (1991) Learning to Live Again: The Process of Adjustment Following a Heart Attack. In J. M. Morse and J. L. Johnson (eds), *The Illness Experience: Dimensions of Suffering* (pp. 13–88). Newbury Park, CA: Sage.
Kaiser, Karen (2008) The Meaning of the Survivor Identity for Women with Breast Cancer. *Social Science & Medicine,* 67: 79–87.
Kelleher, David (1988) *Diabetes*. London: Routledge.
Kenen, Regina, Ardern-Jones, Audrey and Eeles, Rosalind (2007) Family Stories and the Use of Heuristics: Women from Suspected Hereditary Breast

and Ovarian Cancer (HBOC) Families. *Sociology of Health & Illness,* 25(7): 838–65.

Kroll-Smith, J. Stephen (1997) *Bodies in Protest: Environmental Illness and the Struggle over Medical Knowledge.* New York: New York University Press.

Lawton, Julia, Peel, Elizabeth, Parry, Odette and Douglas, Margaret (2008) Shifting Accountability: A Longitudinal Qualitative Study of Diabetic Causation Accounts. *Social Science & Medicine,* 67: 47–56.

Lillrank, Annika (2003) Back Pain and the Resolution of Diagnostic Uncertainty in Illness Narratives. *Social Science & Medicine,* 57: 1045–54.

Lonardi, Cristina (2007) The Passing Dilemma in Socially Invisible Diseases: Narratives on ChronicHeadache. *Social Science & Medicine,* 65(8): 1619–29.

Mathieson, Cynthia and Stam, Henrik (1995) Renegotiating Identity: Cancer Narratives. *Sociology of Health & Illness,* 17(3): 283–306.

Mead, George H. (1934) *Mind, Self and Society.* Chicago: University of Chicago Press.

Meyer, Geralyn A. (2002) The Art of Watching Out: Vigilance in Women Who Have Migraine Headaches. *Qualitative Health Research,* 12(9): 1220–34.

Mishler, Elliot G. (1981) The Social Construction of Illness. In E. G. Mishler, L. R. AmaraSingham, S. T. Hauser, R. Liem, S. D. Osherson and N. Waxler, *Social Contexts of Health, Illness & Patient Care* (pp. 141–68). New York: Cambridge University Press.

Mitteness, Linda S. (1987a) The Management of Urinary Incontinence by Community-living Elderly. *The Gerontologist,* 27: 185–97.

Mitteness, Linda S. (1987b) So What Do You Expect When You're 85?: Urinary Incontinence in Late Life. In J. A. Roth and P. Conrad (eds), *Research in the Sociology of Health Care: The Experience and Management of Chronic Illness,* 6: 1–32. Greenwich, CT: JAI Press.

Moore, Dena L. (2005) Expanding the View: The Lives of Women with Severe Work Disabilities in Context. *Journal of Counseling & Development,* 83: 343–8.

Nack, Adina (2008) *Damaged Goods? Women Living with Incurable Sexually Transmitted Diseases.* Philadelphia, PA: Temple University Press.

Nettleton, Sara (2006) 'I Just Want Permission to Be Ill': Toward a Sociology of Medically Unexplained Symptoms. *Social Science & Medicine,* 62: 1167–78.

Nettleton, S., O'Malley, L., Watt, I. and Duffey, P. (2004) Enigmatic Illness: Narratives of Patients Who Live with Medically Unexplained Symptoms. *Social Theory & Health,* 2: 47–66.

Parsons, Talcott (1953) *The Social System.* Glencoe, IL: Free Press.

Peyrot, Mark, McMurray, James F. and Hedges, Richard (1987) Living with Diabetes: The Role of Personal and Professional Knowledge in Symptom and Regimen Management. *Research in the Sociology of Health Care: The Experience and Management of Chronic Illness,* 6: 107–46. Greenwich, CT: JAI Press.

Peyrot, Mark, McMurray, James F. and Hedges, Richard (1988) Marital Adjustment to Adult Diabetes; Interpersonal Congruence and Spouse Satisfaction. *Journal of Marriage & the Family,* 50(2): 363–76.

Pierret, Janine (2007) An Analysis over Time (1990–2000) of the Experiences of Living with HIV. *Social Science and Medicine* 65:1595–605.

Pinder, Ruth (1988) Striking Balances: Living with Parkinson's Disease. In R. Anderson and M. Bury (eds), *Living with Chronic Illness: The Experience of Patients and Their Families* (pp. 67–88). London: Unwin Hyman.

Pound, Pandora, Gompertz, Patrick and Ebrahim, Shah (1998) *Sociology of Health & Illness*, 20(4): 489–506.

Quint, Jeanne C. (1965) Institutionalized Practices of Information Control. *Psychiatry*, 28(May): 119–32.

Quint, Jeanne C. (1967) *The Nurse and the Dying Patient*. New York: Macmillan.

Radley, Alan (1989) Style, Discourse and Constraint in Adjustment to Chronic Illness. *Sociology of Health & Illness*, 11: 230–52.

Reif, Laura (1975) Ulcerative Colitis: Strategies for Managing Life. In Anselm L. Strauss (ed.), *Chronic Illness and the Quality of Life* (pp. 81–8). St. Louis: Mosby.

Rier, David (2007) Internet Social Support Groups as Moral Agents: The Ethical Dynamics of HIV+ Status Disclosure. *Sociology of Health & Illness*, 29(7): 1–16.

Riessman, Catherine K. (1990) Strategic Uses of Narrative in the Presentation of Self and Illness: A Research Note. *Social Science & Medicine*, 30: 1195–200.

Roberts, Brian (2004) Health Narratives, Time Perspectives and Self-images. *Social Theory & Health*, 2: 170–83.

Roth, Julius A. (1963) *Timetables: Structuring the Passage of Time in Hospital Treatment and Other Careers*. Indianapolis, IN: Bobbs-Merrill.

Salander, Pär (2002) Bad News from the Patient's Perspective: An Analysis of the Written Narratives of Newly Diagnosed Cancer Patients. *Social Science & Medicine*, 55: 721–32.

Sanders, Caroline, Donovan, Jenny and Dieppe, Paul (2002) The Significance and Consequences of Having Painful and Disabled Joints in Older Age: Co-existing Accounts of Normal and Disrupted Biographies. *Sociology of Health and Illness*, 24(2): 227–53.

Sandstrom, Kent L. (1990) Confronting Deadly Disease: The Drama of Identity Construction among Gay Men with AIDS. *Journal of Contemporary Ethnography*, 19: 271–94.

Scambler, Graham (1984) Perceiving and Coping with Stigmatizing Illness. In Ray Fitzpatrick, John Hinton, Stanton Newman, Graham Scambler and James Thompson (eds), *The Experience of Illness* (pp. 203–26). London: Tavistock.

Scambler, Graham and Hopkins, Anthony (1986) Being Epileptic: Coming to Terms with Stigma. *Sociology of Health & Illness*, 8(1): 26–43.

Scheper-Hughes, Nancy (1992) *Death without Weeping: The Violence of Everyday Life in Brazil*. Berkeley, CA: University of California Press.

Schlesinger, Lynn (1996) Chronic Pain, Intimacy, and Sexuality: A Qualitative Study of Women Who Live with Pain. *Journal of Sex Research*, 33(3): 249–56.

Schneider, Joseph W. and Conrad, Peter (1980) In the Closet with Illness: Epilepsy, Stigma Potential and Information Control. *Social Problems*, 28(1): 32–44.

Schneider, Joseph W. and Conrad, Peter (1983) *Having Epilepsy*. Philadelphia, PA: Temple University Press.

Schoenberg, Nancy E., Peters, Jane C. and Drew, Elaine M. (2003) Unraveling the Mysteries of Timing: Women's Perceptions about Time to Treatment for Cardiac Symptoms. *Social Science & Medicine*, 56: 271–84.

Schutz, Alfred (1970) *On Phenomenology and Social Relations: Selected Writings*. Chicago, IL: University of Chicago Press.

Silverman, David (2007) *A Very Short, Fairly Interesting and Reasonably Cheap Book about Qualitative Research*. London: Sage.

Somerville, Claire, Featherstone, Katie, Hemingway, Harry, Timmis, Adam and Feder, Gene Solomon (2008) Performing Stable Angina Pectoris: An Ethnographic Study. *Social Science & Medicine,* 66: 1497–508.

Stockl, Andrea (2007) Complex Syndromes, Ambivalent Diagnosis, and Existential Uncertainty: The Case of Systemic Lupus Erythematosus (SLE). *Social Science & Medicine,* 65(8): 1549–59.

Strauss, Anselm L. (1975) *Chronic Illness and the Quality of Life.* St. Louis: Mosby.

Strauss, Anselm L., Juliet Corbin, Shizuko Fagerhaugh, Barney G. Glaser, David Maines, Barbara Suczek and Carolyn L. Wiener (1984) *Chronic Illness and the Quality of Life,* 2nd ed., St. Louis: Mosby.

Strauss, Anselm and Juliet Corbin (1990) *Basics of Qualitative Research.* Newbury Park, CA: Sage.

Strauss, Anselm and Juliet Corbin (1998) *Basics of Qualitative Research: Grounded Theory Procedures and Techniques, 2nd ed.* Thousand Oaks, CA: Sage.

Suczek, Barbara (1975) Chronic Renal Failure and the Problem of Funding. In A.L. Strauss (ed.), *Chronic Illness and the Quality of Life* (pp. 108–18). St. Louis: Mosby.

Swahnberg, Katarina, Thapar-Björkert, Suruchi and Berterö, Carina (2007) Nullified: Women's Perceptions of Being Abused in Health Care. *Journal of Psychosomatic Obstetrics & Gynecology,* 28(3): 161–7.

Timmermans, Stefan and Freidin, Betina (2007) Caretaking as Articulation Work: The Effects of Taking up Responsibility for a Child with Asthma on Labor Force Participation. *Social Science & Medicine,* 65(7): 1351–63.

Twaddle, A. C. (1969) Health Decisions and Sick Role Variations: An Exploration. *Journal of Health and Social Behavior,* 10(2): 105–15.

Wiener, Carolyn L. (1984) The Burden of Rheumatoid Arthritis. In A. L. Strauss (ed.), *Chronic Illness and the Quality of Life, 2nd ed.* (pp. 88–98). St. Louis: Mosby.

Williams, Clare (2000) Alert Assistants in Managing Chronic Illness: The Case of Mothers and Teen-age Sons. *Sociology of Health & Illness,* 22: 254–72.

Williams, Clare (2002) *Mothers, Young People and Chronic Illness.* Aldershot, England, Ashgate.

Williams, Gareth (1984) The Genesis of Chronic Illness: Narrative Reconstruction. *Sociology of Health & Illness,* 6: 175–200.

Wilson, Holly Skodol (1977) Limited Intrusion: Social Control of Outsiders in a Healing Community. *Nursing Research,* 26: 105–11.

Wilson, Kate and Luker, Karen A. (2006) At Home in Hospital? Interaction and Stigma in People Affected by Cancer. *Social Science & Medicine,* 62: 1616–27.

Wilson, Patricia M., Kendall, Sally and Brooks, Fiona (2007) The Expert Patients Programme: A Paradox of Patient Empowerment and Medical Dominance. *Health and Social Care in the Community,* 15(5): 426–38.

Young, Bridget, Dixon-Woods, Mary, Findlay, Michelle and Heney, David (2002) Parenting in a Crisis: Conceptualising Mothers of Children with Cancer. *Social Science & Medicine,* 55: 1835–47.

3
Medical Sociology and Disability Theory

Carol Thomas

Disablism: refers to the *social* imposition of *avoidable restrictions* on the life activities, aspirations and psycho-emotional well-being of people categorized as 'impaired' by those deemed 'normal'. Disablism is *social-relational* in character and constitutes a form of *social oppression* in contemporary society – alongside sexism, racism, ageism and homophobia. In addition to being enacted in person-to-person interactions, disablism may manifest itself in institutionalized and other socio-structural forms.[1]

Impairment effects: the *direct and unavoidable* impacts that impairments (physical, sensory, intellectual) have on individuals' embodied functioning in the social world. Impairments and impairment effects are always biosocial in character, and may occur at any stage in the life course.[2]

Introduction

As the twentieth century passed its mid-point, populations in the West became increasingly familiar with survivorship associated with chronic disease, traumatic injury and birth 'defects'. As a consequence, impaired family members of any age, but particularly those of third-generation status, made their presence felt in most family structures and community profiles. Survivorship after premature birth and medical diagnoses such as foetal abnormality, heart disease, stroke or cystic fibrosis became relatively commonplace, later joined by extended lifespans associated with more medically challenging neurological and oncology conditions. In the UK, both late twentieth-century *advances in medicine* and government legislation designed to *deinstitutionalize* diverse groups of so-called care-dependent adults and children led to the enhanced public appearance of people living with impairment effects.[3]

This chapter reviews the engagement of two contrasting sociological disciplines with these phenomena: medical sociology[4] and disability studies[5]. These disciplines have been at loggerheads on *the disability question* from the 1980s to the present; the British academy continues to host a rather acrimonious disciplinary divide (Barnes and Mercer, 1997). I declare my allegiance from the start: I lean heavily towards disability studies in my academic work, but, unusually, have had a foot in both camps for more than a decade (see for example, Thomas, 1999). From this vantage point, I have long held the desire to see medical sociologists take the scholarship advanced in disability studies more seriously, and to reconsider the use of ideas that I perceive to be medico-centric and disablist. This was the inspiration behind the writing of my book *Sociologies of Disability and Illness. Contested Ideas in Disability Studies and Medical Sociology* (Thomas, 2007). This chapter picks up the line of argument presented there.

We start by considering the development of ideas about disability and chronic illness in each discipline in turn, then discuss recent changes in approach to these topics and consider whether a *sociology of disablism and impairment effects* might enable scholars in disability studies and medical sociology to cross disciplinary boundaries and work together.

Medical sociology

As chronic illness burgeoned in the twentieth century, it is not surprising that sociologists were drawn to medical sociology from the 1950s. This led, eventually, to the crystallization of a specialist field of sociological scholarship in the US, Europe and other resource-rich regions. Following Talcott Parson's seminal writing on medicine's role in sustaining the functional integrity of *The Social System* (Parsons, 1951), several generations of medical sociologists have studied chronic physical and 'mental' illnesses as matters of social deviance. Indeed, I have argued that a *social deviance paradigm* has remained a remarkably persistent feature of medical sociology for the six decades of its existence. This deviancy paradigm has harboured and nurtured a rich variety of theoretical perspectives applied to the study of long-standing illness and disability. These perspectives, or theoretical groupings, are commonly referred to using the following collective headings: functionalism, interpretative and ethnomethodological theories, conflict-theories and post-structuralism (Gerhardt, 1989; Thomas, 2007).

Moreover, it can be observed that sociologists' long-standing social deviancy conceptualization of chronic illness and disability is the mirror image of modern medicine's *abnormality* and *pathology* under-standing of defective bodily states. Bryan S. Turner noted that both medicine and sociology have dissected abnormality – one biologically and the other socially – with a post-Enlightenment enthusiasm for dif-ferentiating the normal from the abnormal (Turner, 1987). This led him to suggest, contrary to standard genealogical accounts, that sociology itself may be closely bound up with the development of medicine:

> ... my argument considers Foucault's comment that sociology had its origins in nineteenth-century medical practices (in particular med-ical surveys), that sociology and medicine are inextricably linked together, and finally that modern medicine is in fact applied soci-ology, and sociology is applied medicine. (Turner, 1987: 5)

Having made these generalized comments, it is important to distin-guish between the ideas about illness and disability as deviance associ-ated with the different theoretical traditions deployed and to recognize the contrasting moral and political stances taken by the advocates of these traditions. That is, by no means have all medical sociologists advanced medico-centric and normative ideas about chronic illness and disability. Some have *taken the side* of those constituted 'deviant', and come close to naming particular social experiences as examples of dis-ablism (for example, Blaxter, 1976; Goffman,1968; Scott, 1969; Sparkes and Smith, 2003; Williams, 2001).

The medico-centric crown belongs to Parsons' formative structural functionalism; he believed that both acute and chronic illness posed a serious destabilizing threat to society's equilibrium, representing a type of social pathology that should rightly be controlled and regulated by the medical profession (Parsons, 1951; Williams, 2005). Indeed, in Parsonian thinking, the purported unconscious motivations of people to opt out of their social responsibilities by claiming to be seriously ill should be kept continually in check – if not by individuals' own superegos then by stronger external social forces (Gerhardt, 1989).

The *siding with the other* conceptual break came in the 1960s when some American symbolic integrationists began to focus a critical socio-logical lens upon the *social reactions* that designated the particular behaviours and attributes of individuals and groups as 'deviant'. These labelling and other interpretative sociologists – Erving Goffman (1961, 1968) being the most significant for medical sociology – documented the degrading and dehumanizing consequences for 'deviants' catego-rized as 'mentally ill' or 'physically abnormal' through the detailed study of their day-to-day lives. In Britain in the 1980s, a less hard-edged version of interactionist theory laid the foundations for an influential interpretative *sociology of chronic illness and disability*, whose advocates continue to display, in the main, a genuine commitment to understanding and improving the lives of 'sufferers' and their families. Michael Bury's work on *biographical disruption* and *illness management* stands out here (Bury, 1982, 1991) as does Kathy Charmaz's (1983) research on *loss of self* and Graham Scambler's scholarship on *felt stigma*. It is this softer-edged version of interactionist theory that is of particular relevance in this chapter (Anderson and Bury, 1988; Kelly and Field, 2004). Note, in contemporary society both self-identity and ascribed identity are caught up in a complex mix of continuity and change instigated by chronic illness (see also Kelleher and Leavey, 2004).

Less needs to be said here about 'conflict theorists' – a loose mix of Marxists, political economists, critical social epidemiologists, socialist feminists and critical realists. From the 1970s, their ideas have had sustained resonance and relevance in medical sociology (Thomas, 2007). The key point to make is that these perspectives kept alive the 'illness as deviance' mantra – but, once again, theorists and researchers have sided unequivocally with 'deviant groups', especially the socio-economically excluded. Of particular note is that macro-sociological frames of reference have been employed to examine the health-damaging power of capitalist economics and state institutions – including their medical manifestations.

Turning to post-structuralist writers, so popular in the 1990s and 2000s, we find that the *illness as social deviance paradigm* has been infused with fresh vigour. Michael Foucault's name reigns supreme in this connection. Alongside criminality, illness has assumed pride of place in a philosophically driven sociology focused on the social processes involved in the discursive construction and regulation of social deviance. Indeed, in the age of *biopower*, medical discursive practices define normality and abnormality and exert a supreme disciplinary and regulatory force upon 'the body'. However, medical sociologists in this tradition have almost entirely ignored *chronic illness and disability*. And whatever the 'radical' moral pretensions of post-structuralist medical sociology, and its championing of 'the sociology of the body', it has been left to scholars in disability studies to take up the post-structuralist challenge.

Meanwhile, in North America, disability activism and scholarship were beginning to make inroads into the social sciences *and* the humanities. Of particular interest here is the road travelled by Irving K. Zola, known internationally in the academy for his seminal work in medical sociology (Zola, 1966, 1972, 1973). Although Zola was a visibly impaired person, he did not begin to write about disability until he embraced the topic personally and politically in the 1980s (see Williams, 1996). Then he set about writing analytically and autobiographically about the social position of disabled people, switching to the language of social oppression rather than social deviance (Zola, 1982, 1991, 1994).

Disability studies

Just when British medical sociologists were secure and comfortable in the knowledge that their own *social deviance* approaches to chronic illness and disability held monopolistic sway in late twentieth-century sociology, another sociology of disability began to make its presence felt in the 1980s: *Disability Studies*. Like Feminist Studies, its time had come in the wake of civil rights movements in North America and Europe: a movement *of* rather than *for* disabled people.

No doubt, this emerging sociology of disability had an alien and rather uncomfortable feel about it for mainstream medical sociologists in Britain: it was angry, politically charged, materialist and – most notably – articulated by disabled people themselves, or their close non-disabled allies. There was talk, from the start, of *social oppression* rather than social deviance (Hunt, 1966); indeed, ideas that constructed disabled people as deviant were deemed a legacy of the oppressive status quo. A *social oppression paradigm* began to take shape, with the concept *disablism* joining 'racism' and 'sexism'; and chronic illness could be viewed as a category of impairment.

Two wheelchair users, Vik Finkelstein and Michael Oliver, made an early appearance on the academic scene, though their activist roles in expanding the Disabled People's Movement (DPM) always took priority. Finkelstein had forged ideas about disablism with Paul Hunt (1966) and other pioneering activists in UPIAS[6] (1976); Oliver had picked these up and formulated them in a powerfully simplified form known as *the social model of disability* (Oliver, 1983). Finkelstein developed an innovative Open University course in the late 1970s, 'The Handicapped Person in the Community', and Oliver made an impact with his book *The Politics of Disablement* (1990). As most medical sociologists know, the *Social Model of Disability* became the rallying cry and organizing principle of Disability Studies and the DPM:

> In the broadest sense, the social model of disability is about nothing more complicated than a clear focus on the economic, environmental

and cultural barriers encountered by people who are viewed by others as having some form of impairment – whether physical, mental or intellectual. The barriers disabled people encounter include inaccessible education systems, working environments, inadequate disability benefits, discriminatory health and social support services, inaccessible transport, houses and public buildings and amenities, and the devaluing of disabled people through negative images in the media – films, television, and newspapers. (Oliver, 2004: 21)

What is less appreciated is how fast disability studies' influence spread in the university sector in the 1990s under the direction of Colin Barnes (1991, 1996; Barnes and Mercer 1996, 1997; Barnes et al., 1999, 2002; Oliver and Barnes, 1998), Len Barton (1996), and John Swain and Sally French (Swain, French and Cameron, 2003; French, 1994), Paul Abberley (2002), Alan Roulstone (1998), and Jan Walmsley (1993), among others. The ideas of disabled feminist activists and academics took hold too, for example, the arguments and analyses introduced by Jenny Morris (1991, 1996), Mairian Corker (1998, Corker and Shakespeare, 2002), and myself (Thomas, 1999). The volume, range and intellectual sophistication of ideas about disability and disablism that now exists demonstrates that disability studies in the UK, and overseas, have achieved a great deal in a short space of time – retaining, throughout, its commitment to advancing disabled people's social inclusion and citizenship rights.

As in any vibrant academic discipline, debates and arguments about how to take the social oppression paradigm forward have thrived, with contrasting paths taken by materialist, post-structuralist, phenomenological and feminist writers (Barnes, Oliver and Barton, 2002; Priestley 2001, 2003; Thomas, 2007). Ideas about the social manifestation of social oppression and exclusion have ranged from the obvious to the subtle, in line with Iris Marion Young's (1990: 41) generalized understanding of social oppression today:

In [an] extended structural sense oppression refers to the vast and deep injustices some groups suffer as a consequence of often unconscious assumptions and reactions of well-meaning people in ordinary interactions, media and cultural stereotypes, and structural features of bureaucratic hierarchies and market mechanisms – in short, the normal processes of everyday life. We cannot eliminate this structural oppression by getting rid of the rulers or making some new laws, because oppressions are systematically reproduced in major economic, political, and cultural institutions.

Materialist scholars, for example, have theorized disability and disablism as outcomes of the way fundamental social activities are organized – especially, but not exclusively, activities in the economic domain in the early and late capitalist eras. This means that the roots of the social marginalization and spatial segregation of people with impairments are located in the historical development of industrialist capitalist commodity production and exchange (Finkelstein, 1980; Gleeson, 1999; Oliver, 1990). These socio-economic developments gave rise – via early biomedicine and post-Enlightenment forms of political governorship – to social relationships between 'the normal' and 'the impaired' that systematically disempowered and excluded the latter. The foundations were laid for medicalized systems of 'treatment and care' that subjected disabled people to professional control and enforced dependency, first in institutional regimes and later in systems of 'community care'. This gave rise to demands for alternatives to 'care', particularly arrangements for *independent living* and non-oppressive social support. Materialist perspectives served to unleash a great deal of empirical research detailing the *contemporary* social exclusion of disabled people in all social arenas, including employment, housing, education, welfare, health care, leisure and political citizenship (for references, see Swain, French and Cameron, 2003). There has been sensitivity, however, to the charge that the materialist approach ignores or attaches insufficient significance to the role that cultural practices play in shaping disablism. The response has been to insist that attitudes, discourses and ideological representations are critical to disablism, though there is a certainty that these are materialized through the social practices required to meet basic needs.

This acknowledgement of the significance of the cultural has not satisfied those in disability studies who have supported the 'cultural turn' in the social sciences in recent decades. These writers have found post-structuralist theoretical perspectives – particularly Foucauldian, feminist and postcolonial variants – to be of much greater interest and utility (Tremain, 2005). The cultural, the discursive, and the linguistic have assumed pre-eminence in post-structuralist theorizations of disability *and* impairment. Some have dismissed materialist perspectives as modernist grand narratives, that is, systems of thought imbued with conceptual dualisms: abnormal/normal or disabled/non-disabled. It follows that fault is found with the social model of disability for its impairment/disability schism. The deconstruction of such binary thinking has come to the forefront, opening doors to new directions of intellectual travel (Corker and Shakespeare, 2002; Tremain, 2005), though some writers have subsequently re-routed into phenomenology for answers to the conceptual puzzles posed by disability and impairment (Hughes, 1999, 2000). However, whatever direction these deconstructionist turns and twists have taken in disability studies, adherents to perspectives that privilege the cultural have almost invariably stated their commitment to the social emancipation of disabled people on *all* fronts.

As a discipline, disability studies have also encouraged cross-cutting theoretical engagements with key sociological themes, such as social identity and the gendered and queered character of disability and disablism. It followed that the intersection of forms of oppression, and the implications for identity politics, required theorization (Price and Shildrick, 1998, 2002; Shildrick and Price, 1996; Shakespeare, 2006; Thomas, 2007). Feminist writers of all theoretical persuasions have led this work, and in so doing have brought to light new dimensions of disablism. For example, the old insistence on the importance of personal experience, and on the need to transcend the personal/private divide, set the stage for research on so-called private matters: on *psycho-emotional disablism*, and on living with impairment and *impairment effects* (Reeve, 2007; Thomas, 1999, 2007).

Sociologies of disability and chronic illness

The intellectual relationship between representatives of British medical sociology and disability studies in the 1980s and 1990s was tense and distant, with occasional *episodes* of outright clash and contestation. Five of these episodes are discussed in some detail in *Sociologies of Disability and Illness Contested Ideas in Disability Studies and Medical Sociology* (Thomas, 2007). The headlines from the disability studies' point of view were: (a) medical sociologists use definitions of disability that are essentially medico-centric, including the one found in the ICIDH[7], and thus understand impairment to be *the cause* of disability (b) in their interpretative research with chronically ill and disabled people, medical sociologists concentrate on individual *suffering* and personal psychosocial *adaptation* to the *socially deviant* status that living with impairment denotes (c) medical sociologists rarely name or analyse the socio-structural or interpersonal manifestations and consequences of *disablism,* and (d) the *agency* of disabled people has been ignored or narrowly channelled towards notions of adjustment to their fate. From the opposite side of the disciplinary divide, medical sociologists argued that: (a) disability studies advocates have seriously underrepresented the degree to which impairments like chronic diseases *really do cause disablement* by restricting activities and fracturing individuals' social identities (b) research and political advocacy in disability studies have concentrated on younger people in the age spectrum – thus ignoring widespread chronic illness and consequent disablement amongst old people (c) taking their lead from Michael Oliver, disability studies' writers present an over-socialized, reductionist and unidimensional picture of disability, and (d) that analyses in disability studies lack theoretical sophistication (see Bury, 1997; Williams, 2000).

Have these entrenched positions altered in the past ten years or so, particularly in light of the rapid growth and intellectual expansion of disability studies? The national policy scene has certainly changed, suggesting that significant gains have been achieved on the part of the disabled people's movement and its supporters (Cabinet Office, 2004). Successive Labour governments have updated and strengthened the Disability Discrimination Act (DDA, 1995, 2005), set up the Office of Disability Issues (ODI), pledged to work towards a society in which disabled people are equal members and have facilitated meaningful moves towards independent living for disabled people in the form of *individual budgets* or other types of *direct payment*. In short, the social *model of disability* appears to have been adopted, and is regularly endorsed, in official policy circles at central governmental levels.[8] Surely, in this context, medical sociologists have changed some of their thinking about the social character of disability and impairment?

Of course, neither discipline is static: both disciplines live and breathe in national and international policy contexts, and rub shoulders with each other and surrounding disciplines as time moves on. So, the question should really be: have medical sociologists begun to accept and adopt features of the social oppression paradigm when they research disability and chronic illness today? Put another way, do they see the need for *a sociology of disablism and impairment effects* (Thomas, 2007: 182)? I suggest that the answer to these questions is definitely 'no', but that there are signs of movement in this direction.

One obvious example of this movement is that Graham Scambler and Sasha Scambler have seen the need for this book, bringing together a collection of influential writers on both sides of the disciplinary divide. Another related example is that Graham Scambler, a founding figure of the interpretative approach to chronic illness and disability in British medical sociology, has critically revisited his 1980s research on living with epilepsy (Scambler, 1984, 1989, 2004). In *Reframing Stigma*, Scambler explains that his influential *hidden distress model of epilepsy*, which drew heavily on Goffman's analysis of social stigma, should be reformulated. This reformulation is needed, he suggests, to address the model's weaknesses, namely that it:

[1] takes as given the epistemic authority of the biomedical perspective; [2] presumes epilepsy to be a 'personal tragedy'; and [3] intimates a form of fateful passivity conventionally associated with 'victimhood'. (Scambler, 2004: 34)

Scambler acknowledges that arguments in disability studies played a role in suggesting that he rethink stigma, leading him to conclude that the reformulation of his model should demonstrate an appreciation of: (i) the structures of social power involved in the designation and social treatment of 'epileptics' and (ii) the possibility that 'epileptics', individually or collectively, could put up resistance to, and escape from, victimhood (ibid.: 35). Scambler is far from unique in recognizing that the disability studies' critique has something to say to medical sociologists. Moreover, I suggest that medical sociologists new to research on *chronic illness and disability* cannot help but note the relevance and richness of the current literature in disability studies.

However, there have also been recent boundary crossings from the other side. Disability writers such as Nick Watson, Bill Hughes, Tom Shakespeare and myself have, in our different ways, made use of perspectives and concepts elaborated by medical sociologists on *identity, the body*, and *suffering and care* to explore living with disablism and impairment effects (Hughes, 1999, 2000; Hughes and Paterson, 1997; Shakespeare, 2006; Watson, 2002). I, for example, have had some influence in disability studies by putting *the psycho-emotional dimensions of disablism* onto the disability studies agenda (Thomas, 1999, 2007). This refers to the harms that non-disabled people can inflict upon disabled children or adults through their words and actions, sometimes well-intentioned: the undermining of self-esteem, confidence, emotional well-being and willingness to take chances in life. The damage, sometimes profound, might be perpetrated directly by parents,[9] teachers, doctors, or others with authority, or might result through the influence of negative representations of disabled individuals in diverse cultural forms – especially on television and in the printed media (Wilde, 2004). These harms, I argued, constitute forms of *disablism* rather than 'private troubles' (Oliver, 1996) or the inevitable consequence of being impaired. The point to make here is that it was medical sociologists' long-standing interest in interpersonal interactions and individuals' social psychology that influenced my thinking, especially Goffman's work on stigma and total institutions (Goffman, 1961, 1968). My interest was in putting the ideas to work within a social oppression rather than a social deviance paradigm. Donna Reeve has recently used Agamben's ideas on *homo sacer* to push this endeavour further, for example, to explain the existential insecurity that is often associated with psycho-emotional disablism, and the latter's direct and indirect forms (Reeve, 2007).

Another instance of my own boundary crossing is associated with the now widely used concept: *impairment effects* (see definition above; Thomas, 1999). I introduced this concept into disability studies in an attempt to give legitimacy to engagements with the *unavoidably* limiting, though often changing, effects that impairments have on bodily actions, functions and feelings. This legitimacy was necessary because disability studies researchers were often hampered by a common assumption that *we do not 'do' impairment* because allegiance to the social model demands that *we split impairment off, and leave it aside*. The social model had, indeed, severed 'being impaired' from 'being disabled' in an attempt to focus attention entirely on disablism (UPIAS, 1976), and leading social modellists such as Mike Oliver (1996) and Colin Barnes (Barnes and Mercer, 1996) were notoriously fierce in their insistence that impairment was absent from their list of topics to pursue in disability studies. My belief in the need to *bring impairment back in* to disability studies, but in a non-threatening fashion, stemmed from collecting life story data through interpretative research with disabled people, particularly women; I found that experiences of disablism and impairment effects were closely intertwined in their lives, particularly in their encounters with non-disabled people and the structures that inhabit the landscapes of 'normal life'. Indeed, disablism could not be properly understood without engaging analytically with impairment effects. Further thought, assisted by mainstream sociological writing on *the body* (particularly Turner, 1984, 1987, 1992, and Williams and Bendelow, 1998), led me to conclude that

[I]n any 'real' social setting, impairments, impairment effects, and disablism are thoroughly intermeshed with the social conditions that bring them into being and give them meaning. The materiality of the body is in a dynamic interrelationship with the social and cultural context in which it is lived. Moreover, the impaired body is changing and dynamic: whether or not the impairment is 'fixed' (chronic illnesses, for example, are usually marked by flux and change); and the body is constantly ageing. The distinctions made between impairment and disability (disablism) cannot, therefore, be mapped onto familiar biological/social or natural/cultural dualisms, nor should impairment be sidelined as an irrelevant category. In my view, this demands of disability studies that it engages in the full theorisation of 'the impaired body' and its relationship with disablism. (Thomas, 1999: 137)

Might such disciplinary shifts and movements in both disciplines presage the development of a much closer disciplinary alliance?

A test case: Living with cancer

One way of exploring whether the disciplinary shifts and movements described could result in a much closer disciplinary alliance is to consider a test case: *cancer*. That is, if the disciplines can work together on the topic of living with cancer then, in my view, a more comprehensive disciplinary alliance might be possible.

Cancer's quality as a test case resides, I suggest, in the fact that, on the whole, neither of the disciplines consider *lives after cancer* to be territory for pursuing analyses of disability or disablism. From a disability studies' point of view, research and theoretical analyses focused on living with cancer and its impairment effects seem to belong to interpretative medical sociologists, that is, to be territory for exploring *suffering, existential crises, symptom management, coping* and either survival and return to normal life trajectories or a move into the realms of end of life care. Put another way, the disability studies social oppression paradigm appears to be relatively marginal in the struggle to defeat cancer. On the other hand, medical sociologists would rarely concede that the study of living with cancer involves the study of disability – for the same reasons: the social dimensions of cancer appear to be overwhelmingly bound up with traditional concerns: *biographical disruption, loss of self* and *felt stigma* – or, for Foucauldians, the exercise of biopower in the cancer clinic. Put another way, medical sociologists apply their *social deviance paradigm* unquestioningly.

But in recent decades, increasing numbers of *cancers* have become chronic diseases resulting in long-term survivorship with disparate impairment effects (Grinyer, 2008). More effective surgical and drug treatments for childhood and adult tumour types have extended life expectancy considerably, though rarely usher in long lives in full health. As Arthur Frank has put it, cancer survivors now inhabit a *remission society* (Frank, 1995). In this new epidemiological context, many cancers have become chronic illnesses, and thus make everyday living vulnerable to disablism. Policy-makers in the UK have recognized this by extending the provisions of the *Disability Discrimination Act* (1995, 2005) to cover the large number of people who have cancer diagnoses – whilst recognizing that most cancer patients find it very hard to think of themselves as 'disabled'. Can academics in disability studies and medical sociology catch up with these changes by revising their thinking on cancer? And are the conditions now ripe for them to work together in the exploration of cancer survivorship, either directly or indirectly? More importantly, could this branch of sociology sit within a broader *sociology of disablism and impairment effects* – my favoured framework (Thomas, 2007)?

Here I must confess to being one of those who have been tardy in linking living with cancer with living with disablism – although I have researched and written in both areas in the past 15 years. On the one hand, in two quite large-scale interview studies that I directed in the early 2000s on the experiences of cancer patients and their close companions I set about the research design and data analysis phases locked into a traditional interpretative medical sociology mindset (Thomas, Morris and Gatrell, 2003; Thomas et al., 2001). At the same time – but on other days of the week, as it were – I switched mindsets to write about disability and disablism using the social oppression paradigm (Thomas, 1999, 2007).

Fortunately, I am now in a position to close this schism: my current project has allowed me to return to the semi-structured interview transcripts generated in the two cancer studies – involving 88 people with cancer diagnoses and 50 of their main informal carers.[10] Today, I see that people who had survived cancer treatments, and their close companions (spouses, offspring, parents or close friends), often spoke of experiences that I now recognize to be encounters with disablism – though use of the words 'disability' or 'disabled' by respondents was very rare indeed. Now, I recognize the relevance of the social oppression paradigm – to be applied *alongside and in combination with* my original preoccupations with impairment effects: physical and psychological suffering, managing the body and identity change. This recognition is explained by a combination of personal academic circumstances: first, obtaining a more sophisticated understanding of disablism (Thomas, 2007), and second, switching to the use of narrative data analysis methods (Mishler, 1999) rather than retain my original cross-sectional thematic approach to the analysis of the interview data (see Thomas, 2008).

The relevance of material and psycho-emotional disablism in the lives of cancer survivors and their close companions can be illustrated briefly by sketching a few portraits from the dataset (all names are pseudonyms). The experiences described are not unusual among the cancer survivors:

1 *Loss of employment*   Dan, aged 49, was living with the impairment effects that followed treatments for colorectal cancer (transcript B33). A great deal of the interview covered his patienthood experiences – a tale of extreme pain and collapse, misdiagnosis, hospital admissions, treatment regimes, some troubled relationships with health professionals, and post-patienthood bodily and emotional adjustment. But his illness narrative also brought to light the failure of his employer to hold open his job as a chef. Without work, or the prospect of other work, and without workplace-associated accommodation and car use, Dan was living with his mother and was dependent on *Disability Living Allowance* (DLA). He was astonished but grateful to receive DLA – something that had been applied for on his behalf by a Macmillan nurse. In a separate interview with Dan's mother, aged 76, the extreme emotional and physical demands placed upon her as the main informal carer during and after the treatment of a loved one were vividly recounted – but so too were the consequences of Dan's social exclusion and low income. Her own independence was compromised:

> Dan's mother: ... *so he just came here. I mean, he's my son – can't do anything else but take him in, and I don't think he has much money – I mean its been a help for me in a way, but you get a bit of your independence taken away. We get on alright but I just feel that if he'd been on his own he would have had more help.*

2 *Low income, needs and benefits in older years*   A couple in their 60s were interviewed together about life with the wife's impairment effects related to colorectal cancer, and the husband's endeavours to meet her everyday needs (transcript L416). The long transcript was mainly devoted to the telling of illness narratives in the narrow sense – narratives about diagnosis, doctors, nurses, hospitals and treatment regimes. But, once again, there were strong narrative threads relating to the extra expenses that impairment effects brought into their lives, together with the inadequacy of support services and social security benefits. Life after retirement had not worked out as expected, and "being disabled" was an identity that was resisted fiercely:

> Wife: ... *we got a toilet with a high seat because I couldn't get off the loo, and we've just changed the car so as I can get in and out of it – I could get in but I couldn't get out. I can walk down steps but I can't walk up them ...*

I went [to a clinic] with osteoporosis. They told us I could have an orange badge [forerunner of the Blue Badge for disabled people] and I said 'oh, I don't want an orange badge on – I'm gonna be stuck with this orange badge.' Anyway, the doctor said to me 'go and get this orange badge' she said 'its easier for your husband – think about him'. So he got the orange badge and the gentleman at the Social Service has said 'are you not on any benefits?' and I said 'no' and he said 'well you should be because its obvious that you are in pain with walking'. ... I think I get £35 [per week], is it?... Er, £35 and he gets £13 [per week] – something for struggling with me! [laugh]. ... Another lady that came round said 'you should be on a higher percentage of money than this'...

3 Reactions of others   Tom, age 55, describes the reactions of some people that he meets to his lung cancer diagnosis (transcript L125):

I think you come across, in some people, a natural reticence to discuss it, more for my feelings rather than theirs – in that they say 'How are you Chris, how are you doing?' I say 'Well, I've not been so good, I've been having treatment.' 'For what?' 'Cancer'. Step back in amazement and shock! That sort of thing...

I know that people do have reservations. I know that it's a bit like saying 'I've just gone down with leprosy', or something. And they think, well, if they get too near they might catch it. Some people are too sensitive to delve into it, the fact that you've been, you've told them that you have cancer is enough and they recoil, recoil. They say 'Poor old Tom, he's got cancer, and he'll not make Christmas' – that sort of thing. Well in a way they say that.

In retrospect, I see that making use of a *sociology of disablism and impairment effects* framework from the start would have enabled me to cross disciplinary boundaries – that is, to combine the sociological study of chronic illness-related disablism *with* a non-medico-centric study of the impairment effects that cancers leave in their wake.

Conclusion

This chapter has contrasted the use of the social deviance and social oppression paradigms in the sociology of chronic illness and 'disability'. Medical sociology uses the first paradigm – a medico-centric approach, and disability studies the second. A few examples of boundary crossing have been described in brief, and a *cancer test case* has examined a particularly challenging arena for making such crossings.

I offer up *the sociology of disablism and impairment* effects to medical sociologists – as an alternative to their traditional *sociology of chronic illness and disability*. In my view, the former provides an analytical framework that avoids the medico-centric assumption that: 'we study the ways in which people adapt to their socially deviant status caused by diagnoses of chronic illness'. Rather, the emphasis turns to the social negotiation of the lived experience of both impairment effects *and* with encounters with disablism. Only time will tell if medical sociologists take up the offer – laying the foundations for a closer disciplinary alliance.

Notes

1. The meaning of this concept is elaborated at length in: Thomas, C. (2007) *Sociologies of Disability and Illness Contested Ideas in Disability Studies and Medical Sociology.* Basingstoke: Palgrave Macmillan.
2. This simple definition was first introduced in Thomas, C. (1999) *Female Forms: Experiencing and Understanding Disability.* Buckingham: Open University Press.
3. See chapter 4 in Thomas, C. (2007) *Sociologies of Disability and Illness Contested Ideas in Disability Studies and Medical Sociology.* Basingstoke: Palgrave Macmillan.
4. Medical sociology is, of course, a sub-discipline within sociology, but it is helpful to refer to it here as a 'discipline', for ease of discussion.
5. Disability Studies is multidisciplinary, but sociology has remained the dominant discipline.
6. UPIAS: the Union of the Physically Impaired Against Segregation – a forerunner organization of the British Council of Organisations of Disabled People (BCODP).
7. ICIDH: The World Health Organization's (WHO) (1980) International Classification of Impairments, Disability and Handicap. A few medical sociologists helped to formulate the ICIDH – see Bury 1997; the ICIDH has been superseded in recent years by the WHO's International Classification of Functioning (ICF).
8. Whether these developments mark *real* or dangerously partial advances is, not surprisingly, hotly debated within disability studies and the Disabled People's Movement.
9. An example of a well-meaning but undermining parental comment is: 'Well, Sarah, your dad and I think that it would be best if you do as well as you can in education so that you can get a career. I mean, you're not going to marry and have kids, so let's look on the bright side ...' (see Thomas, 1999).
10. ESRC project RES-000-22-2031: Narratives of Living and Dying with Cancer: Sociological Perspectives. For an account of the interview datasets see Thomas (2008).

References

Abberley, P. (2002) Work, Disability, Disabled People and European Social Theory. In C. Barnes, M. Oliver and L. Barton (eds), *Disability Studies Today*. Cambridge: Polity.

Anderson, R. and Bury, M. (eds) (1988) *Living with Chronic Illness. The Experience of Patients and Their Families*. London: Unwin Hyman.

Barnes, C. (1991) *Disabled People in Britain and Discrimination*. London: Hurst and Co.

Barnes, C. (1996) Theories of Disability and the Origins of the Oppression of Disabled People in Western Society. In L. Barton (ed.), *Disability & Society: Emerging Issues and Insights*. London: Longman.

Barnes, C. and Mercer, G. (eds) (1996) *Exploring the Divide: Illness and Disability*. Leeds: The Disability Press.

Barnes, C. and Mercer, G. (eds) (1997) *Doing Disability Research*. Leeds: The Disability Press.

Barnes, C., Mercer, G. and Shakespeare, T. (1999) *Exploring Disability: A Sociological Introduction*. Cambridge: Polity Press.

Barnes, C., Oliver, M. and Barton, L. (eds) (2002) *Disability Studies Today*. Cambridge: Polity.

Barton, L. (ed.) (1996) *Disability & Society: Emerging Issues and Insights*. London: Longman.

Blaxter, M. (1976) *The Meaning of Disability: A Sociological Study of Impairment*. London: Heinemann.

Bury, M. (1982) Chronic Illness as Biographical Disruption. *Sociology of Health and Illness*, 4(2): 167–82.

Bury, M. (1991) The Sociology of Chronic Illness: A Review of Research and Prospects. *Sociology of Health and Illness*, 13(4): 167–82.

Bury, M. (1997) *Health and Illness in a Changing Society*. London: Routledge.

Bury, M. (2005) *Health and Illness*. Cambridge: Polity.

Cabinet Office (2004) *Improving the Life Chances of Disabled People*. London: The Prime Minister's Strategy Unit.

Charmaz, K. (1983) Loss of Self: A Fundamental Form of Suffering in the Chronically Ill. *Sociology of Health and Illness*, 5: 168–95.

Corker, M. (1998) *Deaf and Disabled, or Deafness Disabled?* Buckingham: Open University Press.

Corker, M. and Shakespeare, T. (eds) (2002) *Disability/Postmodernity: Embodying Disability Theory*. London: Continuum.

Disability Discrimination Act 1995. London: HMSO.

Disability Discrimination Act 2005 (Amendment). London: HMSO.

Finkelstein, V. (1980) *Attitudes and Disabled People: Issues for Discussion*. New York: World Rehabilitation Fund.

Frank, A. W. (1995) *The Wounded Storyteller: Body, Illness, and Ethics*. Chicago, IL University of Chicago Press.

French, S. (ed.), (1994) *On Equal Terms: Working with Disabled People*. Oxford: Butterworth-Heinemann.

Gerhardt, U. (1989) *Ideas about Illness: An Intellectual and Political History of Medical Sociology*. London: Macmillan.

Gleeson, B. (1999) *Geographies of Disability*. London: Routledge.

Goffman, E. (1961) *Asylums. Essays on the Social Situation of Mental Patients*. New York: Anchor, Doubleday (first published by Penguin in 1968).

Goffman, E. (1968) *Stigma. Notes on the Management of Spoiled Identity*. Harmondsworth: Penguin (first published in 1963).

Grinyer, A. (2008) *Life after Cancer in Adolescence and Young Adulthood: The Experience of Survivorship*. London: Routledge.

Hughes, B. (1999) The Constitution of Impairment: Modernity and the Aesthetic of Oppression. *Disability & Society*, 14(2): 155–72.

Hughes, B. (2000) Medicine and Aesthetic Invalidation of Disabled People. *Disability & Society*, 15(4): 555–68.

Hughes, B. and Paterson, K. (1997) The Social Model of Disability and the Disappearing Body: Towards a Sociology of Impairment. *Disability & Society*, 12: 325–40.

Hunt, P. (ed.) (1966) *Stigma: The Experience of Disability*. London: Chapman.

Kelleher, D. (1988) *Diabetes*. London: Routledge.

Kelleher, D. and Leavey, G. (eds) (2004) *Identity and Health*. London: Routledge.

Kelly, M. P. and Field, D. (2004) Medical Sociology, Chronic Illness and the Body. In M. Bury and J. Gabe (eds), *The Sociology of Health and Illness. A Reader*. London: Routledge. First appeared in *Sociology of Health and Illness*, 18, 1996: 241–57.

Mishler, E. G. (1999) *Storylines. Craftartists' Narratives of Identity*. London: Harvard University Press.

Morris, J. (1991) *Pride against Prejudice: Transforming Attitudes to Disability*. London: The Women's Press.

Morris, J. (ed.) (1996) *Encounters with Strangers: Feminism and Disability*. London: The Women's Press.

Oliver, M. (1983) *Social Work with Disabled People*. Basingstoke: Macmillan.

Oliver, M. (1990) *The Politics of Disablement*. London: Macmillan.

Oliver, M. (1996) *Understanding Disability: From Theory to Practice*. London: Macmillan.

Oliver, M. (2004) The Social Model in Action: If I Had a Hammer. In C. Barnes and G. Mercer (eds), *Implementing the Social Model of Disability: Theory and Research*. Leeds: The Disability Press.

Oliver, M. and Barnes, C. (1998) *Disabled People and Social Policy: From Exclusion to Inclusion*. London: Longman.

Parsons, T. (1951) *The Social System*. Glencoe: Free Press.

Price, J. and Shildrick, M. (1998) Uncertain Thoughts on the Dis/abled Body. In M. Shildrick and J. Price (eds), *Vital Signs: Feminist Reconfigurations of the Bio/logical Body*. Edinburgh: Edinburgh University Press.

Price, J. and Shildrick, M. (2002) Bodies Together: Touch, Ethics and Disability. In M. Corker and T. Shakespeare (eds), *Disability/Postmodernity: Embodying Disability Theory*. London: Continuum.

Priestley, M. (2003) *Disability: A Life Course Approach*. Cambridge: Polity.

Priestley, M. (ed.) (2001) *Disability and the Life Course: Global Perspectives*. Cambridge: Cambridge University Press.

Reeve, D. (2007) Negotiating Disability in Everyday Life: The Experience of Psycho-Emotional Disablism, unpublished PhD Thesis, Lancaster University: Lancaster.

Roulstone, A. (1998) *Enabling Technology: Disabled People, Work and New Technology*. Buckingham: Open University Press.

Scambler, G. (1984) Perceiving and Coping with Stigmatizing Illness. In R. Fitzpatrick, J. Hinton, S. Newman, G. Scambler and J. Thompson (eds), *The Experience of Illness*. London: Tavistock.

Scambler, G. (1989) *Epilepsy*. London: Routledge.

Scambler, G. (2004) Re-framing Stigma: Felt and Enacted Stigma and Challenges to the Sociology of Chronic and Disabling Conditions. *Social Theory and Health*, 2: 29–46.

Scott, R. A. (1969) *The Making of Blind Men*. New York: Russell Sage Foundation.

Shakespeare, T. (2006) *The Rights and Wrongs of Disability*. London: Routledge.

Shildrick, M. and Price, J. (1996) Breaking the Boundaries of the Broken Body. *Body and Society*, 2(4): 93–113.

Sparkes, A. and Smith, B. (2003) Sport, Spinal Cord Injuries, Embodied Masculinities, and Narrative Identity Dilemmas. *Men and Masculinities*, 4(3): 258–85.

Swain, J., French, S. and Cameron, C. (2003) *Controversial Issues in a Disabling Society*. Buckingham: Open University Press.

Thomas, C. (1999) *Female Forms: Experiencing and Understanding Disability*. Buckingham: Open University Press.

Thomas, C. (2008) Cancer Narratives and Methodological Uncertainties. *Qualitative Research*, 8(3): 423–33.

Thomas, C., Morris, S. M. and Gatrell, A. C. (2003) *Place of Death in the Morecambe Bay Area: Patterns and Preferences for Place of Final Care and Death among Terminally Ill Cancer Patients and Their Carers*. Institute for Health Research: Lancaster University.

Thomas, C., Morris, S. M., McIllmurray, M. B., Soothill, K., Francis, B. and Harman, J. C. (2001) *The Psychosocial Needs of Cancer Patients and Their Main Carers*. Project Report. Institute for Health Research, Lancaster University.

Tremain, S. (ed.) (2005) *Foucault and the Government of Disability*. Michigan: The University of Michigan Press.

Turner, B. S. (1984) *The Body and Society, Explorations in Social Theory*. Oxford: Basil Blackwell.

Turner, B. S. (1987) *Medical Power and Social Knowledge*. London: Sage.

Turner, B. S. (1992) *Regulating Bodies: Essays in Medical Sociology*. London: Routledge.

Union of the Physically Impaired Against Segregation (UPIAS) and The Disability Alliance (TDA) (1976) *Fundamental Principles of Disability*. London: UPIAS.

Walmsley, J. (1993) Contradictions in Caring: Reciprocity and Interdependence. *Disability, Handicap and Society*, 8: 129–42.

Watson, N. (2002) Well, I Know This Is Going to Sound Very Strange to You, but I Don't See Myself as a Disabled Person: Identity and Disability. *Disability & Society*, 17(5): 509–27.

Wilde, A. (2004) Disability Fictions: The Production of Gendered Impairments and Disability in Soap Opera Discourses, unpublished PhD thesis. Leeds: University of Leeds.

Williams, G. H. (1996) Irving Kenneth Zola (1935–1994): An Appreciation. *Sociology of Health and Illness*, 18(1): 107–25.

Williams, G. H. (2001) Theorizing Disability. In G. L. Albrecht, K. D. Seelman and M. Bury (eds), *Handbook of Disability Studies*. London: Sage.

Williams, S. J. (2000) Chronic Illness as Biographical Disruption or Biographical Disruption as Chronic Illness? Reflections on a Core Concept. *Sociology of Health and Illness*, 22(1): 40–67.

Williams, S. J. (2005) Parsons Revisited: From the Sick Role to...? *Health*, 9(2): 123–44.

Williams, S. J. and Bendelow, G. (1998) *The Lived Body: Sociological Themes, Embodied Issues*. London: Routledge.

Young, I. M. (1990) *Justice and the Politics of Difference*. Princeton, NJ: Princeton University Press.

Zola, I. K. (1966) Culture and Symptoms: An Analysis of Patients Presenting Complaints. *American Sociological Review*, 31: 615–30.

Zola, I. K. (1972) Medicine as an Institution of Social Control. *Sociological Review*, 20: 487–504.

Zola, I. K. (1973) Pathways to the Doctor – from Person to Patient. *Social Science and Medicine*, 7: 677–89.

Zola, I. K. (1982) *Missing Pieces: A Chronicle of Living with a Disability*. Philadelphia, PA: Temple University Press.

Zola, I. K. (1991) Bringing Our Bodies and Ourselves Back In: Reflections on a Past, Present, and Future 'Medical Sociology'. *Journal of Health and Social Behaviour*, 32 (March): 1–16.

Zola, I. K. (1994) Towards Inclusion: The Role of People with Disabilities in Policy and Research Issues in the United States – a Historical and Political Analysis. In M. Rioux and M. Bach (eds), *Disability Is Not Measles*. North York, Ontario: Roeher Institute.

4
Beyond Models: Understanding the Complexity of Disabled People's Lives

Tom Shakespeare and Nick Watson

Introduction

The social model approach to understanding disability reflects the growth of the disability movement, and emphasizes the role of discrimination and prejudice in the lives of disabled people. The social model has become more than just a theoretical model or paradigm for research: it has become a litmus test, a means of identifying with a particular disciplinary grouping. Broadly speaking, if you support the social model you are perceived as a disability studies scholar; if you question it you are seen as a medical sociologist.

However, the materialist approach of authors such as Oliver (1990) and Barnes (1991) has been challenged both by disabled feminists (for example, Crow, 1992) and by disabled academics with interests in the sociology of the body and medical sociology (Shakespeare, 2006; Shakespeare and Watson, 2001). Rather than reducing disability to either structural factors ('contextual essentialism', in Morten Soder's terminology) or to medical factors ('biological determinism'), we have argued that it is more helpful to take a complex and nuanced approach to disability (Soder, 1989).

In this chapter, we will draw on several empirical projects, in particular a recent study (Thompson, Shakespeare and Wright, 2008) with adults with restricted growth, and work by Watson (2002) on disabled people and health. These studies complicate understandings of disability, challenge social model and identity politics approaches, and show how 'impairment' and 'disability' entwine in the lives of disabled people. Adopting a critical realist paradigm, we will argue that an adequate sociology of disability will incorporate medical, psychological, social and political dimensions of disabled people's experience. We will conclude by drawing out implications for wider notions of disability identity and disability research.

In challenging the social model and identity politics, we have never intended to throw the baby out with the bathwater. Disability politics in general and disability studies in particular clearly owes a great deal to the pioneer activists of UPIAS, BCODP and other organizations. These 'organic intellectuals' both redefined disability and promoted a civil rights approach, helping end discrimination and achieving independent living. Largely as a consequence of their groundbreaking work, there has been considerable progress in the lives of disabled people both here in the UK and beyond. These improvements are not just confined to developed countries but have also influenced developments in the developing world (Charlton, 1998). Much of this improvement can be attributed to the political pressure, empirical evidence and theoretical analysis developed by social model-wielding disability rights activists backed up by disability studies academics. Moreover, we concur with Carol Thomas (2004), when she celebrates the commitment to equality and social inclusion of materialist disability studies: few medical sociologists could match this level of political engagement, even though the polar dichotomy she establishes between disability studies and medical sociology is overdrawn, and unjust to the world of medical sociology.

Materialist disability studies

The social model of disability is a very simple model. It argues that the disadvantage experienced by disabled people owes nothing to their individual impairment but is the result of a social organization which serves to exclude disabled people. There is no denying that this radical reconfiguration of the disability problem was an important development. It implies that if we want to tackle the problems faced by disabled people we must take a societal approach as opposed to an individual approach. Disability can only be solved through structural change: individual, medical based models are doomed to failure because they do not tackle root problems.

The simplicity which is the hallmark of the social model is also its fatal flaw. The social model's benefits as a slogan and political ideology undermine its contribution as an academic account of disability. A second problem arises from the way that the social model emerged from UPIAS, a narrow cadre of activists, the majority of whom were white heterosexual men with spinal injury or other physical impairments.

Arguably, had UPIAS included people who were more representative of different experiences – people with learning difficulties, mental health problems, or with more complex physical impairments – it could not have produced such a narrow understanding of disability. Certainly, other groups of disabled people that emerged around the same time as the UPIAS, such as the more diverse membership of the Liberation Network of People with Disabilities, produced more nuanced understandings of disability (Shakespeare, 2006).

Among the weaknesses of the social model are

1. The neglect of impairment as an important aspect of many disabled people's lives. Feminists Jenny Morris (1991), Sally French (1993) and Liz Crow (1992) were pioneers in this criticism of the social model neglect of individual experience of impairment:

> As individuals, most of us simply cannot pretend with any conviction that our impairments are irrelevant because they influence every aspect of our lives. We must find a way to integrate them into our whole experience and identity for the sake of our physical and emotional well-being, and, subsequently, for our capacity to work against Disability. (Crow, 1992: 7)

The social model so strongly disowns individual and medical approaches, that it risks implying that impairment is not a problem. Whereas other socio-political accounts of disability have developed the important insight that people with impairment are disabled by society as well as by their bodies, the social model suggests that people are disabled by society not by their bodies. Rather than simply opposing medicalization, it can be interpreted as rejecting medical prevention, rehabilitation or cure of impairment, even if this was never what either UPIAS, Finkelstein, Oliver or Barnes intended.

For individuals with static impairments, which do not degenerate or cause medical complications, it may be possible to regard disability as entirely socially created. For those who have degenerative conditions which may cause premature death, or who experience any condition which involves pain and discomfort, it is harder to ignore the negative aspects of impairment. As Simon Williams has argued,

> ... endorsement of disability solely as social oppression is really only an option, and an erroneous one at that, for those spared the ravages of chronic illness. (Williams, 1999: 812)

The bracketing of impairment has been used to bring in other impairment groups, such as those with a mental health problem or a learning difficulty. Whilst the social model was originally described for people with a physical impairment, subsequent writers have attempted to extend its analysis to all impairment groups. Peter Beresford (2000), for example, argues that all disabled people, whatever their impairment, are

> lumped together within the same externally imposed definitions, administrative categories and statistics. This has important ramifications for all of us, impacting on both our individual and collective identities.

Simone Aspis has made similar points with regard to people with a learning difficulty (in Campbell and Oliver, 1996). The claim is that all people who have an impairment face discrimination and that discrimination constructs their social experience. The focus of research must be to tackle that discrimination. Such lumping together of diverse impairment – and indeed social – experiences overlooks key differences.

Carol Thomas (1999) has tried to develop the social model to include what she calls 'impairment effects', in order to account for the limitations and difficulties of medical conditions. Subsequently, she suggested that a relational interpretation of the social model enables disabling aspects to be attributed to impairment, as well as social oppression:

> once the term 'disability' is ring-fenced to mean forms of oppressive social reactions visited upon people with impairments, there is no need to deny that impairment and illness cause some restrictions of activity, or that in many situations both disability and impairment effects interact to place limits on activity. (Thomas, 2004: 29)

Thomas wants 'disability' to mean social oppression plus social restriction of activity, as distinct from 'impairment' meaning impairment-related restriction of activity. We find this attempt to rescue the social model as creating unhelpful fine distinctions that do not advance the debate. One curious consequence of the ingenious reformulation is that only people with impairment who face oppression or social restriction can be called disabled people. This relates to another problem:

2. The social model assumes what it needs to prove: that disabled people are oppressed. The sex/gender distinction (Oakley, 1972) defined gender as a social category, not as oppression. Feminists claimed that

gender relations *involved* oppression, but did not define gender relations *as* oppression. However, the social model defines disability as oppression. In other words, the question is not whether disabled people are oppressed in a particular situation, but only the extent to which they are oppressed. A circularity enters into disability research: it is logically impossible for a qualitative researcher to find disabled people who are not oppressed.

Linked to this has been the emancipatory research paradigm (Oliver, 1992), which has become synonymous with the social model. This approach has placed demands on researchers to focus solely on the sources of oppression experienced by disabled people. Work that looks at individual, subjective experiences of pain, fatigue or other issue associated with an impairment is discouraged (Barnes and Mercer, 1997). The research must not only concentrate on the barriers faced by disabled people but it must also challenge the social structures that oppress disabled people and bring about change.

Further, the very concept of what oppression is for disabled people remains largely unexplored, a point made by Paul Abberley:

> to usefully apply the notion of oppression to the complex of impairment, disability and handicap involves the development of a theory which connects together the common features of economic, social and psychological disadvantage with an understanding of the material basis of these disadvantages and the ideologies which propagate and reproduce them. (1997: 176)

The complex theorization demanded by Abberley is yet to be developed. But without it, the social model is ahistorical and unsubtle, and built on a series of simplistic dualisms: disabled/non-disabled, oppressed/oppressor. In his development of the social model, Oliver (1990) argues that capitalism is the cause of this oppression This is very hard to support: disabled people are not competing for scarce goods in a market place. Whilst much of the disadvantage encountered by disabled people is experienced economically, at its root, it cannot be explained as economic exploitation. The social model, by seeking to fit the complex actuality of lived experience into narrow formal categories and reducing everything to oppression arising from material social barriers, has created a distance between theory and disabled people's own experiences. Too much is left unexplained. The social model produces generalizations which seek to explain everything and, along the way, homogenize the diversity of disabled people's experience.

3. The analogy with feminist debates about sex and gender high-lights another problem: the crude distinction between impairment (medical) and disability (social). Any researcher who does qualitative research with disabled people immediately discovers that in everyday life it is very hard to distinguish clearly between the impact of impairment and the impact of social barriers (see for example, Sherry, 2002; Watson, 2002). In practice, it is the interaction of individual bodies and social environments which produces disability. For example, steps only become an obstacle if someone has a mobility impairment: each element is necessary but not sufficient for the individual to be disabled. If a person with multiple sclerosis is depressed, how easy is it to make a causal separation between the effect of the impairment itself; her reaction to having an impairment; her reaction to being oppressed and excluded on the basis of having an impairment; other, unrelated reasons for her to be depressed? In practice, social and individual aspects are almost inextricable in the complexity of the lived experience of disability.

From a post-structuralist or post-modernist perspective, the crude dichotomies of the social model conceal another problem. Moreover, feminists have now abandoned the sex/gender distinction, because it implies that sex is not a social concept. Judith Butler (1990) and others show that what we think of as sexual difference is always viewed through the lens of gender. Shelley Tremain (2002) has claimed similarly that the social model treats impairment as an unsocialized and universal concept, whereas, like sex, impairment is always already social, and needs to be problematized.

4. The concept of the barrier-free utopia is problematic. The idea of the enabling environment, in which all socially imposed barriers are removed, is usually implicit rather than explicit in social model thinking, although it does form the title of a major academic collection (Swain, French and Oliver, 1993). Vic Finkelstein (1981) also wrote a simple parable of a village designed for wheelchair users to illustrate the way that social model thinking turned the problem of disability on its head. Yet, despite the value of approaches such as Universal Design, the concept of a world in which people with impairments are free of environmental barriers is hard to imagine let alone operationalize. For example, many parts of the natural world will remain inaccessible to many disabled people, including mountains, bogs, beaches, sunsets, birdsong, depending on the impairment. In urban settings, many barriers can be mitigated, although historic buildings

often cannot easily be adapted. However, accommodations are sometimes incompatible because people with different impairments may require different solutions: blind people prefer steps, defined curbs and tactile paving, while wheelchair users need ramps, dropped curbs and smooth surfaces. Even where individuals share the same impairment, for example visual impairment, they may prefer different accomodations, for example text in braille, large print or audio format. Practicality and resource constraints make it unfeasible to overcome every barrier: for example, the New York subway and London Underground systems would require huge investment to make every line and station accessible to wheelchair users.

Moreover, physical and sensory impairments are in many senses the easiest to accommodate. What would it mean to create a barrier-free utopia for people with learning difficulties? Reading and writing and other cognitive abilities are required for full participation in many areas of contemporary life in developed nations. What about people on the autistic spectrum, who may find social contact difficult to cope with: a barrier-free utopia might be a place where they did not have to meet, communicate with, or have to interpret other people. With many solutions to the disability problem, the concept of addressing special needs seems more coherent than the concept of the barrier-free utopia. Barrier-free enclaves are possible, but not a barrier-free world.

While environments and services can and should be adapted wherever possible, there remains disadvantage associated with having many impairments which no amount of environmental change could entirely eliminate. People who rely on wheelchairs, or personal assistance, or other provision are more vulnerable and have fewer choices than the majority of able-bodied people. When Michael Oliver claims that

> An aeroplane is a mobility aid for non-flyers in exactly the same way as a wheelchair is a mobility aid for non-walkers. (Oliver, 1996: 108)

His suggestion is amusing and thought provoking, but cannot be taken seriously. As Michael Bury has argued,

> It is difficult to imagine any modern industrial society (however organised) in which, for example, a severe loss of mobility or dexterity, or sensory impairments, would not be 'disabling' in the sense of restricting activity to some degree. The reduction of barriers to participation does not amount to abolishing disability as a whole. (Bury, 1997: 137)

Drawing together these weaknesses, a final and important distinction needs to be made. The disability movement has often drawn analogies with other forms of identity politics. The disability rights struggle has even been called the 'Last Liberation Movement' (Dreidger, 1989). Yet while disabled people do face discrimination and prejudice, like women, gay and lesbian people, and minority ethnic communities, and while the disability rights movement does resemble in its forms and activities to many of these other movements, there is an important difference. There is nothing intrinsically problematic about being female or having a different sexual orientation, or a different skin pigmentation or body shape. People with these differences experience wrongful limitation of negative freedom. Remove the social discrimination, and women and people of colour and gay and lesbian people will be able to flourish and participate. But disabled people face both discrimination and also intrinsic limitations. This claim has three implications. First, even if social barriers are removed as far as practically possible, it will remain disadvantageous to have many forms of impairment. Second, it is harder to celebrate disability than it is to celebrate Blackness, or Gay Pride, or being a woman. 'Disability pride' is problematic, because disability is difficult to recuperate as a concept: it refers either to limitation pain and incapacity, or to oppression and exclusion, or else to both dimensions. Third, if disabled people are to be emancipated, then society will have to provide extra resources to meet the needs and overcome the disadvantage which arises from impairment, not just work to minimize discrimination (Bickenbach et al., 1999). To conclude this overview of the materialist approach, a social model forged in the heat of social change and political mobilization is not necessarily adequate or appropriate for theoretical analysis or empirical research: there is a difference between science and ideology (Finkelstein, 1998; Vehmas, 2008).

Building better models

A social approach to disability is indispensable. The medicalization of disability is inappropriate and an obstacle to effective analysis and policy. But the social model is only one of the available options for theorizing disability. More sophisticated and complex approaches are needed, perhaps building on the WHO initiative to create the International Classification of Functioning, Disability and Health. One strength of this approach is the recognition that disability is a complex phenomenon, requiring different levels of analysis and intervention, ranging from the medical to the socio-political, and including the psychological, a dimension which is not adequately addressed in social model approaches. Another is the insight that disability is not a minority issue, affecting only those people defined as disabled people. As Irving Zola (1989) maintained, impairment is a universal experience of humanity.

The social model has also had an important and lasting impact on the way that sociology examines and reports on disability. The origins of the social model lie in part in the way that medical sociologists reported on the disability experience, in particular Miller and Gwynne in their 1972 study on the Le Court Cheshire Home. In medical sociology it is the illness that is the social experience of the impairment, rather than issues of inequality or powerlessness that are placed at the centre of research. Through this analysis various approaches to how people experience an impairment or chronic condition have emerged. These include Charmaz's (1983) association with impairment and loss of self, Bury's (1982) concept of chronic illness as a biographical disruption and Williams' (1984) idea of narrative reconstruction. In stark contrast to the approach favoured within disability studies, which seeks to downplay the importance of individual experience, much of this work has been based on what may be loosely termed narrative research. Kleinman (1988) describes these as illness narratives, through which 'patients order their experience of illness' (49). Whilst some authors have an acknowledgement of conditions of inequality, powerlessness and violence (see for example, Bury (1997: 118–19)), they are rarely placed at the centre of the research or analysis (G. Williams 1996). Even in the work which purports to incorporate or acknowledge wider social issues the focus is still very much on the individual (see for example, Charmaz, 2001). This might go some way to explain some of the animosity felt by disability studies towards medical sociology. Emphasis is also placed on 'coming to terms' with an impairment, hence notions of biographical disruption and of narrative reconstruction: there appears to be little interest in what happens after the biography has been disrupted or the narrative has been reconstructed. In this work there is little attempt to bring in the social and examine the structural issues faced by disabled people. We concur with those approaches, such as the Nordic relational concept, which see disability as an interaction between an individual and their wider social and physical environment. This produces an account such as is represented in Table 4.1.

This appears to be similar, albeit simpler, to the International Classification of Functioning, Disability and Health (ICF) conceptualization.From an ICF perspective, disability is the interrelation of health

Table 4.1   Disability as an interaction

Intrinsic factors	Extrinsic factors
Type of impairment	Physical environments
Severity of impairment	Social arrangements
Motivation, attitude to impairment	Expectations and roles
Self-esteem, confidence	Cultural meanings, representations

Table 4.2   Schema of interventions for the example of spinal cord injury

Domain	Example of intervention
Political	Campaigns for civil rights and welfare services
Culture	Leisure, sport and recreation
Social	Advice, support services and social protection
Education	Going to a mainstream school, accessing FE/HE
Economic	Employment counselling and advice
Environmental	Barrier removal in home and community
Psychological	Counselling and peer support
Technological	Appropriate wheelchair provision
Therapeutic	Rehabilitation, for example, therapies
Nursing	Training in self-care to prevent pressure sores
Medical	Surgical stabilization post lesion
Prevention and public health	Road safety campaigns
Basic science	Stem cell research in pursuit of cure for SCI

condition, personal factors (for example, coping style) and environmental factors (for example, architectural barriers, employment policy, stigma). Given this dynamic and multifactorial model there are a range of options for reducing levels of disability in individuals and in society. For example, combating prejudice and stigma directed towards people who are visibly impaired will reduce the extent to which they are disabled, just as creating accessible workplaces or broadcast media will benefit people with mobility or sensory impairments. A simplified schema of these options is provided for the case of spinal cord injury in Table 4.2.

Traditional biomedical approaches tended to emphasize interventions at the bottom half of this table. With the rise of the disability movement, attention has shifted to structural interventions to improve participation of disabled people, rather than clinical intervention to reduce the impact of impairment. Where disability has been redefined in terms of oppression or discrimination, disability prevention has been reframed in terms of eliminating barriers, reducing poverty and promoting social inclusion. In terms of the intervention schema proposed above, it has been the top half of the table which has been emphasized. However, it seems evident to us that an adequate approach to disability would pay attention to all possible strategies for minimizing the disability problem. In this way, the twin perils of 'biological reductionism' and 'contextual essentialism' are both avoided.

There are limitations and difficulties in the ICF schema. For example, the universal approach means that it covers all health conditions indiscriminately. No distinction is drawn between a temporary illness, such as influenza or a ear infection, and a long-term chronic disease or impairment such as cerebral palsy or deafness. Yet, as Edwards argues, the former will not typically be identity-affecting, whereas the latter generally are. This important social dimension of the disability experience is not adequately conceptualized within the ICF classification.

Different or disabled: The dynamic nature of disability and impairment

The experiences of disablement and impairment are complex and difficult to separate. To explore these complexities we draw on two research projects we have been involved in. One was a project which investigated quality of life for people with restricted growth (Shakespeare et al., 2009; Watson 2002). The other was a study that explored disabled people's views of their body and their perceptions of health. The restricted growth studied employed both quantitative as well as a qualitative methodology: 81 respondents completed a questionnaire, with 50 subsequently taking part in a semi-structured interview whilst the latter study was purely qualitative and the findings are based on a series of semi-structured interviews with 15 men and 15 women with a range of physical impairments.

As could be expected, both groups reported a range of problems and there was a great deal of similarity between the two groups. All reported encountering discrimination. However, in both studies it is difficult to entirely separate impairment from disablement. At times an individual's impairment impacted on their disablement whilst at others disablement impacted on impairment.

In both studies all of our informants reported experiencing discrimination and disadvantage. Our research informants recalled how they had been subjected to violence or abuse, stared at, ridiculed, excluded from buildings and denied opportunities. Whilst there was obviously a great deal of shared experience here, there were also differences between the two groups. People of short stature, for example, were much more likely to report occasions where they were ridiculed or stared at.

I can spend most of the day and not think about it, but something will happen, I'll find people staring at me and I think, what are they looking at? And then I think, it's because it's me. (Female, age 49)

For many other disabled people being stared at is not a major problem:

I don't notice [being stared at]. When I go shopping there are so many people in wheelchairs that, well for example the other day a young friend took me to, it was somewhere off Princes Street. And I thought we were going to a restaurant for some lunch. But they were pretty busy so she said, I'll just go into Crawfords and get us some sandwiches. And I said where do we go to eat them, she said, 'Just here on the street.' Well I had never eaten a sandwich on the street before in my life. But I was starving, so I chomped away on my sandwich and I watched every single person coming up that road, and not one looked at me. (Female, age 46)

Disablement can also impact on impairment.

No matter how many times people say 'Disabled people are not second-class citizens', even just walking down the street and not being able to go into a shop because the door is too narrow says that you are second-class citizen. (Female, age 21)

Experiencing discrimination not only reminds people that they are different but it can also directly affect impairment. Many people reported that when they felt down, symptoms associated with their impairment, such as pain or spasm, became worse. Disabling practices directly impacts on impairment effects. Impairment thus becomes linked to disablement, in that through disabling social relations disabled people become aware of the way that others think about them.

The issues of identity and identification produced interesting responses. Most of the participants in both studies did not see themselves as disabled. As one respondent with restricted growth reported:

I'm just like everybody else, I just see myself as everybody else, I don't class myself as, like, disabled or anything. (Female, age 47)

Informants with other impairments also made similar comments. The following quote from a male wheelchair user is typical:

I don't tend to think of myself as disabled, you know I don't think, oh I'm in a wheelchair, disability's a major part of my life. I tend to try and get on with things. (Male, age 29)

Both of these informants took a broadly barriers-based approach. When discussing disability, the woman quoted above, for example, argued:

I suppose you're disabled by society rather than by the condition. ...I suppose people thinking that you can't do, assuming that you can't do, things that you can do.

However, this woman also referred to disability in terms of the pain and other symptoms she experienced on 'bad days', so was not consistent in her social model approach. The male wheelchair user was similarly ambiguous. For example, he argued:

I don't, or I do produce sperm but it's dead or not as good as an able-bodied person's, but outside that, I'm not really sure. Maybe there's a side of things if you look at man's traditional role in the house, you know, what you would do, perhaps DIY and all the decorating and things like that but I'm limited in what I can do.

Some of the informants were more likely to identify as disabled. These informants tended to see themselves in terms of their incapacity and their inability, adopting a more individual model. For example:

Because we're restricted in what we can do, aren't we? That's the way I look at it, we can't do what everybody else can do. Our height stops us immediately in certain situations. (Restricted-growth male, age 57)

This was particularly associated, in the restricted growth study, with the worsening of physical symptoms as a result of ageing or spinal or joint complications. The experience of having an impairment changed people's ways of thinking about themselves. They all felt that they had to take more care of themselves, as the following quote shows:

> *Well, I'm more conscious about my health because I'm disabled, I've got to look after my body and my health a lot more than [able-bodied people]... When you're able bodied you tend to take if for granted, but when you're disabled, you really, you've really got to watch yourself, cos any signs like if you have an infection you've got to drink a lot and things like that and keep the bladder clear or bowel problems and that, if I have any problems like that then obviously I go to the doctor and see what it is, whereas before I'd maybe ignore it, say, och, it's just nothing, where with being in a chair if there's any problem with bladder or kidneys or any part of the body, then I'll go to the doctors or things like that to get it checked out because it's a more worrying aspect.* (Male, 30-year-old wheelchair user)

They also have to learn about their impairment and how it might impact them. For this reason, some of the informants talked about how they needed to be more in touch, more aware of their body than non-disabled people:

> *I get a lot of different signals, like goose pimples if I've got a bladder problem or a bowel problem, I spasm if there's something going on. Goose pimples, they're a great indication that there's something wrong with my bladder. Unfortunately I get it just as it's started to leak. If I had them just before, the problem could be dealt with – it might just be the position that my catheter's got into, so it's still good in that it has prevented a lot of disasters. I've gone goose pimpled in bed, suddenly realised, had a wee feel down, got it all sorted out, whereas had I not had the goose pimples I could have lain on for another 4 hours and been saturated without knowing it. So I get headaches if there's things going on. I know when I've got a really big, blocked catheter problem because I take that very rare that I get that distroflexia condition and luckily I've got medication for that, I know what I've got to do.*

However this person did not see herself as disabled, nor did she see disability as a major part of her life. She talked as much about barriers as she did about individual impairment issues.

People who are disabled also have to work harder to maintain their sense of normality against daily assaults. Some informants described how much of their life was built around the idea that '*I want to prove people wrong....I want people to listen to me*' (Female, age 23).

People's views of themselves changed over time. With age, for example, comes increasing mobility restriction and pain associated with their impairment. Some respondents in both studies had been forced to redefine their identity and think of themselves as disabled when other problems began to limit their working or social lives. Thus one woman said:

> *Yes, now I would [describe self as disabled]. But 10 years ago, no.* (Restricted-growth female, age 50)

Throughout both these research projects, we were told of many daily, mundane frustrations associated with having impairment. Whilst these are not huge, they increase people's sense of frustration and can impact on their perceived quality of life. The following is a typical example:

> *I have learned to be patient because I can't get quicker. Sometimes it drives me completely bananas. I have learned, it is 12 years now since I had my accident and I have just learned to be patient because the alternative is just too stressful. I know once I have done anything once I know whether or not I am going to be able to do it and therefore with time it will get quicker but I will never be super-fast or I know I am never going to be able to do this and therefore this is something I need to buy in, I will get support to do, and those things one learns.* (Male, age 38)

There are many intrinsic factors associated with an impairment that can impact on an individual's perceived quality of life, but these are usually subjective, and related to the particular personality. One of the research informants we spoke to was a very keen guitarist prior to breaking his neck. His impairment means that he can no longer play the guitar. Another woman described how, prior to her injury, she worked as a translator. During her treatment, her vocal chords were damaged and she was no longer able to speak either French or Spanish.

> *I think – it makes me mad, I spent all these years learning languages and travel and what I can't do now I am losing all my languages.* (Female, age 33)

We have selected these data because they provide evidence of the dynamic and changing nature associated with living with an impairment and the experiences of disability. Some are intrinsic factors – degree of impairment, motivation, emotional well-being – some are extrinsic factors – social participation, discrimination, prejudice. Some are the result of oppressive practices and some are inherent in the experience of impairment. All are involved in the process of disablement and the experience of living with an impairment. If we had only documented experiences of oppression we would not have presented a clear picture of disabled people's experiences.

Conclusion

What conclusions can we draw from these data, and on the basis of the more adequate conceptualization of disability which we have been advocating for some years (Shakespeare, 2006; Shakespeare and Watson, 2001; Watson, 2002)?

First, research should attend to what disabled people say and think, not what we might wish they should say and think. The materialist tradition in British Disability Studies has sometimes been guilty of trying to dissolve the people and elect another (to borrow from a late poem by Bertolt Brecht). Accusing disabled people of false consciousness, or waiting for them to see the light of the social model, is not adequate or appropriate. Researchers and activists alike should be attentive to the ways in which people wish to define their own experience, to what matters to individuals, to the perspectives and choices which people make in their everyday lives.

In particular, we need to offer support and space for disabled people to discuss their impairment and its impact on their lives, on their own terms. Disability studies should not be scared to 'bring the body back in' (Williams, 1999). It is a paradox that disability studies which purports to endorse a disability rights tradition that stresses autonomy, participation and accountability should sometimes have failed to listen to ordinary disabled people. We need to examine all aspects of disabled people's lives, including their engagement with, for example, rehabilitation, assistive technologies and medicine. Only if we do so, can we produce effective research: one indictment of the social model is that it has failed to be operationalized, to generate the desperately needed quantitative and qualitative research into what works in improving the lives of disabled people.

Second, sometimes it is politically and intellectually effective to aggregate the disability constituency and research the experience of barriers, prejudice and oppression. But because disability is such a diverse category, and because many experiences are highly specific – for example, the medical dimensions of particular impairments, the psychosocial subjectivities of different forms of embodiment, the cultural resonances of particular disability labels –there can be a danger of missing the nuance through lumping a disparate group together. People with restricted growth are a small population, easily overlooked in the wider categories of 'disabled people' or even 'people with mobility impairments' or 'people with genetic conditions'. Even the specific diagnoses of achondroplasia and spondo-epiphiseal dysplasia and so on have different natural histories, in clinical terms. Often, researchers should define a narrower group from which to sample, in order to capture the details of what is going on, either socially or medically or psychologically. For example, the headline statistic that disabled people are twice as likely to be unemployed as non-disabled people obscures the nuance that people with restricted growth have good access to employment, but poor career progression: we hypothesize that this is likely to be true of other mobility impairment groups also.

Third, it is clear from many studies including our own that disability is not an identity readily embraced by many people with an impairment. They define themselves in their own terms and under their own terms of reference (Watson, 2002). They all know and are aware of their bodily difference. They do not claim an identity based on their epistemology, but locate one in their ontology. It is an active identity and in challenging an ascribed identity of disability they are displaying both reflexivity and creativity. If we are to generate accounts of the lives of disabled people we need to develop an approach that allows us to capture this element and document the lived experiences of what it is to be a disabled person. A research agenda needs to emerge that provides an opportunity for the stories and narratives of and by disabled people to be heard. Through this, disabled people will be enabled to express the heterogeneity of their lives, the fluid, situated and contextual nature of both disablement and impairment, and the meaning of disability and impairment. This will allow us to develop a value system that represents the diversity of the disability experience. Presenting disabled people's own stories from their own perspective will make possible new forms of distinctive identities which are not based on essentialist characteristics. It will allow for the explorations of the 'real' lives lived by disabled people and an insight into their 'real' worlds. Focusing only on oppression or on disadvantage will not allow for this sort of development and only partial accounts will emerge.

Finally, it is vital that we do not ignore disablement, oppression and disadvantage. Disabled people do face discrimination in their day-to-day lives and we need to continue to document this. Disabled people are more likely to live in poverty than their non-disabled peers, there is a shortage of suitable housing, and sadly, disabled people are denied appropriate care, support and so on. These facts are undeniable and we need to develop a model that allows us to relate the earlier individual experiences in the social, but also, importantly, allow the social to be located within the individual. These relationships are not unidirectional (Williams, 1999).

In conclusion, disabled people need good science, not just inspiring ideology. We need to combine the passion and commitment of the materialist disability studies writers with the scholarship and empirical evidence of the chronic illness perspective. An engaged sociology of disability is indispensable. We need to ensure that disabled academics are well trained in social research, so they can go out and gather the evidence we need to make the argument and achieve the policies which liberate disabled people from the restrictions and oppressions to which their complex and dynamic situation exposes them.

References

Abberley, P. (1997) The Concept of Oppression and the Development of a Social Theory of Disability. In L. Barton and M. Oliver (eds), *Disability Studies: Past Present and Future* (pp. 160–78). Leeds: The Disability Press.

Barnes, C. (1991) *Disabled People in Britain and Discrimination*. London: Hurst and Co.

Barnes, C. and Mercer, G. (1997) *Doing Disability Research*. Leeds: Disability Press.

Beresford, P. (2000) What Have Madness and Psychiatric System Survivors Got to Do with Disability and Disability Studies. *Disability and Society* 15(1): 167–72.

Bickenbach, J. E., Chatterji, S., Badley, E. M. and Ustun, T. B. (1999) Models of Disablement, Universalism and the International Classification of Impairments, Disabilities and Handicaps. *Social Science and Medicine* 48, 1173–87.

Bury, M. (1982) Chronic Illness as Biographical Disruption. *Sociology of Health and Illness* 4: 167–82.

Bury, M. (1997) *Health and Illness in a Changing Society*. London: Routledge.

Butler, J. (1990) *Gender Trouble: Feminism and the Subversion of Identity*. New York: Routledge.

Campbell, J. and Oliver, M. (1996) *Disability Politics: Understanding Our Past, Changing Our Future*. London: Routledge.

Charlton, J. (1998) *Nothing about Us without Us: Disability, Oppression and Empowerment*. Berkeley: University of California Press.

Charmaz, K. (1983) Loss of Self: A Fundamental Form of Suffering in the Chronically Sick. *Sociology of Health and Illness* 5: 168–95.
Charmaz, K. (2001) Experiencing Chronic Illness. In G. Albrecht, R. Fitzpatrick and C. Scrimshaw (eds), *Handbook of Social Studies in Health and Medicine*. London: Sage.
Crow, L. (1992) Renewing the Social Model of Disability. *Coalition*, July: 5–9.
Dreidger, D. (1989) *The Last Civil Rights Movement*. London: Hurst.
Finkelstein, V. (1981) To Deny Or Not to Deny Disability. In A. Brechin, P. Liddiard, and J. Swain (eds), *Handicap in a Social World*. Sevenoaks: Oxford University Press/Hodder and Stoughton.
Finkelstein, V. (1998) Emancipating Disability Studies. In T. Shakespeare (ed.), *The Disability Reader: Social Science Perspectives*. London: Cassell.
French, S. (1993) Disability, Impairment or Something in Between. In J. Swain, S. French, C. Barnes, and C. Thomas (eds), *Disabling Barriers, Enabling Environments* (pp. 17–25). London: Sage.
Kleinman, A. (1988) *The Illness Narratives: Suffering, Healing and the Human Condition*. New York: Basic Books.
Miller, E. and Gwynne, G. (1972) *A Life Apart*. London: Tavistock.
Morris, J. (1991) *Pride against Prejudice*. London: Women's Press.
Oakley, A. (1972) *Sex, Gender and Society*. London: Gower.
Oliver, M. (1990) *The Politics of Disablement*. Basingstoke: Macmillan.
Oliver, M. (1992) Changing the Social Relations of Research Production. *Disability, Handicap and Society* 7(2): 101–15.
Oliver, M. (1996) *Understanding Disability: From Theory to Practice*. Basingstoke: Macmillan.
Shakespeare, T. (2006) *Disability Rights and Wrongs*. London: Routledge.
Shakespeare, T. and Watson, N. (2001) The Social Model of Disability: An Outdated Ideology? In S. Barnarrt and B. M. Altman (eds), *Exploring Theories and Expanding Methodologies: Where Are We and Where Do We Need to Go? Research in Social Science and Disability volume 2*, Amsterdam: JAI.
Sherry, M. (2002) If Only I Had a Brain, unpublished PhD dissertation, University of Queensland.
Soder, M. (1989) Disability as a Social Construct: The Labeling Approach Revisited. *European Journal of Special Needs Education* 4(2): 117–29
Swain, J., Finkelstein, V., French, S. and Oliver, M. (eds) (1993) *Disabling Barriers, Enabling Environments*. London: Oxford University Press/Sage.
Thomas, C. (1999) *Female Forms*. Buckingham: Open University Press.
Thomas, C. (2004) Developing the Social Relational in the Social Model of Disability: A Theoretical Agenda. In C. Barnes and G. Mercer (eds), *Implementing the Social Model of Disability: Theory and Research*. Leeds: The Disability Press.
Thompson, S., Shakespeare, T. and Wright, M.J. (2008) Medical and Social Aspects of Life with Skeletal Dysplasia: A Review of Current Knowledge. *Disability and Rehabilitation* 30(1): 1–12.
Tremain, S. (2002) On the Subject of Impairment. In M. Corker and T. Shakespeare (eds), *Disability/Postmodernity: Embodying Disability Theory* (pp. 32–47). London: Continuum.
UPIAS (1976) *The Fundamental Principles of Disability*. London: Union of the Physically Disabled Against Segregation.
Vehmas, S. (2008) Philosophy and Science: The Axes of Evil in Disability Studies? *J Med Ethics* 34: 21–3.

Watson, N. (2002) Well, I Know This Is Going to Sound Very Strange to You, but I Don't See Myself as a Disabled Person: Identity and Disability. *Disability and Society* 17(5): 509–28.

Williams, G. (1984) The Genesis of Chronic Illness: Narrative Reconstruction. *Sociology of Health and Illness* 6: 175–200.

Williams, G. (1996) Representing-Disability: Some Questions of Phenomenology and Politics'. In C. Barnes and G. Mercer (eds), *Exploring the Divide: Illness and Disability* Leeds, The Disability Press.

Williams, S. J. (1999) Is Anybody There? Critical Realism, Chronic Illness, and the Disability Debate. *Sociology of Health and Illness* 21(6): 797–819.

Zola, I. K. (1989) Towards the Necessary Universalizing of a Disability Policy. *The Milbank Quarterly*, vol. 67, suppl. 2, Pt. 2.: 401–28.

5
'Where the Biological Predominates': Habitus, Reflexivity and Capital Accrual within the Field of Batten Disease

Sasha Scambler and Paul Newton

Introduction

Much of the empirical work within the sociological study of chronic disabling conditions developed, explicitly or implicitly, as a challenge to the dominance of biomedicine. Alongside the work of disability theorists in reincorporating the body into the study of disability (see for example, Lock et al., 2005; Thomas, 2004; Williams, 1999), this chapter addresses the need to re-evaluate the, often negatively portrayed, contribution of biology and biomedicine to the study of chronic disabling conditions. We draw on Bourdieu's concepts of field and habitus to chart the overwhelming impact of the biological on the lifeworld of those living with rare, chronically disabling degenerative conditions and their families. The theoretical framework provided by Bourdieu is used to present data from a recent empirical study to advance the view that for those living with such conditions, the biological can causally 'swamp' the psychological and the social in an extended and pervasive assault on the lifeworld.

In an extension to previous work (Scambler, 2005) the case for giving special empirical and theoretical attention to the growing number of people living with 'rare' conditions entailing both chronicity and profound multiple disability is made. The numbers of children living into adulthood and beyond with profound multiple disability is growing rapidly with biomedical advancements and improvements in palliative care and symptom management. In addition, such conditions offer a glimpse of the full impact of chronic disabling conditions throughout the disease course. The all-pervasive attack on multiple layers of family life from practical, physical and medical issues through to the impact on the development of and challenges to identity can be illustrated through qualitative studies of the families living with diseases of this kind. Drawing on the work of Shakespeare (2006), it can be further suggested that people living with acute, degenerative conditions are far more likely than those living with other types of chronic disabling condition to view the search for a cure as a central and essential cause (see Shakespeare, 2006). To extend the terminology of 'assault' borrowed from the title of this collection, the biological sphere can thus be seen as: the aggressor (in the form of the disease); the victim (in the form of the body); the occupier (through the pervasive influence of the disease on the lifeworld); the means of defence (through symptom management); and the potential victor (through the search for a cure).

One such biologically 'overwhelming' rare and chronically disabling degenerative condition is Batten disease. Batten disease (Neuronal Ceroid Lipofuscinoses) comprise a group of metabolic diseases which are both rare and the most common inherited neurodegenerative disorders of childhood (Siintola, Lehesjoki and Mole, 2006). Batten disease are part of a group of approximately 50 genetic Lysosomal Storage Disorders which share common clinical and biomedical characteristics. The worldwide prevalence of the group of diseases is thought to be approximately 1:12,500 (Hofmann and Peltonen, 2001) although this may be an underestimation due to poor recording in many countries. When considered as a group, however, the prevalence of the Lysosomal Storage Disorders as a whole is closer to 1:5000 (Global Organisation of Lysosomal Diseases, 2008) giving the experiences of people living with diseases within this group much wider application. This chapter starts then with an outline of the key characteristics of Batten disease in its various forms and a review of the, albeit limited, literature on rare disabling conditions of this kind. The key aspects of Bourdieu's concepts of field and habitus are then explicated and used to frame empirical data on families' experiences of living with Batten disease to encapsulate the complexity of the biologically determined 'assault' that they face.

Batten disease: The biological weapon of 'assault'

Batten disease is the common name for the group of diseases known alternatively as the neuronal ceroid lipofuscinoses, a group of rare, genetic, neurodegenerative, metabolic diseases which can be found in both children and adults across the world (Batten Disease Family Association, 2008). At present, nine different forms of Batten disease have been identified with four main types, four variants and a congenital form of the disease. The different types of Batten disease are usually classified by age of onset and are as follows:

Infantile – onset between 6 months and 2 years. Death can occur in mid-childhood.

Late infantile and variant late infantile – onset between 2 and 4 years. Death can occur between the ages of 5 and 15.

Juvenile – onset between 5 and 9 years. Death can occur from the late teens to the mid-thirties.

Adult – onset normally before the age of 40. Shortened life expectancy (Batten Disease Family Association, 2008).

Whilst age at onset, life expectancy, progress of symptoms and genetic causes vary by disease type, the group of diseases share broadly similar symptoms. Common symptoms include epilepsy, visual impairment, cognitive and motor degeneration (including the loss of the ability to walk, eat and talk) and a shortened life expectancy (Scriver et al., 2001). Work is well underway to develop gene therapies for some variants of Batten disease; however 'at present there is no cure or treatment that makes a significant impact on the progressive decline in bodily functions and inevitable early death' (Batten Disease Family Association, 2008).

The past two decades have seen great changes in the care available for children and young people with Batten disease. There have been vast changes in the mechanisms through which these conditions are diagnosed, the drugs available for seizures and other symptom control and nutritional management strategies. There have also been developments in the provision of care with the introduction of specialist medical and support services together with greater involvement of families and carers in decision-making processes. Attitudes of the wider society towards children with life-limiting neurological disorders and the quality of care to which they are entitled are also evolving with time. Most children with Batten disease in the UK receive medical care from their local paediatric services with some input from a regional paediatric neurology service, especially around the time of diagnosis. Because of the rarity of these diseases, few UK paediatricians will have seen more than one case in their professional career and paediatric neurologists are likely to have seen only a small number of cases over short periods. In other European countries, the pattern of service provision is different and experience in the management and care of families with Batten disease is concentrated in one or two multidisciplinary teams, for example, in Finland, the Netherlands and Germany. The families in these countries have established active support networks. With the increased availability of internet resources and national support groups, families are likely to become more aware of differences existing in provision of care both between and within countries.

Reviewing the literature and setting the scene

Multiple literatures are obliquely relevant to the experiences of families living with Batten disease although there is limited work relating specifically to the disease itself. To make sense of the data presented in the next section we are going to explore the relevance of a range of different literatures building to an argument that it is both necessary and timely for disciplines that have long worked in parallel with one another to come together and share their knowledge and expertise.

There is a very limited pool of literature relating specifically to Batten disease, the experiences of the families and the provision of care and services for children and adults with Batten disease. There is a raft of literature covering the provision of support to families of children with a range of other chronic and multiply disabling conditions. Most majority of this literature, however, is care oriented and/or biomedical and there is a dearth of theoretically driven, social research. In addition, most of the literature that is available focuses on juvenile Batten disease. Two studies have focused on the social implications of the disease. Labbe (1996) studied the impact on the families of caring for a child with juvenile Batten disease focusing on the issue of stress. In addition, in an earlier study, one of the present authors (Sasha Scambler) looked at the wider implications of the experiences of families living with juvenile Batten disease on our understanding of disability within society, positing that conditions of this kind pose a challenge to the more extreme versions of the social model of disability (Scambler, 2005). This thesis will be expanded in this chapter in light of the new data.

Available studies looking at the treatment of children and young adults with Batten disease focus on medical treatments, symptom control and the potential development of therapies rather than psychosocial. The initial study carried out by SeeAbility (Scambler, 1999) focusing on juvenile Batten disease, and the 'Family Support Study' commissioned by the Batten Disease Family Association (Scambler and

Williams, 2008), remain the only in-depth studies of the social care/ support needs of this group as seen through the eyes of both families and professionals in the UK. Whilst there is a lack of written/published information, there is an accumulation of knowledge, particularly around the key professionals working in the area. Much of this information remains at an informal level and is not published and in the wider arena. Any review of the literature, therefore, is a reflection of the lack of published material and not necessarily a reflection of knowledge.

A good sample of current, published and non-published, expertise can be found in the proceedings of the first International Education Conference on Batten Disease which was held in Orebro, Sweden, in 2006. This conference reflected current research and best practice in the provision of care for children and young adults with Batten disease and is the largest body of written, published and unpublished, expertise reflecting the range of issues from laboratory-based gene manipulations to care strategies and education. Amongst the scientific papers, Cooper (2006) outlined developments in the understanding of where and how the brain is effected in juvenile Batten disease, whilst Mole (2006) focused on the need to carry out complete genetic analysis of each person with Batten disease so that 'diagnostic approaches can be appropriately modified and extended' (Mole, 2006: 2). This is a further step in the process of moving towards a therapy or therapies. The education stream focused on education strategies, locations and common misconceptions. Johnston (2006) explored the issues from a parents' perspective whilst behaviour management issues (Bills and Calvert, 2006) and individual needs (Punkari, Eskonen and Hietaharju-Mölsä, 2006) were also addressed. Other issues covered included parent-support groups (Houen and Munkholm, 2006), disclosure (Willers, 2006) and web resources (Mole, 2006; Schultz and Kohlschutter, 2006). This gives a flavour of the papers that came out of the conference, and illustrates the fact that whilst there is little published on Batten disease, there is much knowledge and experience that could and should be pooled.

In a study carried out in 2002, Brett asked parents to think about the relationship between themselves and the various professionals involved in the care of their child. She suggests that the role of parents, particularly where children have severe disabilities, is crucial: 'I consider that parents hold the key to their child's communication and offer that by "ignoring" the experience of these "others", the social model may miss the "voice" and thus the experience of the child.' (2002: 831). Brett focused on the need for a partnership between parents and professionals. She highlights the many and varied medical tasks taken on by the parents of children with severe disabilities and the many new skills which need to be learned in order to carry out these tasks. A lack of support was highlighted. Murray (2000) also looked at the provision of care and specifically at special education. She suggested the need for a parent-professionals partnership if the best possible care is to be provided. This is a view echoed by Spiegle and van den Pol (1993) who suggest that where a child has total or almost total communicative inability, parents hold the key to accessing their personal experiences and background. Brown (1998) takes this further to suggest that parents offer a context through which meanings can be attached to the child's experiences and actions, particularly where the child does not have the communication skills or short-term memory to do this themselves.

The idea of 'discursive othering' (Dowse, 2001) or the use of parents' views on their children's wants and needs as a proxy for the child's own voice has been seen as problematic. It has been suggested that focusing on the interface between parents and professionals can effectively exclude the voice of the child from the equation (Cocks, 2000; Shakespeare, 1999). Murray (2000) deals with this criticism directly, however, when she talks about a parent-professionals partnership:

> In using the term here, I am referring to relationships within which my son was positively valued in addition to being central and of foremost importance; where, in the light of his medical condition, his learning and communication difficulties, my parental knowledge was seen as crucial to forming and maintaining a relationship with him; where different roles with regard to my son were recognised and the boundaries between those roles respected by all parties; and finally, and most importantly, they were relationships with which my son was happy.

She suggests that most parents automatically work from the viewpoint that the child is of primary and central importance.

A range of papers also look at the parent-professional partnership. Baxter (1989) looked at the experiences of parents of children with learning difficulties and suggested four main parameters through which the attitudes of professionals are perceived by parents of disabled children: helpfulness; professional interest (in all aspects of child's health, life, family etc.); consideration and respect; and professional commitment. Baxter found that service delivery was more likely to be successful if professionals displayed helpfulness in facilitating access to the services that parents need. Showing an interest was deemed as important – even where services were well designed, they were less well rated if the professionals showed little interest. Case (2000) takes this a step further suggesting that professionals continue to control the parent-professional relationship. He makes the case that families need to play a greater role in the decision-making process when looking at the care needs of their children. A related point is made by Brown (1998) who notes that families are unique in terms of their child's specific problems – BUT they share a commonality of experience in their conflictual, unsatisfactory relationships with professionals. Dissatisfaction with the parent-professional relationship seems to be a common theme in the literature, and one which fits well with the experiences of the families in this study.

Finally, a number of other issues are covered. Dowling and Dolan (2001) look at the financial implications of having a disabled child. They suggest that families of children with disabilities experience a range of inequalities which families of non-disabled children do not. These include financial hardship, stress and anxiety as a result of social barriers, prejudices and poorly conceived service provision. Similarly, Higginson (2003) suggests that not only do parents sit in the middle trying to achieve the best care for their children, but they often have care needs of their own. Informal carers offering palliative care often have needs unmet and suffer psychological morbidity. Few interventions targeted at this group are reported in the carer literature. Whilst there is little doubt that Batten disease offers a particularly extreme example of a chronic disabling disease, the rarity of the disease, combined with a lack of research, necessitates drawing conclusions from a wider literature.

Linking the literatures

Theorizing a biological assault on the lifeworld

What can be seen from the literature is the all-encompassing impact of Batten disease on the lifeworlds of all those it touches. There is a multifaceted and multilayered effect which can be causally attributed to the biological attributes of the disease but is biological, social and psychological in its impact. The biological impact of the disease is both direct in its determination of the symptoms of the disease itself and the nature of the trajectory, and indirect in its impact on every, or almost every, aspect of daily life. Even the direct biological impact of the disease spreads far beyond the affected, diagnosed individual. The hereditary nature of Batten disease spreads the direct biological impact to siblings and extended family members as well as potentially to future generations through a network of carrier, post and prenatal testing. To begin to understand the multi-level factors at play within Batten disease a theoretical means for framing the experiential level web of interrelated experiences, choices and actions that occur is needed along with a means to chart the flows of capital through which these experiences are shaped and the context in which they occur. One possible means for gaining this wider picture is through the use of Bourdieu's concepts of field and habitus along with economic, social, cultural and symbolic capital (1990, 1992, 1999). Using the work of Bourdieu allows us to encapsulate the causal swamping of the lifeworld by the biological within the field of Batten disease whilst acknowledging both capital flows and individual agency.

The field refers to a social arena, bounded in an experiential context, which 'calls forth' the need to respond and attend to the self and/or a given situation. For Bourdieu a field is '...a relational configuration endowed with specific gravity which imposes on all the objects and agents which enter into it' (cited in Adams, 2006: 514). Thus, fields both prompt and orientate certain behaviours from the agents entering them. By envisaging Batten disease as a field with biologically determined parameters, we can explore the ways in which the disease and all it entails impose on all of the objects and agents which find themselves within it. The parameters of the field are temporal and temporary in that they are dependant on the changing and developing realms of biological and biomedical research into both the genetic makeup and mechanisms of the disease itself and the development of potential therapies to 'treat' it. Thus, we can chart the changing nature of behaviour exhibited by families on entering the field. Further, although fields are generated in any circumstances where practices are performed – inherent within them is a structured system of social positions and power relations formed by the interplay and distribution of various species of capital, some of which may cut across multiple fields. These positions develop because positions occupied within the field afford or deny access to the distribution of resources within a field.

> [A] field may be defined as a network, or a configuration, of objective relations between positions. These positions are objectively defined, in their existence and in the determinations they impose on their occupants, agents and institutions, by their present and potential situation in the structure of the distribution of the species of power (or capital) whose possession commands access to the specific profits

that are at stake in the field, as well as their objective relations to other positions... (Bourdieu and Wacquant, 1992: 94)

An exploration of the capital controlled by families would then allow us to explore the relationship between families and the social world in which they find themselves, incorporating parent/professional power relations, family relations, career choices, educational decisions and all of the minutiae of daily life affected by the disease onset, trajectory, prognosis and outcome.

Bourdieu distinguishes four key form or species of capital which operate throughout fields: economic, cultural, social and symbolic. In addition, we draw on the work of Williams (1995), who suggests a further form of capital, 'physical capital' which is particularly relevant to those existing in a field with biologically determined parameters.

- Economical capital is directly convertible to commodity forms for example, money, and is institutionalized, for example, property rights. In the field of Batten disease, economic capital can refer to the money available to families to adapt to and combat the disease, through personal wealth, benefits and state intervention. This economic capital is institutionalized through the health and welfare systems.
- Cultural capital is based on socially 'legitimated' knowledge and practices (including 'distinctions in taste'), which in certain circumstances is convertible to economic capital and is institutionalized through educational qualifications. Families entering the field of Batten disease may face a challenge to their cultural capital reserves and their ability to build more capital as they face the challenge of developing new knowledge and practices around the disease process.
- Social capital refers to affiliations and obligations in relations pertaining to social obligations and quality of relations with others, which may also be convertible to economic capital, and is institutionalized through social networks. This type of capital can be found in the formal and informal support networks available to and drawn on by families and may be challenged by the loss or non-repetition of previous forms of support.
- Symbolic capital relates to the prestige and honour ascribed to significant institutions, groups and relations with people which in certain circumstances is convertible to economic capital, and is institutionalized through systems of status for example, peerage systems

and parental authority. In the field of Batten disease, parents find their symbolic capital in the form of parental authority challenged by a multitude of professional experts with higher levels of symbolic capital within the field. New avenues for collecting this type of capital are needed as parents develop and extend their parental authority into biomedical decision-making, practice and potentially an altogether new status as an expert patient by proxy.

- Physical capital relates to the health, fitness for purpose and aesthetic quality of the body through which actors embody habitus within the field. In the field of Batten disease, the body of the actors is only relevant in so much as it holds up to the strain of providing care. We suggest that a more relevant form of physical capital in this field is the loss or challenge to physical capital by proxy by the impact of the disease process on the lives of the children and young adults living with Batten disease.

All of these forms of capital are explored through the experiences of families living with Batten disease in the next section. The relative confluences, disjunctions or homologies between positions in the field determine the configuration of forces within the field, and the inter- and intra-balances of power within and between species of capital and fields. In Batten disease the configuration of forces within the field are controlled by biology and the professionals who are seen as legitimate holders and keepers of capital within the field. Thus, for families entering the field they must compete not just to accrue capital but to have their capital resources legitimated by those who hold dominant forms of capital within the field. Although the accrual of capital yields power, capital requires a field in which to operate. As such, primary aims of agents in the field is maintaining and improving (or preventing a devaluation) of their position. This may lead to a position where families fight to gain capital and legitimation for that capital, and professionals fight to prevent legitimation of types of capital which threaten their pre-existing positions and power within the field, leading to the types of relationships highlighted in the work of Murray (2000). Similarly, cultural commonalities, repeated social hierarchies and even patterns of bodily form and deportment are reproduced through practice and evaluated and accorded differential status and social, cultural and economic values in a pre-existing field; thus it is not just symbolic and cultural capital that may be challenged.

Like Giddens (2005), Bourdieu focuses on the unthinking everyday, taken-for-granted practices of actors. Thus, habitus – the agentic aspect of Bourdieu's approach – pertains to the stocks of acquired knowledge (Layder, 1994) or a received system of generative dispositions (Williams, 1995) malleable by the conditions (field/s) in which they are constituted. Bourdieu argues that not only does the habitus form and set embodied dispositions (presenting and maintaining the body and its deportment), but it also sets the parameters (through contact with the orienting and mediating nature of fields) of behaviour and social/personal expectation. Thus, field, habitus and capital serve to condition the individual and maintain structures through repeated social practices. Following Bourdieu, the families of those with Batten disease, as agents, move through a variety of fields in their conduct but tend to attract or move within fields common to their social groupings, thus developing a tacit, non-consciously realizable competence in these given fields – 'le lens pratique...(feel for the game)' (Bourdieu, cited in Adams, 2006). Further to this, Bourdieu (1990: 20) refers to 'doxic experience' where '... objective structures and internal structures...' are mutually constitutive and complementary, thus describing the unthinking nature of practices whilst showing how more deliberated and intentional actions will still be located in logic of their social practices and orientated towards the individual's experiences of reality (via doxic habitus). As Bourdieu states 'Each agent, wittingly or unwittingly, willy nilly, is producer and reproducer of objective meaning...it is because the subjects do not, strictly speaking, know what they are doing that what they do has more meaning than they know' (cited in Williams, 1995: 582). Hence, families fighting for control over their children's illness and working within incomplete knowledge about the disease structure and an uncertain trajectory add to and transform the parameters of the field in which they are acting as they add to biological knowledge about the disease both directly through research and clinical trials and indirectly through experiential developments and the sharing of ideas and actions. The structurally positioned effect precedes and determines any autonomous action. Bourdieu describes this succinctly in his assertion that '...people's wills adjust to their possibilities' because 'they have a taste for what they are anyway condemned to' (Bourdieu, 1990: 216; Bourdieu cited in Williams, 1995: 594).

> [W]hat Bourdieu described are subconscious culturally determined templates or dispositions which inform behaviour and importantly generate different forms of capital for an individual in different settings (Bourdieu, 1984). He also typologised these cultural templates on the basis of class and argued that the characteristics of those

templates inform and reinforce inter-class power relations together with facets such as health behaviour. When a person's habitus and field are congruent they develop important social, economic and psychological capital which provide the resources of life. If, however, something interferes with that congruence their capacity to develop such capital is compromised. (Forbes and Wainwright, 2001: 806)

This is particularly relevant here as we present a field which changes the social world in which families find themselves and not only destroys, albeit temporarily, their capacity to produce capital but also assaults reserves built up in other more congruent fields. This can include the loss of reserves of social capital through the loss of friendship support networks, and the loss of economic and symbolic capital through the curtailment or cessation of careers and the status they ascribe.

The final part of Bourdieu's theory relevant to us here is the reference to an individual's capacity for reflexivity. Bourdieu portrays reflexivity as a form or aspect of habitus, or a required constituent of a given field. In scientific and academic study as a field, for example, reflexive awareness is actively encouraged. Similarly, the awareness felt and acted upon when moving through non-doxic fields is seen as reflexive – for example, a situation where a non-clinically trained person attempts self-consciously to adapt their behaviour to their understandings of the clinical environment they have found themselves in. Reflexivity is also seen to arise in crisis or new situations, and in the awareness required to manage the self (habitus) when moving between various fields. All of the above examples highlight that reflexivity is formed in response to the requirements or procedures of the field, and in some instances it can be converted into forms of capital (Adams, 2006). Field as aspirational, or as exigent in the practices of state institutions, for example, active citizenry, becomes ascriptive or productive upon habitus through becoming positioned within exigent requirements of forms of capital. For example, considering parents' attitudes towards the transmission of cultural values through involvement in their children's education from a Bourdieuan perspective, Reay (1998) concludes that 'middle class women are predominantly engaging in a process of replicating habitus while their working class counterparts are attempting a much harder task; that of transforming habitus'. Hence, Bourdieu addresses Bauman's (2003) assertion that choices (as structured by the dynamics of field) may be meaningless, even oppressive, without the resources and conditions to follow them through, or exclude and alienate those who do not understand or have the 'feel for the game'.

Theoretical modelling of the empirical data: Living in the field of Batten disease

The data presented here are part of a study funded by the Batten Disease Family Association (BDFA) through 'Jeans for Genes' to look at the support needs of families of children and young adults with Batten disease in light of existing services. Participants were recruited from the Batten Disease Family Association (the largest charity for families with Batten Disease in the UK). Data were collected through in-depth semi-structured interviews with 17 families of children and young adults with Batten disease, and the interviews covered the 3 most common forms of Batten disease. All interviews were recorded and transcribed verbatim and thematic analysis was conducted. Ethics approval for the study was gained from Kings College London Ethics Committee.

Defining the field

From symptom onset through the often lengthy pre-diagnosis period to the confirmation of diagnosis and the start of the process of reorientation, reconstitution and adjustment, Batten disease has a profound impact on the lifeworld of both the affected child and his/her family. The impact of the disease moves beyond the multiple challenges of daily life to incorporate, often complex, biomedical knowledge based activities and decision-making procedures. The daily lives of families with Batten disease are irrevocably bound to biomedicine regardless of the lack of a cure and the essentially palliative nature of the care required. Further, the process of negotiating the lifeworld necessarily combines the social, emotional and biological consequences of living with a disease of this type and can be understood only as a bio-psycho-social interaction. The starting point for an analysis of the impact of Batten disease on the lifeworld is the point of symptom onset. It is at this point that families enter the 'field' of Batten disease. As suggested previously, the parameters of the field are biological and both temporal and temporary. Parameters change over time with the development of new knowledges, technologies and therapies, and the entire 'field' only exists in its present form as long as there is no cure.

The field is entered through the formal process of diagnosis where affected children receive the requisite label and families receive the legitimation of their place within the field. The process of diagnosis is not a straightforward one however, and may take a period of months or years and involve a number of misdiagnoses. Families could find themselves lingering on the periphery of the field, sometimes for extended periods, whilst awaiting the legitimation required to fully enter the field and be formally recognized, and in the interim facing potential challenges to their right to even linger on the periphery:

> *We had lots of investigation, people coming back saying they couldn't find anything wrong.* (006: 1)
>
> *Basically she was treated as if she was a naughty girl.* (004:1)
>
> *[He] referred us to the local general hospital who basically told us there wasn't a problem; they just found he was lazy.* (013:1)
>
> *I was referred to a consultant and was told I was neurotic and imagining things.* (012:1)

The most common biological marker heralding a diagnosis was the onset of seizures although initial symptoms such as visual impairment and a decrease in motor ability often preceded this. Initial problems were most likely to be picked up in school and viewed initially as behavioural. Accounts given also suggested an element of luck in being referred to a professional with some knowledge of the disease and, where this occurred, the diagnosis followed relatively quickly. What can be seen from this is that whilst the parameters of the field are biological, the gatekeepers are biomedical utilizing the biological to generate and maintain their power. Theirs is the position at the top of the hierarchy to which all other positions are ultimately answerable, and yet, the experiences of the families interviewed suggest that due to the rarity of the disease, it is a position often characterized by ignorance and insouciance.

Whilst parents fight to gain entry to the field and access to the positions within it, it is clear that the field is one to which they would rather not belong. Entry to the field is both shocking and traumatizing, and it also radically changes the lifeworld of those entering it, attacking the very notion of 'normality'.

> *Between four and nine we thought we were going to have a child that was going to grow up and live a normal life but would be blind. But all that changed when he was diagnosed with Juvenile Battens. It's changed everything basically.* (013:2)

Then from the perfect child, you knew there was something wrong, it was serious. I think it was so hard to think about, especially when your child's born healthy, and you tend to think everything will be all right, it makes you realise that – And you think she's fine, she'll be OK. (011:2)

I think we felt afterwards that everything we believed was totally undermined and had gone. ... We have no one else in the family so she's the last one. (002:7)

You came away thinking there was nothing, and you felt despair, you felt they didn't give you any hope, they didn't give you anything constructive that you could work with. And yet you had been delivered with a double whammy of a bombshell and that was it. (004:3)

it was just like [she] had died, that's what it, because I've lost people close to me before, and that's what it felt like, she'd died, someone had told me she'd died. (014:2)

We have got to be positive because we have got to live with this every day. You don't just live with it at the time of diagnosis, every minute, every hour, every day. So for our sanity we have to, not lie, but live a level of normality somehow. (002:4)

Entry into the field of Batten disease is thus a traumatic and life-changing event through which the very notion of normality is challenged. When coupled with the loss of the 'dreams' that parents so often have for their children, this represents a reorientation of both present and future realities and suggests a changed or reconstituted sense of the reality within the lifeworld.

Habitus and reflexivity

Habitus emerges at the point that parents move on from reacting to the diagnosis and start to 'cope' with or respond to it. It could be argued, however, that at least in the early stages of entry into the field of Batten disease, the majority of actions represent not just habitus but reflexivity as reflexivity is seen to arise in crisis or new situations, and this is clearly both. In this sense reflexivity is a process of seeking a context for the content of their experiences. Diagnosis puts some perspective on experiences to date, providing a brief sense of clarity, but the 'causal swamping' of biology leaves them with a certainty of more uncertainty rather than their previous (uninformed) uncertainty. This ties in with the idea of reflexivity being a necessity, a blessing, and a curse where the habitus is removed from its field, as for Bourdieu the very awareness felt and acted upon when moving through a non-doxic, or alien, field such as Batten disease is seen as reflexive; thus, parents have to find a way of negotiating an unknown field with little knowledge about the resources which are needed or how they might accumulate them. Parents use the 'acquired knowledge' (Layder, 1994) that they have brought into the field to shape the ways in which they respond, drawing on the capital that they have already accumulated whilst developing an understanding of the capital that they are going to need in order to 'act' effectively within the field, and of how that capital might be accrued. For those willing and able to exercise reflexivity, this process started at or before the point of diagnosis and would carry them throughout their visit to the field.

> *It's just so numbing that you really need to go away to then just look at it, and we'd look at it and we'd look at it, to stop ourselves going into denial, yea, because this is the reality, you know, that is highlighted as well, the reality of what it is, you know, you can't change it, but if you didn't have anything in black and white you can change your mind, but this is black and white, and that was very important.* (015:2)

For others, habitus in the form of the unthinking everyday, taken-for-granted practices of actors identified by Bourdieu was reflected in the initial reaction on entry to the field.

> *Saying really not more than half your family are going to survive, so we both felt suicidal really. Kind of the thought process went through our minds – you know, shall we drive in the lake all of us together. But having a new baby was a practicality for keeping going.* (001:3)

Unthinking exercising of habitus here can still be seen to represent a move to a way of coping and the start of the process of reintegration into the lifeworld and of both habitus and the possibility of more obvious reflexivity. Reflexivity in its positive form, when relating to the ability to demonstrate awareness through planning and organization, is the key to the successful negotiation of the field of Batten disease and lies in the ability to be proactive. One father described the point at which he made this substantive change through the realization that the diagnosis was not an end point, and that he still had many years with his son.

> *[He] was diagnosed when he was nine and you don't realise at the time, you know, that with some luck your child can live 18, 20 and probably beyond*

that and still have a reasonable and enjoyable life. And that's more time that you've got with your child. (013:5)

This was a sentiment echoed by a number of parents who talked about experiencing relief at meeting other parents with older children and seeing children who were still enjoying their lives five or more years on from diagnosis. Reflexivity here represents the positive choice to enjoy the time available and the awareness that in order for this to happen parents have to act to accumulate and spend the necessary capital to provide that 'reasonable and enjoyable life'.

So really from September to Christmas, we were going through sort of looking at is there any ray of hope, and at the same time, parallel with that was – OK you now have – what do you do, what do you do, and I felt I like to have a plan, if I have a plan, then at least I'm following a train track, I've got a guide, I've got a mission. I've got a direction to follow. If I don't have a plan I found my emotions were going all over the place, they were, they were just all over the place. (015:2)

It is at this stage that the need to negotiate, accumulate and spend the appropriate types of capital becomes apparent. In order to 'have a plan' and follow it to fruition parents need to first discover what actions they need to take to successfully negotiate the field of Batten disease, the capital needed to perform these actions and where or how this capital might be accumulated. It is in the negotiation that takes place around capital that the permeation of the biological becomes apparent in this field, moving from the determination and policing of the parameters of the field itself to control of the transactions that take place within it.

Capital accumulation and transactions

All five of the forms of capital identified in the previous section are utilized by families negotiating their way through this field. Whilst the successful conclusion of their actions may be beyond the individual (although many can and do take an active part in basic and clinical research) the ability to carve out a positive lifeworld experience and forge the necessary relations within and across positions in the field is dependent on capital. Physical capital is central to the nature of the actions and transactions taking place within the field and is as yet separated from all but the affected children and young adults. The parameters of the field necessitate the inevitable, gradual and complete loss of physical capital for those affected and the loss of this physical capital by proxy for the families living with and managing the disease process. Thus, physical capital is central to the field through its permeation of all else rather than in and of itself. The impact of physical capital in this field can be seen through its ramifications for all other forms of capital.

Cultural capital and symbolic capital

Cultural capital is the key to successful negotiations with the multitude of professionals encountered within this field. The professionals' legitimacy stems from their symbolic capital within biomedicine and cemented through the accreditation and qualifications gained through cultural accumulation. Whilst for the professionals within the field the symbolic status that they maintain assists with their cultural capital and vice versa, for parents moving into and exerting habitus within the field the symbolic capital that they have through their status as parents may actually damage their ability to accumulate cultural capital. A whole range of biomedical expertise in symptom control, therapies, pharmacy, palliative care and knowledge of the disease and research developments are developed and yet parents fight to be 'taken seriously' in their dealings with biologically legitimated professionals.

> *If it's a ... like a weekend for example and you got up at 5, give them the drugs, give them their breakfast, every two hours it's either a feed, or a water, or a bonus feed, or drugs ... and obviously it's moving them backwards or forwards or into a room or position, because obviously they can't stay in the same position all the time, and obviously pad changes regularly, especially with [my son] because he's ... he does like to wee a lot (laughs). It's worse with him and he is so heavy it involves a lot of hoisting because I can't lift him any more ... it's a case of personal hygiene, mouth care all the time ... keeping an eye on, that they keep their feeds in. You can't just, like with a normal child you would give them their dinner and they would eat their dinner and that would be it. You have to keep an eye on it, you have to let out wind because if you don't do that they will vomit their food back up. And the vomit then goes onto their ... so there is all that to contend with. In between sort of dealing with the rest of the family as well. Come the evening time it's feeds again. The last feed is at ... between six and half six. This is all recorded in the book so that we both know, because you're doing it with two children as well we write it in the book, all the time, what we do with them. Feeds and drugs for the night, you have to wait for those to*

settle and then move them back into the bedroom again and change them, which is not easy because they're not easy children because of the condition they're in now. And then it's a case of getting them into a comfortable position through the night. And then you're up and down through the night anyway repositioning, or if they cough you're using suction because they can't swallow, and [my daughter] now, regrettably is having oxygen therapy all the time, she's constantly on oxygen. (012:10)

This type of daily routine served as a backdrop to any activities undertaken by the family and limits their participation in the lifeworld. Parents battle to get legitimation for their multiple expert roles within the care and have to balance this with their roles as parents.

I just feel I'm playing this role of God, you know, I'm deciding do I give her another one or not, without fully knowing all the effects of what I'm giving her. So, I suppose from that point of view, I just feel terribly, terribly responsible ... it would be nice if someone, if we didn't have to make that decision. If someone just said – right give her this. (014:20)

For all of the families living and acting within the field of Batten disease, medication and the management of a complex and often uncertain medical regimen has simply become part of daily life and of the fabric of their lifeworlds. This requires them to develop a detailed and advanced knowledge of medical issues which they would not otherwise have had to have as parents. Whilst this is clearly cultural capital it lacks the legitimation taken for granted by biomedical and allied professionals. Parents are neither experts in the professional sense of the term, nor expert patients. They could be viewed as expert patients by proxy but as of yet gain no cultural or symbolic capital for this status.

Social capital

Social capital in the field of Batten disease takes two forms: it is evident in the informal support networks developed by and around families and in the formal support structures mitigated by the institutions of health and social care and education. Support, when offered, was rarely turned down, although there was also a need to control the care and support offered, particularly where it related to a multitude of different people coming in to the home and/or to providing assistance with personal care. This led to parents having to make decisions about the number of people that they wanted coming into their home on a regular basis and, thus, the level of support received.

> *Yes. I was satisfied. They all wanted me to have more and I said 'no thank you'. (004:14)*

> *We've never ... wanted or requested any external support although it has been offered on lots and lots of occasions ... We're a close knit family as in me and my wife and my kids and then [my wife's] mum and dad, we're really close as well, we just wanted to look after them ourselves. And if we were ever going to get into a state where we couldn't look after them then we'd have asked but it's never got to that. We've never needed respite care for them or anything ... that's basically down to being able to pack in work and look after them both. (16:4)*

Here, the accumulated economic capital was seen as mitigating the need for formal social capital, whilst informal social capital was highly regarded, accumulated and used.

> *Money wise, thankfully the State provided an income that we were able to live on and look after our children 24 hours a day, so ... and it wasn't as if it was a ... it wasn't hard to look after them. A lot of families have a lot of kids who are problematic and need a lot of energy to look after them. But with [our daughters] there was, the period where they could still walk aided was hard work where you had to sort of physically support them and they would try to walk because they still wanted to play and wanted to be able to run around, that period was hard work. But as soon as they couldn't walk it was just a case of having them sat on your knee or taking them for walks in their pushchairs and that. It wasn't as physically demanding. We didn't get to a point where we couldn't mentally cope with them at all. (16:5)*

Two types of 'non-professional' or informal social capital were used by families taking the forms of kinship and friendship networks and the specific social capital gained through links to other affected families within the field.

> *We don't get any professional support, but obviously we've got network and family – extended family that will have her for a couple of hours for a break. (014:19)*

> *We tend to use grandparents ... the problem is the grandparents, you know they're all in their seventies, but they'll come round here and sit with him*

in the evening so if we want to go for a curry we can do. And they're quite comfortable doing that. (013:14)

Again the essentially messy nature of social interactions within the lifeworld can be seen here as the social capital gained through close family ties with grandparents is threatened by the physical capital being lost to the grandparents through the ageing process. This serves to illustrate the point that all transactions are interlinked, and that even where not directly linked to the disease itself, the influence of biology can be seen. In addition, whilst informal social capital was seen as invaluable it was not available to all families through lack of kinship networks, geography or prejudice.

Different forms of social capital are used for different purposes.

I've got a network of friends and family who not necessarily support me in the Batten's, but just support me as a person. (014:17)

The nature of the disease and its impact on the family can have an effect on the ability to accumulate or maintain social capital, however.

I think what you actually rapidly find is that you can have a bunch of friends out there, and some are born to be compassionate, and some are not, and you find that your structure of friends changes and some of your valued friends you find yourself losing because they are just not into disability or whatever, um. (015:4)

Friendships survive but may take on different forms, particularly in the development of new friendship networks through the disease itself. A positive effect of membership of a biologically determined and controlled field is the presence of similar others. Friendship relations with other Battens families were seen as particularly important in combating isolation as well as in sharing knowledge and experiences.

Formal social capital takes the form of the social relationships forged with professionals positioned within the field and the support or care they provide. This incorporates medical and nursing care, the therapies and institutions such as social services. Formal social capital was broadly inadequate, difficult to accumulate and of poor quality. Most families could, however, identify particular professionals or strains of formal social capital that were knowledgable, adaptive and supportive. A lack of knowledge on the part of the professionals, due again to the biological nature of the disease and its rarity, was identified as the main cause, confounded by a lack of social and communication skills and constraint within a wider, less responsive health and social care system. The level of cultural and social capital displayed by those providing formal care is key.

> *We were then sent to see a consultant..., who clearly had no idea what Battens was but she was willing to get herself up to speed on it and she did that very quickly and she's proved a real help. And also she asked that we could give her all the information that the BDFA had given to us, which we did, and still do. She still asks for, anything new that the BDFA produces she likes to get a copy.* (013:4)

> *We were surprised that we were dealing with something they hadn't heard of and also that when we went back they didn't seem to know any more. It took us a long time before we met somebody who knew a bit more about it.* (008:2)

Here parents' reactions, reflexivity and their ability to utilize stores of social, cultural and symbolic capital can assist.

> *We used to go in from school with a little folder that actually told them the sort of things that were actually wrong with [our daughter] and how to talk to her. But yes, nursing staff, some of them did need a bit of a kick.* (004:13)

> *We used a communication tool to try to keep everybody up to date – an all about me book, which works – you know it just kept everybody up to date. You know the condition changes very quickly, you might get a report from a dietitian or a speech therapist one day and it would take two weeks for that report to reach the school and also the change needed to happen the next day if it was to involve swallowing or diet etc.* (001:10)

Others organized regular meetings with key professionals to ensure that all were up to speed, not just with the disease itself but with the specific needs of their child. Again, the essential biological nature of the disease is the key and even those in 'powerful' positions with the appropriate types of symbolic and cultural capital may not be of use to the families.

> *I just think they've got no idea what they're doing, what they're dealing with... the whole thing is just a charade. They deal with us because they have to deal with us because obviously it's bad professionalism not to. I've had too many bad experiences with all of them. And it's as soon as you've*

got the word 'terminal' next to you you're written off. You really are written off. You've got no future so why bother. (012:18)

What is apparent from the quotes above is that the situations which families and, to a lesser extent, professionals find themselves in in this field is one where their habitus is not congruent with the field and the very nature of the field curtails the numbers of people in positions higher up the hierarchy who are able to act to full capacity within this field. The nature of the field devalues the capital of almost all of those who find themselves within it and renders them relatively powerless.

Economic capital

The role of economic capital within these transactions can be illustrated through two aspects of the experiences of families: the impact of the disease on the career and aspirations of the parents and their earning potential, and the all-encompassing need for equipment and the necessary funding to purchase that equipment. The nature of Batten disease and the care it entails impacted on all parents' ability to accumulate personal economic capital. Biologically determined impact ranged from career choices, flexibility, progression and in some cases, being compelled to give up work. Whilst clearly social processes and wider issues around gender relations and the position of care and carers within society need to be taken into consideration here, these social factors act on a backdrop of the essential biological determinants of the field.

I've tried to get work since but I can't find an employer who's sympathetic to the amount of time off and the unpredictability. (006:5)

I used to work. I had to give work up because every time I had a job I would get an emergency call and people just didn't consider me to be reliable enough. So I had to give up my ... [children's father] managed to keep his job. He's had a few warnings where he's had to rush off to be there for them, but even he's ... I mean he got his holiday and it's all gone, already. He uses his holiday up to care for them so he doesn't even get holiday time. (012:12)

My career has now really been terminated, so I'll probably get a job but it won't be well-paid. (009:5)

I went for another position and I was basically told, even though it's prejudice, I was told that I can't have it because of my children, because they would interfere with my work. (012:12)

Over half of those interviewed had been forced to give up, or seriously curtail their work. Clearly, the government's plans for flexible family-friendly working, along with the anti-discrimination legislation, are not doing the job they were developed for.

The personal economic capital accumulated by the families is balanced against the institutionalized economic capital that they may be able to access through health and social care funding streams and the welfare system. Here the dearth of money within the system itself caused access problems for families, ranging from lack of access to services to the cessation of funding for necessary equipment.

> *I think the difficulty was that social services, education and health, the only real difficulties was getting them to work together was to do with the funding, and who would fund what. And I know that's a political issue as much as anything else. (014:7)*
>
> *From when [my daughter] was diagnosed I had the counsellor. And it's finished because they've run out of money. (011:8)*
>
> *People that don't live with it don't realise just how housebound you become if you haven't got the equipment. (001:11)*
>
> *They couldn't be hoisted onto the sofa or sit with us on a chair. They have to be in a wheelchair all the time. So they can't sit and have a cuddle with their parents unless my ex-husband lifts them for a cuddle. Which is quite strenuous. His back's nearly gone now. It's a bit of a joke really. (012:15)*

The ability to apply for, fight for and eventually access funding depends on the availability of cultural, symbolic and social capital reserves. Where institutional level funding is inaccessible, personal economic capital again comes into play.

> *You know the financing you can get doesn't cover what you need a lot of the time, so lots of families go down the route of fundraising for themselves so you know, family, friends and local people do that so that's quite challenging in itself, when you are used to being self-sufficient financially. To actually have to ask for help from friends and neighbours to get through the day is really difficult. (001:7)*

What also becomes clear, when talking to families, is that there are benefits available to families which can be accessed if parents know about them and have the energy, wherewithal and cultural capital to jump through all of the hoops necessary to secure them. Here capital is used in the form of organizational skills.

We've got the hospice, social services, occupational therapists, charities in terms of – various charities provide various bits of equipment which the health service doesn't provide, or social services don't, bereavement support, play schemes, and then you've obviously got a financial sort of back-up which you sort of then need to deal with, which is your dis-ability living allowance which is filling in a form and on an annual basis confirming it, mobility allowance for [my son's], carers allowance, council tax reduction if you've got somebody in a wheelchair and you've had adaptations to the home you have one band council tax reduction, car tax reduction they pay your car tax on the car, you have a blue badge for parking, TV licence reduction, for visual impairment in the household you get your TV licence for 50% of the fee. Transport reductions – [my son] is free along with his carer on almost all the transport. In London also we have about £500 of taxis a year, different grant schemes if you have to start adapting your home, obviously, so co-ordinating all that, and therefore, on average, you have certainly got two meetings or three or four, a week. On top of your normal routine. And if you are setting up something new, you've got much more. So that's just your average dealing. (015:19)

Clearly, a huge amount of energy is expended in setting up and main-taining these services and funding sources, requiring massive amounts of cultural capital, reflexivity and organization. It clearly also helps to have a store of symbolic capital transferred through from previous fields.

One of my rules now, is I have always said, generally is it takes a year to get something. If I have to help someone – a new person, I always tell them everything takes a year. If it takes you six months, then great. If it takes 18 months your expectation is not far wrong, but it takes a lot of time to get professionals wound up or charities wound up to give you pieces of kit or what have you – yes it takes a year. (015:9)

The examples given above are only some of the many actions and transactions that take place within the field of Batten disease and are given to illustrate the biologically shaped nature of this lifeworld rather than to illuminate the minutiae of daily life with the disease. What they do is show the complex, messy nature of the lifeworld in which families find themselves and give a taste of the arena in which they have to enact habitus, display reflexivity and manage multiple capital transactions with players and institutions occupying various positions within the hierarchy of the field and themselves constrained by the very nature of the field in which they are all present.

Some final points

Exploration of the lifeworld of families living with Batten disease illustrates the multiple impacts of living with a chronic multiply disabling condition of this type and the all-encompassing implications across the family. What you have is a complex web of interrelated factors necessitating a sophisticated understanding of the ways in which they interact with one another. As the data here illustrate, the lifeworld of these families, and thus the impact of Batten disease on daily life, cannot be understood solely through exploration of the biological, social or psychological impacts of the disease process. In the words of Law (2004) the lifeworld and people's lives within it are 'messy' and cannot be understood in their entirety through neat structured qualitative studies and recourse to a single discipline or literature. In attempting to constrain and compartmentalize the lifeworld we run the risk of losing the essence of that messiness and compromise our understanding of its multifaceted nature. In the same way, immersion in a single means of understanding the lifeworld loses the sense of the whole. What is needed to aid in understanding is a theoretical framework which allows us to unpick this messy whole without losing its essential messiness. Bourdieu's concepts of field and habitus are one way of doing this, allowing for the messiness of the lifeworld within the constraining parameters of a biologically shaped and controlled field.

Arguments for the inclusion of impairment as a category are not addressed in this chapter as they are explored in detail elsewhere (Shakespeare, 2006). What we seek to do here is to use the theory of Bourdieu to encapsulate the inherently biological assault on the lifeworld caused by chronic disabling conditions which result in profound and/or multiple disabilities. To use the more traditionally fought dichotomy between impairment and disability, we suggest that in these extreme conditions, both impairment and social oppression play a role in the assault on the lifeworld, but that the impairment is predominant and shapes even the experiences of social oppression.

Shakespeare suggests that there are two important features of impairment which need to be addressed when looking at the wider picture.

First, there is a hierarchy of impairment: different impairments have different impacts, and the same impairment can have different effects. Second, mild to moderate impairment may not be a difficulty for anyone, given supportive and flexible environments prepared to respect and value difference. However, severe forms of impairment will often cause considerable problems and limitations and sometimes suffering and distress for individuals and their families. The goal of promoting cultural respect and social acceptance for people with impairment should not distract us from the importance of mitigating or preventing impairment via individual medical or psychological therapies. (Shakespeare, 2006: 116)

We contest that Batten disease is one such 'severe form of impairment' and would go so far as to suggest that the social effects of the oppression are, in this case, secondary to the biological effects of the disease itself.

References

Adams, M. (2006) Hybridizing Habitus and Reflexivity: Towards an Understanding of Contemporary Identity? *Sociology* 40(3): 511–28.

Bauman, Z. (2003) *The Individualised Society*. Cambridge: Polity.

Batten Disease Family Association (2008) *What Is Batten Disease Information*. http://www.bdfa-uk.org.uk/about_batten_disease.htm.

Baxter C. (1989) Parent-Perceived Attitudes of Professionals: Implications for Service Providers. *Disability, Handicap and Society* 4(3): 259–69.

Bills, W. and Calvert, E. (2006) The Effects of Comprehensive Behavioural Support Strategies on Behavior Problems Associated with Batten Disease. Paper presented at the First International Education Conference on Batten Disease, 3–6 May, Örebro, Sweden.

Bourdieu, P. (1990) *The Logic of Practice*. Cambridge: Polity Press.

Bourdieu, P. (1999) *The Weight of the World: Social Suffering in Contemporary Society*. Cambridge: Polity Press.

Bourdieu, P. and Wacquant, L. J. D. (1992) *An Invitation to Reflexive Sociology*. Cambridge: Polity Press.

Brett, J. (2002) The Experience of Disability from the Perspective of Parents of Children with Profound Impairment: Is It Time for an Alternative Model of Disability? *Disability and Society* 17(7): 825–43.

Brown, S. (1998) The Orchestrated Body: An Anthropology of Embodiment and Experience in Brain Injured Children. PhD. University of Edinburgh.

Case, S. (2000) Refocusing on the Parent: Social Issues for Parents of Disabled Children. *Disability and Society* 15(2): 271–92.

Cocks, A. (2000) Respite Care for Disabled Children: Macro and Micro Reflections. *Disability and Society* 13: 507–19.

Cooper, J. (2006) Moving towards Therapies for Batten Disease. Paper presented at the First International Education Conference on Batten Disease, 3–6 May, Örebro, Sweden.

Dowling, M. and Dolan, L. (2001) Families with Children with Disabilities – Inequalities and the Social Model. *Disability and Society* 16(1): 21–35.

Dowse, L. (2001) Contesting Practices, Challenging Codes: Self-advocacy, Disability Politics and the Social Model. *Disability and Society* 16: 123–41.

Forbes, A. and Wainwright, S. (2001) On the Methodological, Theoretical and Philosophical Context of Health Inequalities Research: A Critique. *Social Science and Medicine* 53: 801–16.

Giddens, A. (2005) *Modernity and Self-Identity: Self and Society in the Modern Age.* Cambridge: Polity.

Global Organisation of Lysosomal Diseases (2008) *Disease Information.* http://www.goldinfo.org.

Higginson, I. (2003) Priorities for End of Life Care in England, Wales and Scotland. National Council for Palliative Care, London.

Hofmann, S. L. and Peltonen, L. (2001) In C. R. Scriver, A. L. Beaudet, W. S. Sly, B. Childs and B. Vogelstein (eds), The Neuronal Ceroid Lipofuscinoses. New York: McGraw-Hill, 8, pp. 3877–94.

Houen, J. and Munkholm, C. (2006) Parents Influence in the Spielmeyer-Vogt Work. Paper presented at the First International Education Conference on Batten Disease, 3–6 May, Örebro, Sweden.

Johnston, L. (2006) Parent Perspectives on the Education of Individuals with Batten Disease. Paper presented at the First International Education Conference on Batten Disease, 3–6 May, Örebro, Sweden.

Labbe, E. E. (1996) Emotional States and Perceived Family Functioning of Caregivers of Chronically Ill Children. *Psychology Report* 79 (3pt2): 1233–4.

Law, J. (2004) *After Method.* London: Routledge.

Layder, D. (1994) *Understanding Social Theory.* London: Sage.

Lock, S., Jordan, L., Bryan, K. and Maxim, J. (2005) Work after Stroke: Focusing on Barriers and Enablers. *Disability and Society* 20(1): 33–47.

Mole, S. E. (2006) Update on the Molecular Genetics of Batten Disease and Its Implications for Patient Care. Paper presented at the First International Education Conference on Batten Disease, 3–6 May, Örebro, Sweden.

Murray, P. (2000) Disabled Children, Parents and Professionals: Partnership on Whose Terms? *Disability and Society* 15(4): 683–98.

Punkari, L., Eskonen, T. and Hietaharju-Mölsä, H. (2006) The Model for Working for Individuals with Neuronal Ceroid Lipifuscinosis in Finland. Paper presented at the First International Education Conference on Batten Disease, 3–6 May, Örebro, Sweden.

Reay, D. (1998) Rethinking Social Class: Qualitative Perspectives on Gender and Social Class. *Sociology* 32(2): 259–75.

Scambler, S. (1999) Care in Partnership – Caring for Young Adults with Juvenile Batten's Disease, *Research Trust for Metabolic Diseases in Children* 6(1): 17.

Scambler, S. (2005) Exposing the Limitations of Disability Theory: The Case of Juvenile Batten Disease. *Social Theory and Health* 3: 144–64.

Scambler, S. and Williams, R. (2008) Support Needs of Families with Batten Disease: Research Report. Batten Disease Family Association: Hampshire.

Schultz, A. and Kohlschutter, A. (2006) NCL-Net: An Information Network for Families and Professionals. Paper presented at the First International Education Conference on Batten Disease, 3–6 May, Örebro, Sweden.

Scriver, C. R., Beaudet, A. L., Sly, W. S., Childs, B. and Vogelstein, B. (eds) (2001) *The Neuronal Ceroid Lipofuscinoses*, New York: McGraw-Hill.

Shakespeare, T. W. (1999) Losing the Plot? Discourses on Genetics and Disability. *Sociology of Health and Illness* 21(5): 669–88.

Shakespeare, T. (2006) *Disability Rights and Wrongs*. London: Routledge.

Siintola, E., Lehesjoki, A.-E. and Mole, S. E. (2006) Molecular Genetics of the NCLs – Status and Perspectives. *Biochimica et Biophysica Acta* 1762: 857–64.

Spiegle, J. A. and van den Pol, R. A. (1993) *Making Changes: Family Voices on Living with Disabilities*. Cambridge: Brookline books.

Thomas, C. (2004) How Is Disability Understood? An Examination of Sociological Approaches. *Disability and Society* 19(6), October.

Willers, R. (2006) Do We Talk about the Disease with the Children and If So, How Do We Talk about the Disease? Paper presented at the First International Education Conference on Batten Disease, 3–6 May, Örebro, Sweden.

Williams, S. J. (1995) Theorising, Class, Health and Lifestyles: Can Bourdieu Help Us? *Sociology of Health and Illness* 52(5): 577–604.

Williams, S. J. (1999) Is Anybody There? Critical Realism, Chronic Illness and the Disability Debate. *Sociology of Health and Illness* 21(6): 797–819.

6
Discerning Biological, Psychological and Social Mechanisms in the Impact of Epilepsy on the Individual: A Framework and Exploration

Graham Scambler, Panagiota Afentouli and Caroline Selai

Introduction

There are very few scientists or clinicians who would deny that a proper grasp of the 'whys' and 'hows' of the insinuation of epilepsy into individuals' lives calls on contributions from a growing range of disciplines. These range from genetics at what might be regarded as one end of the spectrum to anthropology at the other. In this chapter we refer to *biological, psychological* and *social* mechanisms in full realization that this represents a kind of shorthand for the gamut of discipline-based inputs into any comprehensive understanding of epilepsy and its effects. Our purpose is not to review this extensive and fragmented literature (again), but to explore the possibility of moving on conceptually and scientifically and to offer some empirical illustrations.

We start by reaffirming the causal salience of biological, psychological and social mechanisms for any appreciation of why and how epilepsy frequently comprises an unwelcome assault on the lifeworlds and sense of well-being of many of those affected. We then draw on the realist philosophy of natural and social science of Roy Bhaskar to sketch a conceptual framework allowing for the recognition that biological, psychological and social mechanisms are all typically, *and simultaneously*, implicated in this 'assault', although which if any biological, psychological and/or social mechanism holds causal sway varies by context or 'figuration'. Having, hopefully, made a plausible *prima facie* case for the (cross-disciplinary) adoption of this framework, we report on a small exploratory study which offers material illustrative of our argument. We commit the rest of the chapter to demonstrating how, as a kind of case study, our framework might be used to reorientate future *sociological* investigations of the impact of epilepsy on people's lives.

It is, of course, possible to argue that the study of epilepsy and its impact is best served by maintaining rather than overcoming disciplinary exclusivity. One of us (Graham Scambler) has suggested elsewhere that scientists from the many disciplines with mechanisms on offer might with intellectual profit fight it out rather than seek to collaborate: sociologists might yield ground in the face of biological advance and *vice versa* (Scambler and Scambler, 2003). This chapter explores the obverse possibility of fruitful cross-disciplinary, scientific collaboration.

Background

That epilepsy genetics is already an important contributor to our understanding of epilepsy is beyond dispute, even if its contribution is less decisive than some of its proponents suggest. Research has tended to focus on the analysis of rare families with autosomal dominant powers of transmission, leading to a number of gene discoveries in non-symptomatic epilepsy; but genes have also been identified in a number of Mendelian symptomatic epilepsy syndromes (for example, progressive myoclonic epilepsies (Shahwan et al., 2005)). Sufficient evidence has accumulated to suggest tangible progress towards the identification of genes that: (a) cause epilepsy via monogenetic inheritance; (b) are associated with increased susceptibilities to epilepsy (including possible genetic predispositions to developing epilepsy after central nervous system trauma); and (c) influence differential responses to medications (Berkovic et al., 2006; Mullay et al., 2005; Tate et al., 2005, 2006). Genetic screening and counselling for people with epilepsy and their families have become a salient issue (Winawer and Shinner, 2005), although one which has as yet to be properly assessed (Shostak and Ottman, 2006).

For the purposes of this chapter the category of the biological extends well beyond genetic mechanisms. Congenital malformations present at birth but not inherited can lead to epilepsy. For example, an angioma can starve neighbouring neurones of oxygen, providing a seizure focus in the process. Anoxia may occur at birth, in febrile convulsions or following stroke; in each case neurones die or are damaged in such a way that they may paroxysmally discharge later. Neurones may also be damaged as a consequence of physical trauma, either at birth or later, due, for example, to head injury from a road accident. Intracranial surgery is another source of trauma associated with subsequent epilepsy. To this list might be added other biological progenitors of epilepsy, including brain tumours, infectious diseases like bacterial meningitis, acquired metabolic diseases like hypoglycaemia and hypocalcaemia, chronic alcoholism, and degenerative disorders like Alzheimer's.

In as many as 40–70 percent of cases, the aetiology of epilepsy remains uncertain, although this may in part be a function of under-investigation. Further, biological mechanisms leading to epilepsy must be distinguished from 'precipitants' of seizures, the latter referring to short-term stimuli like exposure to flashing lights in susceptible people. Already, well within the parameters of the biological, there is significant complexity, the more so if the category of the biological is taken – as it is for present purposes – as embracing the taking of antiepileptic drugs (AED), together with their iatrogenic effects. Hopkins (1987: 124–5) captures something of this complexity in a vivid hypothetical case study that comfortably survives 20 years of scientific advance:

> Take a man with a moderate genetic predisposition to seizures. Add the effects of a moderate cranial injury some two years before. Add also the effects of 'stress' at the office during the preceding month. Add also the effects of amitriptyline prescribed to help with the depression associated with this stress. If this man then has a seizure after consuming a moderate amount of alcohol the night before, what caused it – the genetic propensity, the cranial injury, the stress, the alcohol and associated metabolic changes, the disturbance of sleep associated with the depression, or the amitriptyline? Depending upon the perspective of the world of both patient and neurologist, agreement may be reached to blame just one of all these factors, quite illogically.

Hopkins' case study also implicates 'stress' in the aetiology/precipitation of seizures, and this introduces psychological mechanisms.

Psychology as a discipline ranges from the biological to the social. The literature is replete with studies of epilepsy's associations with psychological disorder and distress, even if myths like that of the 'epileptic personality' have long since been debunked and abandoned. Learning and educational problems, changed affect, personality and behaviour difficulties, in addition to assorted psychiatric disorders, have all been associated with epilepsy. Aldenkamp and Hendriks (2000) offer useful distinctions. They distinguish, first, between indirect and direct effects of epilepsy. Indirect effects embrace the stress induced by living with epilepsy (or other chronic conditions) and may be sufficient to explain anything from mild depression to paranoid delusions. Direct effects allude, for example, to neuropsychological-neurochemical mechanisms like those reflecting limbic system dysfunction. The temporal lobe, together with the limbic structures contained within it, is of known importance in the mediation of emotional and social behaviour. It is not surprising therefore that people with epilepsies originating in the temporal lobe show a high incidence of emotional disorders. The location of the epileptogenic focus, in other words, can exercise an unmediated bearing on psychological/psychiatric disorders.

A second distinction separates ictal/peri-ictal from inter-ictal effects of epilepsy. The former may be observed as direct aftermaths of the ictus or seizure, while the latter occur in the periods between seizures. Like Hopkins, however, the authors are at pains to emphasize that these 'sets of factors' are rarely independent of each other: limbic system dysfunction may be an inter-ictal factor predisposing people with epilepsy to emotional and behavioural disorders, but in individual cases the form and severity of these disorders is likely to depend on other 'indirect' or contextual factors.

Such contextual factors may well be social (Scambler, 1989). Although funding has to date privileged biological (an easy first) and psychological (second, but a long way adrift), over social investigations of what it is to have and live with epilepsy, there is unequivocal evidence that the circumstances of epilepsy's intrusion into and accommodation within people's lifeworlds are crucial components of what is increasingly being referred to as epilepsy-related quality of life (ERQOL). Thus negative cultural stereotypes, social stigma, family antagonism or over-protectiveness, truncated social networks and diminished work opportunities, extending readily to the internalization of discriminatory attitudes and practices, have all been implicated in reduced well-being. Unsurprisingly, it is no easy task to undo negativity of context or experience (Birbeck, 2006).

Since this contribution concentrates on the social, there is no need to comment further on the literature at this point. It is worth noting, however, that any sense that the move from the biological via the psychological to the social reflects a parallel move from 'hard' to 'soft' science is simplistic. Arguably it is the geneticists and neurologists/epileptologists who most often advocate the positivist concept of science that we seek here to question and supersede, although, as will be seen, quasi-experimental 'closures' may be more accessible to them than to psychologists or sociologists.

A realist framework

The propensity for geneticists to utilize the putatively scientific method of positivism to seek out laws governing inheritance is understandable (witness monogenetic inheritance, for example). In much of genetics, most of biology, and routinely within the behavioural and social sciences, however, adoption of precisely *this* 'one true scientific method' constitutes their partial undoing. Bhaskar (2008) advances the sensible argument that natural/life and social scientists are convincing *to the extent to which in practice they abandon the positivism they often espouse in favour of what he calls 'critical realism'*.

Bhaskar's (1978, 1989) distinctive philosophical approach might be interpreted as emerging out of a critique of Humean empiricism in general and the regularity theory of causation in particular (Archer et al., 1998). Bhaskar deploys a Kantian transcendental argument to insist that, given the developments in human knowledge that have *in fact* occurred, there *must* exist real – that is, mind-independent – 'objects' of that knowledge, possessed of certain properties and emergent powers, which argument leads to a postulate of ontological stratification. Bhaskar contends that if, as Humean empiricism would have it, human knowledge were restricted to atomistic events given in experience, then something akin to the regularity theory of causation would obtain. However, the world is, and must be, stratified: it is *not* comprised merely of events (the *actual*) and experience (the *empirical*), but also of underlying mechanisms (the *real*). These mechanisms are 'intransitive' (that is, they exist whether or not they are detected); 'transfactual' (that is, they are enduring not transitory); and they govern events. This is as true for knowledge of the social as for knowledge of the natural world.

In the social world most conspicuously, but by no means exclusively, events tend to be 'unsynchronized with the mechanisms that govern them', and 'conjointly determined by various, perhaps countervailing influences so that the governing causes, though necessarily "appearing" through, or in, events can rarely be read straight off' (Lawson, 1997: 22). The governing causes, in Bhaskar's terminology *generative mechanisms*, can rarely be 'read straight off' because they only manifest themselves in *open systems* (that is, in circumstances where numerous mechanisms are simultaneously active and there is therefore limited potential for experimental *closures*). They cannot be identified independently of their effects. Sociology differs from biology, however, in that the objects of its enquiries not only cannot be identified independently of their effects, but they do not *exist* independently of their effects. Furthermore, sociology must accept an absence of spontaneously occurring, and the impossibility of creating (for example, through laboratory experiments), closures. This denies sociologists, 'in principle', decisive test situations for their theories. Since the criterion for the rational confirmation of theories in sociology cannot – after the positivist injunction – be 'predictive', it must be 'exclusively explanatory' (Bhaskar, 1989). Thus explanation displaces prediction; and to *explain* a phenomenon is to provide an account of what might be termed its *causal history* (Scambler and Scambler, 2003).

Society does not exist independently of human activity, nor is it simply the product of it. Thus, 'social structures are both the necessary conditions for and the reproduced outcomes of human action. Structures pre-exist and hence shape and determine human action, but at the same time, the continued existence of these structures depends upon the activities of the agents they govern' (Joseph, 2002: 32).

One of us (Graham Scambler) has argued that the objects of enquiry of biology, psychology and sociology are *real* (in Bhasker's sense) and *different* (Scambler and Scambler, 2003). Creaven (2000) draws on the work of Archer (1995) to contend that a 'strong explanatory account of human nature, and of the non-social subject' is indispensable in providing 'micro-foundations' for the theory of social structures and human agency. He develops this transcendentally, arguing that human nature and the non-social subject denote 'an ensemble of species powers, capacities, dispositions and psycho-organic needs and interests' that 'logically must be held to exist in order to account for the existence of human society' (Creaven, 2000: 139).

Creaven steers clear of what Bhaskar calls the 'naturalistic fallacy' (namely, collapsing society into human biology or human nature). Given the argument of this chapter, he warrants extended quotation at this point:

> At the same time as humanity's species-being and attendant powers and capacities are transmitted 'upstream' into social interaction and socio-cultural relations (supplying the power which energizes the social system, constraining and enabling socio-cultural production and reproduction, and providing a certain impetus towards the universal articulation of particular kinds of cultural norms or principles), structural-cultural and agential conditioning are transmitted 'downstream' to human persons (investing in them specific social interests and capacities, shaping unconsciously much of their psychological and spiritual makeup, and furnishing them with the

cultural resources to construct personal and social identities for themselves). At the 'micro' level, the result of this complex dialectical interaction between these *distinct layers of human and social reality* is precisely the individual as the bearer or embodiment of a complex articulation of psycho-organic and socio-cultural properties. That is to say, human persons are simultaneously constituted as the concrete bearers of the specific social relations, agential collectivities and institutional roles of which they are a part (social being), of the capacities, powers, needs and interests inherent in them as members of a particular biological species (species-being), and of the process which yields these human and social elements together in the life of the individual (personal biography mediated by social and non-social experience). (Creaven, 2000: 140–1)

Williams (1999) develops Creaven's argument in a direction of relevance here. He reminds sociologists inclined to forgetfulness that the body, 'diseased or otherwise', 'is a real entity, no matter what we call it or how we observe it'. It has 'its own mind-independent generative structures and causal mechanisms', and, as such, 'it has an ontological depth independent of epistemological claims, right or wrong, as to its existence' (Williams, 1999: 806). Disease labels, diagnostic categories like 'epilepsy', are 'merely *descriptive*, not *constitutive* of disease itself'.

Translated into the brief of this chapter, the impact of epilepsy on quality of life typically constitutes: (1) a mix of the biological, psychological and social (causality travelling both upstream and downstream); (2) the 'interaction' of biological, psychological and social generative mechanisms; (3) variously and variably the 'primary' product of biological *or* psychological *or* social mechanisms; and (4) an experience more accessible to a critical realist, multidisciplinary analysis oriented to open systems than to a discipline-specific positivistic variable analysis presuming the possibility of experimental closure. Further, there is a need to factor in agency, or the capacity individuals have to act in wilful defiance of the mechanisms that otherwise structure their actions, and contingency, or the arbitrary intrusions of the unpredictable.

Further reflection on (1) to (4) is in order. If the focus of interest is ERQOL, then definitional differences arise. While some investigators insist there can be *objective* markers of ERQOL, others regard it as an inherently *subjective* notion. Clearly objective and subjective ERQOL need not correspond: epilepsy pursuant on severe brain injury might by common consent be associated with poor objective ERQOL without this translating into a poor subjective ERQOL. Clinicians and natural/

life and social scientists would in all probability agree that biological, psychological and social mechanisms have a potential bearing on both objective and subjective concepts of ERQOL, even if they are likely to go on to diverge on effective interventions.

The causal history of a phenomenon, in this case ERQOL, can be complex. Consider the following, for example. Deleterious effects of epilepsy can be present in the absence of *any* salient biological structures or mechanisms. This is the rule rather than the exception when epilepsy is *mis*diagnosed (Benbadis, 2007; Chadwick and Smith, 2002); application of the diagnostic label to a person-as-patient can itself trigger (psychological and/or social) mechanisms to negative effect (Scambler and Hopkins, 1986). If epilepsy is but one symptom of a particularly severe underlying pathology, biological mechanisms can cancel out or override the causal potential of psychological and social mechanisms: this is the case with the rare juvenile Batten disease, for example (Scambler, 2005). Genetic predisposition and brain insult can be mediated by psychological mechanisms that over time 'decide' ERQOL. The causal efficacy of psychological mechanisms like internal versus external locus of control can themselves be dependent on contexts shaped by social mechanisms, or, for that matter, agency or contingency.

What these credible if 'hypothetical' scenarios commend is scientific caution. Biological, psychological and social structures or mechanisms can vary in their causal efficacy from individual to individual as well as by context or figuration. Moreover, they can and frequently do interact: one genus, acting upstream or downstream, can 'cancel out' or ameliorate the impact of others. Critical realism allows for this fluidity. At this point, however, its conceptual offerings require some refinement. Distinctions elaborating on our previous explication can usefully be made between 'objects', 'structures', 'powers', 'mechanisms' and 'tendencies':

> The objects have the powers they have by virtue of their structures, and mechanisms exist and are what they are because of this structure; this is the nature of the object. There is an internal and necessary relation between the nature of an object and its causal powers and tendencies. This can also be expressed as follows (Collier, 1994: 43): 'things have the powers they do because of their structures ... Structures cause powers to be exercised, given some input, some 'efficient cause', eg the match lights when you strike it'. This in turn is an example of a mechanism having generated an event. A mechanism is that which can cause something in the world to happen, and in this

respect mechanisms can be of many different kinds. (Danermark et al., 2002: 55)

So a generative mechanism operates when it is being triggered. Unlike the internal and necessary relation between objects and their causal powers, however, the relation between causal powers or mechanisms *and their effects* is external and contingent. The reason for this is that, underlying phenomena in the domain of the actual, there are many biological, psychological, social mechanisms that are concurrently active. Thus ERQOL is a complex effect of influences emanating from an array of multi-level mechanisms, where some mechanisms reinforce while others frustrate others.

> Taken together this – that objects have powers whether exercised or not, mechanisms exist whether triggered or not and the effects of the mechanisms are contingent – means we can say that a certain object *tends* to act or behave in a certain way. (Danermark et al., 2002: 56)

Inconveniently for those inclined to positivism, numerous and fortuitous circumstances can play their part in determining whether a specific causal power will manifest itself or not.

Exploratory data

The interview material drawn on intermittently in the remainder of this contribution affords only illustrations of how a critical realist framework of the kind we have sketched might be of value. *It cannot bear the full weight of our arguments.* Abductive inference from the empirical (approached qualitatively rather than quantitatively) via the actual to generative mechanisms in Bhaskar's stratum of the real is a precarious if vital step. The investigation was conducted by one of us (Panagiota Afentouli) and was written up as a Masters dissertation in clinical neuroscience (Afentouli, 2008). The general aim of the study was to elicit and explore any critical events or moments *thought to have to shaped* ERQOL. A small sample of ten adults with epilepsy attending the outpatient clinic of a London teaching hospital was recruited. Ethical approval for the project was granted by the University College London Hospitals/National Hospital of Neurology and Neurosurgery (UCLH/NHMN) Ethics Committee.

Semi-standardized interviews, conducted around a series of topics and probes but allowing for flexibility, adjustment and divergence, were chosen. The topics and probes ranged over:

- socio-demographic circumstances, including family and household characteristics, education and work histories;
- medical histories, including origins, course and treatment of epilepsy, incorporating side-effects of medical regimens;
- history of patient careers, including assessments of medical encounters and service delivery;
- coping strategies in the domains of the household, relationships and work, extending to personal aspirations and sense of fulfilment;
- information on biological, psychological and social factors bearing on epilepsy-related quality of life.

The interviews were recorded and transcribed prior to processing and analysis. Grounded theory provided the framework for the analysis (see note at end of chapter). The characteristics of the ten participants are summarized as Table 6.1A.

Nine core categories pertinent to critical events or moments emerged from the processing and analysis of the material. We comment briefly below on each of these categories before turning specifically to social mechanisms and ERQOL, and to the parameters for a sociology orientation to epilepsy set within a critical realist framework.

1 Medical state (diagnosis, prognosis, number of seizures, AED). A considerable range of types and syndromes of epilepsy was found even in this small sample. Five participants expressed a general optimism about the future based on AED, while three appeared quite negative, for example:

I am stuck with this... There is no way to be improved (ninth patient).

If this battery (of AED) doesn't work it will be left as it is, which I am actually quite scared of, because if it stays that way I won't be able to work... my life is ruined! (Tenth patient)

One person emphasized stress as a seizure precipitant and mediating agent, but intimated an external locus of control (fifth patient). While seizure frequency was often a factor in optimism/pessimism, remission did not guarantee a positive orientation: the phrase 'touch wood' featured even after seizure-free periods in excess of six years (seventh patient). Certainly not all interviewees were equally affected by their medical state, which they often interpreted and appraised via considerations of the nature and past and present frequency of seizures, treatment, prognosis, stress and lifestyle restrictions.

2 Diagnosis/reaction to diagnosis   Half those interviewed described being told the diagnosis as a traumatic and pivotal event:

> *I know normally perhaps you would think I was relieved because at least you knew what it was, but I don't remember that...I don't remember feeling relief...horrible...then, obviously I wanted them to go away.* (Fourth patient)
>
> *I didn't like it really because I thought I was going to fall to the floor and shake, its epilepsy, so I would be ruined!* (Tenth patient)

Others, particularly those who had 'grown up with it' alongside parents who hadn't 'overreacted' (third patient), were able to take it in their stride. Reactions to diagnosis were typically influenced by age of diagnosis, family attitudes, stock of knowledge, treatment options, satisfaction with medical care and public perceptions.

3 First seizure/reaction from family and friends   Recollections of first seizure were linked for most people with reactions to it by family, friends or the public. Six experienced their first seizure in public places in the company of others:

> *At that time I was driving the car...I just stopped what I was doing...blackout...I didn't crash the car, I stopped the car...my friend that I had in the car, she stepped out ... She didn't want to come in the car with me; she realized that something wasn't right...but I came to within five minutes, and I panicked: I thought 'where's my friend gone?' I didn't realize that anything was wrong because I didn't collapse on the floor. I just had this blank look on my face, it's what I've been told. I don't get any warning, anything.* (First patient)
>
> *I was in the post office and I couldn't cope with what I was doing, and I felt ill: I started sweating and feeling very unwell, and somebody gave me a chair and a glass of water and I recovered very quickly.* (Fourth patient)
>
> *Just loss of speech...I was in the middle of a conversation and I knew exactly what I wanted to say, it was all in my head, and I could not connect...brain*

could not connect with speech...and I could not physically talk, nothing, I couldn't form a word at all. (Eighth patient)

Half those interviewed remembered their first seizure as sudden and unexpected, sometimes leading to denial. The clear memories many had of this 'event', however, had become coloured by its context and the degree of intimacy shared with any witnesses.

4 Disclosure (timing and context) The major barrier to an open and mutual understanding of epilepsy seemed to be a putative fear of seizures on the part of others. In only nine out of the ten cases the family were judged wholly supportive, although two of these nine reported family and friends as uncomfortably 'over-protective'. One man had lost contact with both family and friends from the time of diagnosis (ninth patient). The prevailing sense was one of open disclosure in principle but wariness in practice. The reason given was learned or anticipated scepticism about others' reactions. Three said they had lost friends as a result of their epilepsy. When it occurred, disclosure tended to be reluctant, selective and prompted:

Well, because it's called epilepsy or whatever, they said 'Oh God, that's awful!', that kind of thing...but it's not like saying cancer. I think perhaps four or five close friends...maybe more because just explaining why I have been in hospital...you know, that kind of thing...it wasn't a secret. (Fourth patient)

Exceptionally, one woman refused to be defensive:

It didn't bother me...I never let it bother me...people accept me for who I am...maybe actually it made me a stronger person, a better one. (Seventh patient)

If most seemed predisposed to concealment, *de facto* decisions were often fashioned by the quality of personal relationships, on the one hand, and fear of prejudice and discrimination on the other.

5 Employment/studying Work and study were primary foci of concern and sources of self-affirmation. Three interviewees felt they had not been affected by their epilepsy, but four claimed their studying had been disrupted and six that they had experienced epilepsy-related work problems.

I left it ... first because of epilepsy ... I couldn't cope with the fits, couldn't study and go there ... I was tired. (Ninth patient)

I thought they would fire me because the fits were scaring them ... I left ... I chose to leave ... the fits have ruined me. You can't get a job can you? (Tenth patient)

Other obstacles in the workplace included lack of concentration, memory difficulties, stress, fear of seizures and medical advice. Four people felt 'less capable', 'useless', 'unwanted', 'depressed' or 'ruined' as a result of their seizures:

I can't think. I forget things as well, and it affected my study ... that's the reason I changed it to part-time. (First patient)

One young man, currently unemployed, said employers were often discriminatory (tenth patient), and one woman blamed her school for not picking up her epilepsy earlier, thereby imperilling her future (seventh patient).

6 Discrimination/stigma   Seven of the ten interviewed told of facing discrimination. Four of these attributed this behaviour to ignorance, popular misconceptions, fear or simple lack of concern:

Of course, other people, they don't know what epilepsy is, they might think it's HIV or, I don't know, completely different stuff. (First patient)

They didn't want to know ... they were scared. (Second patient)

People don't care. (Tenth patient)

One 65-year-old man dwelt on the perils of being a person 'who is not perfect', intimating cumulative disadvantage (ninth patient). Clusters of factors, ranging from seizure severity and frequency to the iatrogenic effects of AED to the need for time off to visit hospital clinics to embarrassment in social settings, were implicated in others' proneness to discriminate and stigmatize.

7 Public understanding/social support   Reportage of lay ignorance was unanimous. Many emphasized that epilepsy is an umbrella term covering a diversity of (observable) phenomena, and that members of the public have a propensity for 'tunnel vision': stereotypically, they presume grand mal or tonic-clonic seizures (fifth patient). Faith in the effectiveness of educating the public varied. Only two interviewees inclined to toleration of ignorance, one remarking:

> So the public don't fully understand yet...but I think epilepsy is quite well hidden...is not always open. (Fifth patient)

8 Critical turning point Turning points are here understood as challenging experiences with either moral or affective personal referents (King et al., 2006). When asked about turning points, seven of the interviewees recalled a particular epileptic seizure (dwelling variously on the experience itself, the shock or its aftermath), one reported the moment of diagnosis, while another selected being unable to drive. For eight of the ten the turning points were defined in negative terms. Two, however, called to mind positive experiences, one involving contact with an epilepsy specialist:

> I think there is probably a beneficial one (critical moment)...I was being referred to the care of Professor...He is very helpful...I couldn't ask for more. (Ninth patient)

The other positive experience came with an opportunity to do media work around disability issues (third patient). For some a turning point was associated with feelings and sensibilities, for example, a fear of permanent disability:

> I suppose the turning point was the fear that I felt, 'Oh my God, what's going on?'...and also when I first lost my speech: I was home on my own trying to call my husband...thank God he understood me, and thank God he came home. (Eighth patient)

Another arose with the acceptance of epilepsy as a chronic complaint:

> I have learned to live with it, and that's what everybody should do. (Seventh patient)

For a third person the feeling concerned the likely severity and unpredictability of seizures. Despite the fact that most participants (7/10) identified a seizure as the turning point, the seizure type, context and others' reactions were complicating factors: there is a relatively unexplored hermeneutics of seizures here.

9 Patients' perceptions of epilepsy and its impact   Objective/subject-ive ERQOL can be consequent on biological, psychological or social mechanisms, or, more likely, a mix of all three. As much was impli-cit in what a number of interviewees said. Most acknowledged being affected by the nature and complexity of underlying biological proc-esses, their symptoms, their personal decision-making and their rela-tionships with family, peers, teachers, employers and others comprising their lifeworlds. Sleep deprivation, fatigue and cognitive deficits such as impaired concentration and memory were stressed by four:

> *I can't sleep. I am weak during the daytime and I can't put all my effort into my work; I can't do daily activities; I can't drive; I can't do the normal stuff that I used to do. I forget!* (First patient)

Inability to drive was lamented by five participants, while inhibitions in relation to swimming and leisure also got mentions:

> *I used to drink a lot...I stopped drinking three years ago...I used to drink quite a lot and get drunk and had a great time.* (Fourth patient)
> *I just couldn't swim or drive or anything like that...it would be nice to have that choice.* (Sixth patient)

Day-to-day decision-making and activities were disrupted or made awkward, sometimes because of others' tendency to intervene or over-protect:

> *Well, I lost my independence, they are treating me like a child all the time.* (Second patient)

Three people complained of social isolation and loneliness:

> *It stops me being social and it has had a big impact that way...I wouldn't go out on my own...I wouldn't go away from home and I wouldn't go to big parties, unless it was close friends.* (Eighth patient)

For one man of 26:

> *It has ruined my life...I hate it...I hate it. Everyone is scared and don't want to be with me, and they don't understand what I am going through all the time...I just say 'You don't understand, it's hard, it's awful': I can't drink, have fun...I hate it.* (Tenth patient)

The particular concerns were diverse if concern itself was standard. The restrictions and limitations associated with epilepsy evidently emanated from a variable mix of the biological, psychological and social.

How might these exploratory data be summarized? We have seen that in the event of misdiagnosis, ERQOL can become negative even in the absence of requisite biological mechanisms. Typically, however, biology *matters*. The material sampled here frequently 'implicates' biological mechanisms via events like first or public seizures. Epileptic seizures may not be of prior import if they are the by-product of severe abnormalities, but typically, they too matter. The nature or type of epilepsy, seizure severity and frequency, inter-ictal phenomena, seizure predictability, AED, and so on are all of likely salience to ERQOL, even if only as conditions for or precipitants of psychological and social mechanisms.

Psychological mechanisms, causally indebted or not to biological mechanisms, *condition* people's handling of epilepsy. Some interviewees construct their seizures as external, intrusive, biological events, while others emphasize a capacity to assume personal control; such differences bear testimony to tendencies alluded to in psychological theories of personality, attributions, coping, locus of control, and so on.

Social mechanisms provide the *contexts* that seem so often to be sites of life events as critical turning points for ERQOL. Both the exploratory study reported here and the published literature on living with epilepsy are replete with examples of how the real or imagined responses of others to a particular witnessed seizure or diagnostic disclosure fundamentally diminish their prospects for a decent job or career, a close relationship, personal equanimity, or even happiness. Such negative impacts on ERQOL can be self- or other-generated, a finding reflected in Scambler and Hopkins' (1986) distinction between *felt* and *enacted stigma*. Felt stigma refers to a sense of shame and an associated fear of meeting with stigmatization, while enacted stigma refers to actual instances of stigmatization. Felt stigma can be every bit as intrusive and debilitating as enacted stigma, independently of factors like seizure frequency (Scambler, 1989).

The final section of this chapter focuses on the ways in which a heterogeneous array of social mechanisms can causally affect ERQOL, amounting to an agenda of sorts for a continuing research programme.

A social research programme for studying ERQOL

Discussion to this point has left no doubt that ERQOL cannot be understood or explained solely in terms of social mechanisms governing context. Not only do biological mechanisms typically matter, but psychological mechanisms typically condition people's handling of biologically induced 'impairment effects' (Thomas, 2007) in socially induced contexts. Further complications arise with unannounced *contingency* in human affairs and the play of human reflexivity and *agency*. In short, these closing paragraphs only address one of several research programmes relevant to ERQOL, and even were they to address the totality of relevant (biological + psychological + social) research programmes, the explanatory power generated would not be matched by an equivalent predictive power: people and their circumstances can and do defy science.

The sociology of epilepsy does not begin and end with individual impairment or coping, or even the social contexts in which 'embodied' coping occurs. As Temkin's (1945) historical research demonstrates, the authoritative categorization and labelling of phenomena by healers is subject to continuous change. Thus *our* 'taken-for-granted' diagnosis of epilepsy is historically recent, specific to the Occident (within which there remains considerable variation in definition and practice), *and will without doubt mutate in ways we cannot second guess*. The first plank of a sociological research programme, then, is an ongoing investigation of how social mechanisms influence the social construction of the biological sciences and the use to which they are put in theory and practice by professions of medicine. This extends also to the social construction of the psychology of the individual and its scientific and therapeutic application to epilepsy.

A second topic of study concerns to what extent and how people's social locations and the contexts in which they live and work contribute to the causation of epilepsy. It is a socio-epidemiological commonplace, for example, that those in lower socio-economic groups tend to experience weaker – biological, psychological, social, cultural, spatial and material – 'assets flows' known to be conducive to health and longevity (Scambler, 2007). A child from a low-income household, for example, is more likely than his or her counterpart in a moderate to high-income household to grow up in an environment where early illness and accidents in the home and neighbourhood are not uncommon, thus increasing the likelihood of epilepsy.

A third set of questions concerns the degree and nature of any correspondence between current professional constructions of epilepsy based on expert knowledge and phenomenological constructions arising out of lay or experiential knowledge. It cannot be presumed that the former provides the impetus for lay understanding or action. The concept of illness behaviour subsumes the empirical study of how people yet to become patients (if they ever do) construct understandings – typically in conjunction with their lay referral networks – of any perceived threats to good health and what (if anything) they opt to do about it (Freidson, 1970). Social mechanisms, in other words, are pivotal for grasping the 'whys' and 'hows' of people's use of the 'popular', 'folk' and 'professional' sectors of what Kleinman (1985) usefully calls their 'local health care system'. Those with medically defined epilepsy who do not find their way to the professional sector not only miss out on any costs and benefits of clinical treatment and care but also remain immune from medical labelling.

A fourth area for investigation focuses on the encounters between people with epilepsy *as patients* and their doctors. Once in the professional sector of their local health-care system, whether via a general practitioner (GP) or nurse consultation, leading to a referral to a neurology outpatient clinic, or an ambulance pick-up to a hospital accident and emergency department, patients become involved in novel 'definitions of their situations'. Such definitions are never cut and dried and always involve negotiation. Patients require multiple working definitions forself and for-others: their roles, reference groups and the particular contexts in which they find themselves can all require re-negotiation.

Doctors are likely to feature in a fifth and related area, that of social aspects of coping. The sociological literature on the 'biographical disruption' occasioned by chronic illness is considerable (Bury, 1982, 1991). It covers the 'loss of self' that often follows diagnosis (Charmaz, 1983), the 'narrative reconstruction' that this requires (Williams, 1984), and the altered interactions with others, be they family, friends, employers or 'the public' (represented by Mead's notion of the 'generalized other'). Issues of coping loom large in the comments of interviewees cited earlier. Particularly pertinent is the concept of stigma, denoting the shame often associated with epilepsy. As already noted, norms of shame can be acted out in the form of discrimination by others ('enacted stigma'), or can lead people with epilepsy to withdraw into themselves or act defensively out of a fear of discrimination ('felt stigma') (Scambler and Hopkins, 1986).

A sixth and as yet under-investigated domain involves the embedding of norms of shame, and its sometime companion blame, in the structures and institutions of a society. It is not possible to grasp relations of stigma (shame) and deviance (blame) in a societal vacuum. Any taint attached to epilepsy has roots also in the 'layering' of society, that is, it reflects the multiplicity of ways in which people are valued and consequently classified and processed (Scambler, 2004). As a topic requiring empirical study this is far removed from conventional sociological as well as psychological concerns with an individual's biographical disruption and coping, as disability theorists have noted (Thomas, 2007). It offers the prospect of a meta-theory of the structural and cultural parameters and contexts within which individual coping occurs.

Concluding comments

This account of a possible research programme for the sociological study of objective and subjective dimensions of ERQOL remains skeletal. It needs, of course, to be complemented by comparable accounts for the biological and psychological study of ERQOL. In other words, within each of the biological, psychological and social there exist multiple objects with causal powers or generative mechanisms, issuing in tendencies. Whether or not tendencies affect events is an external or contingent matter. We inhabit ineluctably dynamic and complex natural and social worlds, as is apparent in our interviewees' narratives (see especially remarks under 'critical turning points' and 'patients' perceptions of epilepsy and its impact'). This has important ramifications for research on phenomena like ERQOL. An event of special or critical salience for ERQOL is unlikely to be amenable to *either* biological *or* psychological *or* sociological explanation; and this is without factoring in contingency and agency.

A critical realist orientation of the sort characterized here yields an immediate threefold return. First, it recognizes and allows for an adequate ontology of objects, powers/mechanisms and tendencies in open systems, and does so without falling foul of the naturalistic fallacy. Second, it requires and facilitates a move beyond the positivist pursuit of statistical associations between variables, be they biological, psychological, social or, more rarely, some combination of these. And third, it calls for methodological rigour even as it denounces positivist 'textbook' emphases on measurement via operationalization and quantification using ever more advanced forms of multivariate analysis. The denunciation is not of these positivist accessories per se, but rather of the underlying assumption that phenomena can be predicted, and therefore explained, given 'empirical' study of the 'actual', that is, without resource to Bhaskar's 'real'. The potential for experimental closure in open systems is grotesquely exaggerated.

It does not follow from our advocacy of a critical realist as opposed to a positivist concept of science that the findings reported on behalf of the latter are redundant. Indeed, much of the substantive material utilized in this chapter is of positivist origin, whether the product of (biological, psychological, sociological) quantitative or (psychological, sociological) qualitative research. Such findings are grist to the mill, as 'cues', in that they often favour particular retroductive/adductive inferences to 'real' objects and their causal powers/generative mechanisms and tendencies. Moreover, more than science is at stake. Much of the research literature from epilepsy genetics to epilepsy's psychosocial sequelae is driven by an instrumental concern to improve objective and/or subjective ERQOL. In this vein we close with the outline of a science-based intervention model which is, we believe, both consonant with research to date and worthy of attention.

It is a model that arises out of an embryonic 'hidden distress model of epilepsy' published two decades ago (Scambler, 1989). Using our earlier terminology, this acknowledges that biological mechanisms, extending from genetics to the neuropharmacology of AEDs, typically *matter* in relation to ERQOL, deeper understanding typically mitigating epilepsy's assault on people's day-to-day lives via more effective treatment. *But even severe biological assaults may not be relevant for ERQOL.* Psychological mechanisms typically *condition* people's handling of epilepsy's assault, and therefore its impact on ERQOL, independently of its biological severity or intractability. There is considerable scope for counselling, targeting the interface between enduring psychological traits and coping styles. *Yet psychological mechanisms too may not be relevant for ERQOL.* Social mechanisms typically provide people with *contexts,* some of which prove decisive for ERQOL. Spontaneous reactions to a witnessed seizure can be pivotal in the long as well as the short term.

In line with the hidden distress model, which accords primary significance to felt stigma and a concomitant urge to fearful secrecy and compromised aspiration, it might reasonably be hypothesized that what might be called after Bourdieu (1977) an *epilepsy habitus* is key. This refers to an enduring, context-induced mindset, with felt stigma at its core, which predisposes to acquiescence or passivity with regard to socially disadvantaging difference. Anticipating discrimination, people with epilepsy (learn to) do to themselves what they anticipate others would 'inevitably' do to them. An epilepsy habitus can form independently of either biological or psychological tendencies, *although it too may lose relevance for ERQOL, for example in the presence of prepotent biological mechanisms (for example, severe brain injury).* Clinical and public health interventions might reasonably aim to curtail or constrain an epilepsy habitus.

Table 6.1A Appendix: Study participants' characteristics

	Gender	Age	Type of epilepsy	Current state	Age of onset	AED therapy	Marital status
1st patient	F	24	Partial absence epilepsy	Active	20	Yes	Single
2nd patient	F	38	Complex partial epilepsy	Active	18	Yes	Single
3rd patient	F	40	Complex partial epilepsy	Active	1	Yes	Single
4th patient	F	62	AVM (with auditory hallucinatory seizures)	Active	30	Yes	Single
5th patient	M	34	Myoclonic juvenile epilepsy	Active	6 weeks	Yes	Married
6th patient	M	26	Grand mal seizures	In remission	15	Yes	Single
7th patient	F	36	Myoclonic juvenile epilepsy	In remission	13	Yes	Married
8th patient	F	42	Grand mal & petit mal seizures	In remission	39	Yes	Married
9th patient	M	65	Nocturnal epilepsy	In remission	26	Yes	Widower
10th patient	M	26	Simple partial epilepsy	Active	School age	Yes	Single

Note

1. The data were analysed according to their iterative nature and the constant comparative approach. The application of grounded theory allowed for a range of productive interrogations: 'why', 'where', 'when', 'how', 'under what circumstances' and 'with what consequences' do causally efficacious experiences for ERQOL occur? During coding, transcripts were subjected to line-by-line analysis to generate meaningful coding categories. Axial coding was then deployed to identify codes and sub-codes of critical events or moments, leading to a reduction to nine 'core' categories (Strauss and Corbin, 1990). These processes of category-generation were conducted independently by Panagiota Afentouli and Caroline Selai, who subsequently compared and cross-verified their results, exploring and evaluating any differences and similarities.

References

Afentouli, P. (2008) The Impact of Epilepsy: Developing More Robust Models of Causality, unpublished dissertation for the M.Sc. in Clinical Neuroscience, UCL.

Aldenkamp, A. and Hendriks, M. (2000) Managing Cognitive and Behavioural Consequences of Epilepsy. In G. Baker and A. Jacoby (eds), *Quality of Life in Epilepsy: Beyond Seizure Counts in Assessment and Treatment*. Amsterdam: Harwood Academic Publishers.

Archer, M. (1995) *Realist Social Theory: The Morphogenetic Approach*. Cambridge: Cambridge University Press.

Archer, M., Bhaskar, R., Collier, A., Lawson, T. and Norrie, A. (eds) (1998) *Critical Realism: Essential Readings*. London: Routledge.

Benbadis, S. (2007) Errors in EEGs and the Misdiagnosis of Epilepsy: Importance, Causes, Consequences and Proposed Remedies. *Epilepsy and Behaviour* 11: 257–62.

Berkovic, S., Harkin, L., Mcmahon, J., Pelekanos, J., Zuberi, S., Wirrell, E., Gill, D., Iona, X., Mulley, J. and Scheffer, I. (2006) De-Novo Mutations of the Sodium Channel Gene Scnia in Alleged Vaccine Encephalography: A Retrospective Study. *Lancet Neurology* 5: 488–92.

Bhaskar, R. (1978) *A Realist Theory of Science* (2nd ed.). Brighton: Harvester.

Bhaskar, R. (1989) *The Possibility of Naturalism* (2nd ed.). Hemel Hempstead: Harvester Wheatsheaf.

Bhaskar, R. (2008) Grounds for Critique. Plenary Lecture. International Association for Critical Realism Annual Conference, King's College London.

Birbeck, G. (2006) Interventions to Reduce Epilepsy-Related Stigma. *Psychology, Health and Medicine* 11: 364–66.

Bourdieu, P. (1977) *Outline of a Theory of Practice*. Cambridge: Cambridge University Press.

Bury, M. (1982) Chronic Illness as Biographical Disruption. *Sociology of Health and Illness* 4: 167–82.

Bury, M. (1991) The Sociology of Chronic Illness: A Review of Research and Prospects. *Sociology of Health and Illness* 13: 167–82.

Chadwick, D. and Smith, D. (2002) The Misdiagnosis of Epilepsy: The Rate of Misdiagnosis and Wide Treatment Choices Are Arguments for Specialist Care in Epilepsy. *British Medical Journal* 324: 495–6.

Charmaz, K. (1983) Loss of Self: A Fundamental Form of Suffering in the Chronically Ill. *Sociology of Health and Illness* 5: 168–95.

Collier, A. (1994) *Critical Realism: An Introduction to Roy Bhaskar's Philosophy*. London: Verso.

Creaven, S. (2000) *Marxism and Realism: A Materialist Application of Realism in the Social Sciences*. London: Routledge.

Danermark, B., Ekstrom, M., Jakobsen, L. and Karlsson, J. (2002) *Explaining Society: Critical Realism in the Social Sciences*. London: Routledge.

Freidson, E. (1970) *Profession of Medicine*. New York: Dodds, Mead & Co.

Hopkins, A. (1987) The Causes and Precipitation of Seizures. In A. Hopkins (ed.), *Epilepsy*. London: Chapman Hall.

Joseph, J. (2002) Five Ways in Which Critical Realism Can Help Marxism. In A. Brown, S. Fleetwood and J. Roberts (eds), *Critical Realism and Marxism*. London: Routledge.

King, G., Willoughby, C., Specht, J. and Brown, E. (2006) Social Support Processes and the Adaptation of Individuals with Chronic Disabilities. *Qualitative Health Research* 16: 902–25.
Kleinman, A. (1985) Indigenous Systems of Healing: Questions for Professional, Popular and Folk Care. In J. Salmon (ed.), *Alternatives Medicines: Popular and Policy Perspectives*. London: Tavistock.
Lawson, T. (1997) *Economics and Reality*. London: Routledge.
Mulley, J., Scheffer, I., Petrou, S., Dibbens, L., Berkovic, S. and Harkin, L. (2005) Scnia Mutations and Epilepsy. *Human Mutations* 25: 535–42.
Scambler, G. and Hopkins, A. (1986) 'Being Epileptic': Coming to Terms with Stigma. *Sociology of Health and Illness* 8: 26–43.
Scambler, G. (1989) *Epilepsy*. London: Tavistock.
Scambler, G. (2004) Re-framing Stigma: Felt and Enacted Stigma and Challenges to the Sociology of Chronic and Disabling Conditions. *Social Theory and Health* 2: 29–46.
Scambler, G. (2007) Social Structure and the Production, Reproduction and Durability of Health Inequalities. *Social Theory and Health* 5: 297–315.
Scambler, G. and Scambler, S. (2003) Realist Agendas on Biology, Health and Medicine. In S. Williams, L. Birke and G. Bendelow (eds), *Debating Biology: Sociological Reflections on Health, Medicine and Society*. London: Routledge.
Scambler, S. (2005) Exposing the Limitations of Disability Theory: The Case of Juvenile Batten Disease. *Social Theory and Health* 3: 144–64.
Shahwan, A., Farrell, M. and Delanty, N. (2005) Progressive Myoclonic Epilepsies: A Review of Genetic and Therapeutic Aspects. *Lancet Neurology* 4: 239–48.
Shostak, S. and Ottman, R. (2006) Ethical, Legal, and Social Determinants of Epilepsy Genetics. *Epilepsia* 47: 1595–602.
Strauss, A. and Corbin, J. (1990) *Basics of Qualitative Research: Grounded Theory Procedures and Techniques*. Newbury Park, CA: Sage.
Tate, S., Depondt, C., Sisodiya, S., Cavalleri, G., Schorge, S., Soranzo, N., Thom, M., Sen, A., Shorvon, S., Sander, J., Wood, N. and Goldstein, D. (2005) Genetic Predictors of the Maximum Doses Receive during Clinical Use of the Anti-Epileptic Drugs Carbamazepine and Phenytoin. *Proceedings of The National Academy of Sciences USA* 12: 5507–12.
Tate, S., Singh, R., Hung, C., Tai, J., Depondt, C., Cavalleri, G., Sisodiya, S., Goldstein, D. and Liou, H. (2006) A Common Polymorphism in the Scnia Gene Associates with Phenytoin Serum Levels at Maintenance Doses. *Pharmacogenetic Genomics* 16: 721–6.
Temkin, O. (1945) *The Falling Sickness*. Baltimore, MD: Johns Hopkins University Press.
Thomas, C. (2007) *Sociologies of Disability and Illness: Contested Ideas in Disability and Medical Sociology*. London: Palgrave.
Williams, G. (1984) The Genesis of Chronic Illness: Narrative Reconstruction. *Sociology of Health and Illness* 6: 174–200.
Williams, S. (1999) Is Anybody There? Critical Realism, Chronic Illness and the Disability Debate. *Sociology of Health and Illness* 21: 797–819.
Winawer, M. and Shinnar, S. (2005) Genetic Epidemiology of Epilepsy or What Do We Tell Families? *Epilepsia* 46, Supplement 10: 24–30.

7
Retheorizing the Clinical Encounter: Normalization Processes and the Corporate Ecologies of Care

Carl May

Introduction

The clinical encounter fascinates sociologists because it is a tremendously rich source of empirical knowledge about the conduct and character of contemporary societies. It is a vehicle for both macro-sociological interests about the social distribution of material resources and cultural capital, mapped along the axes of ethnicity, gender, class, age and religion, and at the same time a locus for micro-sociological investigations of the accomplishments of knowledge and practice, the making of meanings and identities, the relations between persons and technologies, and the narratives by which everyday life is socially constructed. Not only that, but in the clinical encounter chemistry, biology and psychology appear not as collaborative or competitor disciplines of enquiry, but as embodied and embedded realities that must be pragmatically negotiated by its participants, and interpreted sociologically. Thus, the clinical encounter is easily assigned the status of a technical and moral 'special' place where deep existential questions and troubling experiential elements of human life get played out.

I cannot hope to capture the range of these encounters, or review their treatment in sociological theory and research in this chapter. But my brief from the editors of this collection was to draw on my own work to 'retheorize' the clinical encounter. My approach to this has been to think about some of its meso-level aspects – not so much about what sets it apart, as what makes it *like,* other episodes of social action – from a starting point that in some ways the clinical encounter is not 'special' at all. Like many institutionally framed and organizationally enacted encounters, it is the site of *work*. It is the work of the clinical encounter that I wish to explore in this chapter. In turn this gives me the opportunity to think through some aspects of Normalization Process Theory (May, 2009; May and Finch, 2009), a theoretical model that focuses on how material and symbolic practices are organized into the work of everyday life, and so become routinely embedded and integrated in their social contexts.

The 'special character' of the clinical encounter

Medical sociology has long conceptualized the clinical encounter as a site of hierarchical asymmetries of knowledge and practice – in which doctors, nurses and patients play out complex exchanges within autonomous and private social spaces (Heritage and Maynard, 2006; May, 2007). The earliest sociological accounts of doctor-patient interaction stressed their status as social systems bounded off from the rest of the world by the space assigned to autonomous professional knowledge and self-regulated institutional forms (Hall, 1951; Henderson, 1935). This remains a kind of 'ideal type' of professional-patient relationship, not simply for medicine but also for other health professions, including nursing and dentistry. My interest in this chapter is to explore the theorization of the clinical encounter in sociology, but to do so inevitably involves some consideration of the ways that the health professions theorize their social relations. In 1935, as Lawrence J. Henderson wrote the first 'medical sociology' paper for the *New England Journal of Medicine*, the British general practitioner Henry Britten Brackenbury (1935) was developing a view of clinical encounters that drew on the emerging discipline of social psychology and which articulated clinical work to privatized social relations and 'good' communications.

This functional perspective is most rigorously developed in Parsons' analysis of medicine in *The Social System* (Parsons, 1951) in which professional and patient roles are conceived in terms of privatized and proximal relations, and in which the moral qualities of these roles rest on the capacity of doctors to maintain the direction and boundaries of the clinical encounter itself. Parsons points to the way in which these activities rest on the 'segregation of the context of clinical practice from other contexts' (1951: 457). Unlike almost everything else that Parsons wrote, his account of medical practice is derived from fieldwork, undertaken in the private Boston hospital where his brother-in-law (a consultant physician) worked during the 1940s (Parsons, 1977). His later writings on medicine and health – especially those on chronicity – were also profoundly influenced by his experiences of medical responses to the depression, panic disorder and subsequent suicide of his daughter Anne Parsons (Orr, 2006).

The ideal type clinical encounter specified in the work of Talcott Parsons has enormous resonance with the aspirations of both professionals and patients. Underpinning these aspirations – and perhaps also the interests of sociologists, then and now, that have studied the clinical encounter – is the notion that it is in some way *special*. This is not so much a question of the 'black box' of biomedicine, as much as one of the existential importance of the encounter. It is one where awareness of the fragility of things looms and lingers in the application of medical concepts, the naming of parts and the materiality of the body. Elsewhere (May, 2007), I have outlined the 'Parsonian Paradigm' running through contemporary medical sociology, pointing to the ways that this has framed analysis of the 'relationship' between doctor and patient as an essentially private one characterized by affective neutrality (Cockerham, 2005; Parsons, 1951). However, over a period of approximately 50 years this notion of neutrality has broken down in the face of shifts in professional knowledge and practice that have emphasized the importance of subjectivity and experience of illness and the possibility of therapeutic alliance.

In Parsons' account, medical practices are seen to be organizationally and professionally located, but these locations are secondary to the privatized – mainly dyadic – social relations through which they are mobilized and enacted in the clinic. This private dyad has subsequently formed a basic unit of analysis for medical sociology. Elsewhere, I have argued that it retains paradigmatic force precisely because of its continuing claim of individualization (May, 2007). The Parsonian paradigm has been heavily criticized, especially by sociologists concerned with chronic illness (Gerhardt, 1989), but its continuing effects have been argued to represent under-theorization from within sociology itself (Scambler and Britten, 2001) and it has continuously sedimented into sociological research and practice. But crucially, it has retained its analytic force because it permits a set of reciprocal relations across boundaries. This, in turn, supports an alliance between the social and clinical sciences (O'Neill, 1986; Timmermans and Haas, 2008). It is also the case that in the second half of the twentieth century, medical knowledge and practice increasingly sought to include elements of the patient's subjectivity by individualizing experience and meaning (May et al.,

2006), while at the same time massive global processes of *biomedicaliza-tion* have reconstructed health-care institutions and their organizing impulses (Clarke et al., 2003). Indeed, health technologies of different kinds have become important actors upon the bodies of the sick, and intermediaries between the sick and those who seek to care for them.

The specialness of the encounter between medicine, nursing, the other health professions and sick people is opened up by sociological analyses that take Parsons' dyadic and private relationship as the starting point. These analyses fly off in different directions. Some sociologists are increasingly influenced by perspectives from Science and Technology Studies (Langstrup, 2008). Others – for example, Timmermans and Haas (2008) – argue for an even greater integration between the specialness of medicine and the specialness of its study by sociologists, suggesting that medical sociology should reorient itself to the study of objective biomarkers.

I am going to take a completely different line in this chapter, by suggesting that there is nothing 'special' at all about the clinical encounter. In asserting this I am not, of course, saying that it is not important. The conduct and consequences of these encounters often matter a great deal to their participants, and to those around them. They are sometimes matters of life and death. Often they are the site of complex asymmetries of power and knowledge and negotiations that stem from these (Salmon, 2000). But they are also very much like other kinds of social encounters in which complex patterns of knowledge and practice are operationalized and negotiated – often with the assistance of technical algorithms, managerial directives, cost controls and electronic intermediaries – in which trajectories and circumstances are translated into a *management problem* for corporate entities, and the consequent harnessing of experiences and subjectivities to divisions of labour and labour processes. Parsons saw the working out of relations between doctor and patient as the ideal type of professional encounters. He set it out as a matter of neutrality and privacy in its conducts and contexts. However, in the conditions of late modernity, the construction of privatized professional space and autonomous professional action is collapsing in the face of systemic corporate intrusions that have reshaped professional-patient relations.

These are areas of sociological enquiry that raise important questions about subjective self-identity, narrated meanings and epistemological communities. But they also raise important questions about action, and it is this problem that I want to focus on in what follows. So, this chapter pursues the implications of the argument advanced in the introduction – that the intrusion of corporate organizing impulses into the clinical encounter assaults its special moral character as the ideal type of professional-patient interaction.

Forming and framing the clinical encounter

Timmermans and Haas (2008) are the latest in a long line of critics of medical sociology who have pointed to the purposive nature of medicine, and its normative focus on doing *for* the patient. But as Parsons noted, just at the point when his theoretical star was beginning to wane, medicine did not shoulder this burden alone (Parsons, 1965), for the patient had become a participant in this process – and participation in sickness and recovery was 'a *job* to be done' to reach 'achievement capacity' and 'overcome dependency' but in 'co-operation with those technically qualified to help' (ibid.: 286–7). The work of his contemporaries added a temporal element to this, in the concept of the illness career (Glaser and Strauss, 1965; Roth, 1963; Twaddle, 1980), as a set of phases and transitions characterized by sequences of decisions and actions and consequent patterns of changing interactional forms, roles and attributions of status.

Of course, the business of cooperating with 'technically qualified' health professionals, and the concomitant problem of legitimately occupying the sick role, raised objections. Principal amongst these was that in some illnesses whether or not the sick person conformed to normative expectations of the sick role was irrelevant. Such diseases included chronic illnesses (the 'long-standing conditions' of contemporary health policy), mental health problems and malignant neoplastic or neurodegenerative diseases. Uta Gerhardt (1989) has charted the emergence of these sociological criticisms of the 'sick role' as it was conceived by Parsons. However, it is important to remember that such objections emerged during a period in which the epidemiological landscape underwent massive changes, because profoundly important developments in clinical medicine meant that in the advanced economies many dangerous and acute diseases were displaced by chronic health problems associated with an affluent and ageing population. At the time at which Parsons formulated the 'sick role', cooperation with recovery was at issue, and recovery itself was more often than not in doubt. The epidemiological transition from acute to chronic illness has changed this, and for most of us our encounters with medicine will be about palliating symptoms, managing decline and delaying death – not saving life.

As we have seen, Parsons focused on the 'special' character of clinical encounters as the site in which social roles were manifest and the moral qualities of actors were played out. To fully understand the clinical encounter, we need to think of it as Parsons seems to – as a place where a job gets done – and consider the nature of work. Normalization Process Theory can help us think about this because it provides a framework for thinking about how the 'work' of doing and being is brought forth in practice – and emphasizes the importance of social *action* in such contexts. If what I have claimed earlier is true, and the privatized relation between professional and patient is now an instance of a set of corporate impulses, we must begin by defining the clinical encounter as distributed and reciprocal rather than singular relations, thus:

i. The clinical encounter consists of socially patterned components of *work* through which participants are *organized into* and *embedded in* a distributed network of organizational and institutional relations.
ii. The work of organizing and embedding participants into the clinical encounter is operationalized through generative mechanisms that form relations of *coherence*; *cognitive participation*; *collective action*; *reflexive monitoring*.
iii. The production and reproduction of the clinical encounter requires continuous investments by participants in ensembles of *action*. These investments are carried forward in time and space, and the products of this work may eventually become routinely integrated in the lifeworlds of participants.

From these postulates, as we shall shortly see, stem a set of theoretical hypotheses about the form and direction of sickness work.

The corporate and distributed character of the clinical encounter has important implications. The first of these is that when we speak about 'participants' in the clinical encounter we are not necessarily referring solely to doctors or patients, but rather to many actors whose work connects with the encounter. Nor should we see the patient as solely the object of work. They *do* the work too – a point consistently made in sociological studies of the experiences of illness, for example, by Charmaz (2006), Corbin and Strauss (1988) and Cornwell (1984). Patients *enact* the business of sickness by doing work that establishes themselves and others in illness careers, and just as the business of bio-medicalization (Clarke et al., 2003) and medicalization (Conrad, 2007) form frameworks for patienthood, so the work of doing patienthood and being ill reciprocally forms the business of professional action and the everyday negotiation of professional identities. Twaddle's (1980) observation that 'no patient comes to the health professional with a disease' fully formed (112), ought to have its counterpart in the notion that no doctor comes to the patient with a fully formed body of medical knowledge and practice. Ruth Graham has observed that it has long been a criticism of medical sociology that it treats illness and patienthood as something that is *done to* people by a medicine that takes the form of an impersonal, impassive, institutional thing – neglecting the human qualities of individual clinicians and the dilemmas that they face (Graham, 2006). Clinicians appear in such accounts as representatives of institutionalized knowledge and practice, often resisting narrated and embodied expressions of identity. We need to remember that doctors and nurses are also *working* (Melia, 1987), and that they are pushing to get through work that is 'hard' and 'heavy'.

Embedding the work of sickness

In the first part of this chapter, I argued that the clinical encounter is temporally and spatially distributed and that it is the site of multiple forms of work, through which sickness is enacted, embedded and integrated into the lifeworld. The clinical encounter can thus be considered a *field* rather than a *thing*. Rapley has offered a rigorous theoretical and empirical analysis of the problem of the distribution of decision-making work across such fields (Rapley, 2008). One way to see the clinical encounter, in this context, is to locate it in a *corporate ecology*, an organizing terrain in which the *co-production* of health and health care is at issue, but which includes many social actors – individuals and groups – who contribute individually and collectively to the processes of co-production by their actions (and sometimes inaction). This process of co-production may involve innumerable others and, in the end, may have very little to do with the doctor and patient around whom it is formed.

All of this involves looking at sickness as a job to be done, and to the view that I have outlined earlier that this work is framed and constrained by corporate impulses rather than privatized roles. It shifts attention away from a set of experiences and identities that are attributed to and by sick people, and involves us in looking at the *coherence* of the symbolic and material resources that are mobilized to form the objects of work; the patterns of *cognitive participation* and *collective action* that are implicated in being and doing the work of being sick; and the means of *reflexive monitoring* by which that work is made sense of and appraised.

Coherence

The notion of coherence draws into view work that defines and organizes the practices of sickness as embeddable in the lifeworld. We can draw this out as a formal hypothesis:

(H1) *Coherence is dependent on work that defines and organizes the elements of sickness as a cognitive and behavioural ensemble.*

Coherence means that the work of co-producing sickness – the ensemble of beliefs, behaviours and acts that manipulate or organize its objects – is made possible by a set of ideas about meanings, uses and utility; and by socially defined and organized competencies. These meanings and competencies hold the sickness together, and make it possible to share and enact it. This leads to a second hypothesis that:

(H2) *Sickness work is shaped by factors that promote or inhibit participants' apprehension of it as meaningful.*

Studies of the differentiation of sicknesses have focused on nosology (Bowker and Leigh-Star, 1999) more than distinctions between bodies of work, but the nature of this differentiation is sometimes in doubt. The complex interweaving of chronic pain, so-called medically unexplained symptoms, and depression, that is sometimes a problem for people in pain (May, Rose and Johnstone, 2000) and doctors (May et al., 2004) is the focus of different kinds of work that promote or inhibit different frames of meaning. In this context, co-production requires work that differentiates and specifies personal experiences of the body in pain that belong to both doctor and patient, and the socio-technical categories that they can place these in. Central to the work of making sickness meaningful are the practices of joining individual experiences – pain, distress, incapacity – to communally specified categories. Membership of these categories permits both of the parties immediately involved (doctor and patient), along with many others, to do the work that goes along with sickness. These practices are more than a set of acts that are externally defined and normatively constrained. They have meanings that are learned, shared and experienced by actors in specific social contexts, as they work the practice through. These meanings are internalized and contribute to anchoring sickness in the lifeworld. This leads to a further hypothesis:

(H3) *The coherence of sickness work requires that actors collectively invest in its meaning.*

Cognitive participation

Sickness requires symbolic and real enrolments and engagements of human actors that position them for interactional and material work. From this stems the hypothesis that:

(**H4**) *Cognitive participation is dependent on work that defines and organizes sickness into networks of actors.*

Work that defines and organizes human engagements with sickness runs through long interaction chains which bind different categories of actors together. Such chains can involve highly focused work for and on the body, or more diffuse patterns of activity – the practices of management and self-management that have become so important in policy around chronic sickness. This leads to the hypothesis that:

(**H5**) *Sickness work is shaped by factors that promote or inhibit actors' participation.*

Participation in sickness work requires that actors initiate a practice. That is, they possessed powers of invention and agency that lead to their enrolment into social and socio-technical networks. There is now a great deal of work that points to the impacts of biographical disruptions (and consequent socialization processes) experienced by sick people (Bury, 1982; Charmaz, 2006; Pilgrim and Rogers, 1993), as they enter into sickness. There is a parallel literature on the occupational socialization of doctors (Good, 1994; Sinclair, 1997). These form quite distinct spheres of sociological interest and practice. But an approach that looks at the co-production of sickness work draws them together. In this context, studies of disputed enrolments – for example, of chronic fatigue syndrome (Clarke, 2000; Ware, 1999) – are sociologically interesting because they are deviant cases. Deviance calls into question legitimacy of an illness identity, and in doing so, the warrantability of enrolling *all* of its participants is thrown into doubt.

Social constructionist approaches that have (rightly) emphasized the contested nature of much medical knowledge and practice are important. But these also serve to distract attention from the more mundane, but still deeply problematic, contests over participation that stem from inequalities of understanding and access. In this context, enrolment involves work that brings about and organizes sickness into communities of practice. These may be characterized in many different ways: through attributions of shared identity or difference (Whelan, 2007), within patient groups, for example; or through the closely framed interactions that derived from shared knowledge about disease that bring together families and their genetic counsellors (Chapple, May and

Campion, 1996). But for many people doing sickness work, contests over the legitimacy of sickness identities or over the warrantability of symptom expressions are matters for the margins. The work that they face is work of enrolment and activation, bringing forth the cultural and material resources that make sickness work possible, and which engage them in overlapping networks of norms and conventions by which they can, in turn, enact sickness. This leads to a further hypothesis, that:

(**H6**) *Cognitive participation requires that actors invest commitment in sickness work.*

Collective action

The chains of interactions around which cognitive participation in sickness work is framed and performed are simultaneously the sites of *enacting* sickness. It is important to emphasize that just as cognitive participation requires that people are *organized in* to sickness work, so collective action is required to express that participation in a set of relationships and practices. This leads to a hypothesis that:

(**H7**) *Collective action is dependent on work that defines and operationalizes sickness.*

If we take the notion that sickness work really is work seriously, then this is the site of its most visible elements. It is about framing identities (mobilizing attributions about selves), measuring and managing the body (the peak flow meter and the urine test; the handkerchief and the syringe driver), and the organizational contexts in which actors are located. Salmon et al.'s work on patient controlled analgesia in hospitals (Chumbley, Hall and Salmon, 1999; Salmon and Manyande, 1996) and Ong et al.'s on experiences of musculosketal pain in the community (Ong and Hooper, 2006) are important British examples of research that draws out the multiple forms of public work that stem from enacting sickness work in clinical encounters. This work is not unproblematic, however, and this takes us to our next hypothesis:

(**H8**) *Sickness work is shaped by factors that promote or inhibit actors' enacting it.*

Four sets of factors shape collective action around sickness work. First, problems of *interactional workability* shape the way that sickness attributions and connected symbolic and material tasks can be mobilized in practice, both to solve problems and secure agreements about the nature of those problems and solutions. This is the *doing* work of sickness, the point at which the body and mind are worked out. This work may be to manage and measure bodies, to employ objects or artefacts, or to assemble accounts of feelings and sensations, and it may be to reorganize relationships and contexts – with the self (in response to biographical disruption) and with others (in response to the requirements of sick roles) – but however it is formed, this is the visible domain of sickness work. It is not exclusive to patients, doctors or others. Instead it is distributed across broad (and multiple) networks, and embedded in the application of techniques and technologies. Almost all sickness work is now distributed in part to the patient – only the most seriously ill are completely relieved of their normative responsibilities.

Second, *relational integration* is about the social organization of trust through the social networks in which sickness work is operationalized. Here, asymmetries in knowledge and practice between different categories of actors are important elements of practice, but as Beutow and colleagues (Buetow, Jutel and Hoare, 2009) point out, there is increasing homologization amongst participants in sickness work. Patients have increasing technical knowledge and expertise and vastly improved access to information. In this context, sickness work may include resistance, subversion or reinvention, as well as affirmation, and compliance – on all sides – but it always involves work around confidence and accountability between network members. The redistribution of information – and also the capacity to interpret this knowledge – is one of the key elements of sickness work in late modernity. But there is simply too much information to manage, and so new techniques and technologies for securing confidence in this knowledge need to be embedded in sickness work. New domains of *technogovernance* are forming in which the affordances of information and communications technologies are played out in the service of rationalizing the relationships between participants in sickness work (May et al., 2006), and a regulatory science of codified health-care information is also emerging in the production of clinical guidelines. These manage spending decisions, constraining the previously autonomous decisions of the private clinical encounter according to corporate norms.

If there is too much information to manage in the distributed elements of the clinical encounter, then there may be also be too much work. All but a tiny proportion of the burden of sickness work has always fallen outside the formal boundaries of health-care systems. In the past decade or so, however, formal health-care agencies have sought to find ways to shift some of their burden elsewhere. This not just a matter of cost control. It also reflects the increasingly routine nature of much health-care work (May, 2009). This shift demands workers, and so the doing of sickness work is shaped, third, by its *skill-set workability.* This describes the conduct of work that distributes sickness work across a division of labour and defines elements of its performance. Anne Rogers' programme of critical research on 'expert patient' programmes has shown how shifting the burden of this work to sick people is an important underpinning for policies of empowerment and consumerism that underpin the political programmes of New Labour in the UK (Gately, Rogers and Sanders, 2007; Kendall and Rogers, 2007; Rogers et al., 2005) and the advanced economies.

Finally, this work must possess *contextual integration.* Collective action in this context not only includes the material work of sickness, but also the work of controlling the burdens of sickness – the patterns of self-governance and preventative regulation that are a commonplace of Foucauldian analyses of the discipline of health (Petersen and Lupton, 1996). These seek to individualize both responsibility and costs. However, socially patterned sickness work needs to be linked to cultural and material resources. To be fully realized, this work must have those resources flowing through it. That sickness work is labour intensive is not in doubt. Expenditure of money and effort is distributed horizontally across networks, and vertically through policy structures. This tends to be seen as a political or policy problem about money (in which the growing *costs* of health care are construed as a burden on the reducing population of young healthy taxpayers), rather than a political or policy problem about labour processes and markets (in which the increasing effort required to manage and do sickness work is a burden on the increasing population of mainly older, less healthy, tax-beneficiaries).

Taken together, the operation of the four factors that frame collective action lead us to the hypothesis that:

(**H9**) *Collective action requires that actors collectively invest effort in the production and reproduction of sickness work.*

Reflexive monitoring

To this point I have argued that sickness work is defined by practices that organize it as a coherent ensemble of beliefs and actions; that it is formed through practices of cognitive participation; and that it is made manifest in socially patterned collective action. Further, I have argued that sickness work is horizontally distributed across social networks, and distributed vertically in a set of relations between persons and policies. The fourth and final domain of sickness work that I wish to consider here is the work of *reflexive monitoring.* By this I mean socially patterned mechanisms for making sense of meaning of work and its objects, patterns of participation and action, and their outcomes. From this stems the proposition that:

(H10) *Reflexive monitoring is dependent on work that defines and organizes the everyday understanding of sickness.*

Reflexive monitoring may involve judgements about the value, utility and effectiveness of elements of sickness work. These are made with reference to socially patterned beliefs about desirable states, configurations of practices, and their outcomes. This leads to a further proposition:

(H11) *Sickness work is shaped by factors that promote or inhibit appraisal.*

One way of characterizing late modernity would be as an epidemiological epoch, in which sickness is constantly measured and monitored – what Armstrong (1995) has called 'surveillance medicine' – in which sickness work is accomplished by large-scale social institutions (in which Universities, government departments, health-care agencies and pharmaceutical companies all play important parts). *Systematization* is central to this process, and it refers to the methodological formality of these judgements and the rationalities that underpin them.

But while regular and organized procedures for monitoring and ongoing assessment of the process and impact sickness work may involve highly structured and formal mechanisms, this need not be at a societal level. Instead, monitoring individuals is now a crucial component of sickness work. As Pascale Lehoux (2008) has shown, technologies of knowledge production and interpretation that serve this purpose proliferate, distributing information across networks. The rise of the 'wireless patient' is one of the important features of late modern sickness work (May et al., 2005), because it is framed by patterns of *communal appraisal* in which the work of monitoring no longer sits in one place, but can be distributed according to available bandwidth (Percival and Hanson, 2006). Of course, communal appraisal coexists with *individual appraisal* that relies on experiential and unsystematic practices of judging the value and outcomes of sickness work, and from which stem individual commitments to its conduct and performance – for example, in work around assessing blood sugar levels and dietary management in diabetes (Bissell, May and Noyce, 2004). More immediately, both communal and individual appraisal may lead to attempts at *reconfiguration* in which ideas about the use and utility of elements of sickness work are subverted, modified or reconstructed, for example, in the reorganization of activities that engage symptoms and services simultaneously (Mair, Hiscock and Beaton, 2008). This leads us to a final proposition:

(H12) *Reflexive monitoring requires that actors invest in understanding sickness work and its implications.*

Conclusion

My brief in this chapter was to 'retheorize' the clinical encounter, and to do this I have applied a theoretical model of the work of embedding practices in the lifeworld to the business of sickness work. In doing so, I have extended a set of generic theoretical proposals about normalization processes (May and Finch, 2009) and specific propositions about the management of chronic disease (May, 2009) into a general account of sickness work. Further, I have offered 12 hypotheses about the forms, constraints and investments through which such work is operationalized and accomplished. There is an important general sociological point here, which is that the routine embedding and accomplishment of practices is one of the primary means by which social structures are produced and reproduced (Huber, 1991).

Like Buetow et al. (2009), and other proponents of 'convergence' hypotheses, my account rests on the work of clinicians and their patients – the constituents of the clinical encounter – being increasingly intimately linked in late modernity. In this chapter, I have tried to show how this work is not just a matter of convergent technical knowledge and the delegation of decisions to patients. Instead, I have tried to show how 'retheorizing' the clinical encounter at the beginning of the twenty-first century actually requires us to take note of sometimes mundane, but sometimes very complex and demanding, *work* that is increasingly distributed rather than delegated. One striking feature of the analysis offered above is that nowhere in it is this work specifically attributed to patients or doctors. This is because I have argued that sickness work is distributed horizontally and vertically through networks that extend a long way from the doctor's office.

There are obvious parallels between the view that I take in this chapter and actor-network theory in its classical formulation (Latour, 2005). However, although I have drawn on the sociology of science and technology (Jensen, 2008; Webster, 2007), I have aimed for a sociological account that emphasizes agency and action, rather than actor-networks. Sickness work is truly agentic, and it involves the production and investment of meaning, participation, action and understanding. All of this takes place through highly differentiated symbolic processes and equally variable material contexts. It belongs to both professionals and patients, and to extended networks who may be both or none of these things, who are here conceived as agents, doing work. As they do this work, they contribute to the production and reproduction of social structures, and they do so in a highly dynamic way – illness is not something that is *done to* sick people, but rather sickness is co-produced as people *work together* across the terrain of an increasingly corporate ecology.

References

Armstrong, D. (1995) The Rise of Surveillance Medicine. *Sociology of Health and Illness* 17: 393–404.

Bissell, P., May, C. R. and Noyce, P. R. (2004) From Compliance to Concordance: Barriers to Accomplishing a Reframed Model of Health Care Interactions. *Social Science and Medicine* 58: 851–62.

Bowker, G. and Leigh-Star, S. (1999) *Sorting Things Out. Classification and Its Consequences*. Cambridge, MA: MIT Press.

Brackenbury, H. (1935) *Patient and Doctor*. London: Hodder and Stoughton.

Buetow, S., Jutel, A. and Hoare, K. (2009) Shrinking Social Space in the Doctor-Modern Patient Relationship: A Review of Forces for, and Implications of, Homologisation. *Patient Education and Counseling* 74: 97–103.

Bury, M. (1982) Chronic Illness as Biographical Disruption. *Sociology of Health and Illness* 4: 167–82.

Chapple, A., May, C. and Campion, P. (1996) Predictive and Carrier Testing of Children: Professional Dilemmas for Clinical Geneticists. *European Journal of Genetics in Society* 2: 28–38.

Charmaz, K. (2006) *Good Days, Bad Days: The Self in Chronic Illness*. New Brunswick, NJ: Rutgers University Press.

Chumbley, G. M., Hall, G. M. and Salmon, P. (1999) Why Do Patients Feel Positive about Patient-Controlled Analgesia? *Anaesthesia* 54: 386–9.

Clarke, A. E., Mamo, L., Fishman, J. R., Shim, J. K. and Fosket, J. R. (2003) Biomedicalization: Technoscientific Transformations of Health, Illness, and U.S. Biomedicine. *American Sociological Review* 68: 161–94.

Clarke, J. N. (2000) The Search for Legitimacy and the 'Expertization' of the Lay Person: The Case of Chronic Fatigue Syndrome. *Social Work in Health Care* 30: 73–93.

Cockerham, W. C. (2005) Medical Sociology and Sociological Theory. In W. C. Cockerham (ed.), *The Blackwell Companion to Medical Sociology* (pp. 3–22). Oxford: Blackwell Publishing.

Conrad, P. (2007) *The Medicalization of Society: On the Transformation of Human Conditions into Treatable Disorders*. Baltimore, MD: Johns Hopkins University Press.

Corbin, J. and Strauss, A. (1988) *Unending Work and Care: Managing Chronic Illness at Home*. San Francisco, CA: Jossey-Bass.

Cornwell, J. (1984) *Hard-Earned Lives: Accounts of Health and Illness from East London*. London: Routledge.

Gately, C., Rogers, A. and Sanders, C. (2007) Re-thinking the Relationship between Long-term Condition Self-management Education and the Utilisation of Health Services. *Social Science and Medicine* 65: 934–45.

Gerhardt, U. (1989) *Ideas about Illness: An Intellectual and Political History of Medical Sociology*. Basingstoke: London.

Glaser, B. G. and Strauss, A. (1965) *Awareness of Dying*. Chicago, IL: Aldine.

Good, B. J. (1994) How Medicine Constructs Its Objects. In B. J. (ed.), Good *Medicine, Rationality and Experience* (pp. 65–87). Cambridge: Cambridge University Press.

Graham, R. (2006) Lacking Compassion: Sociological Analyses of the Medical Profession. *Social Theory and Health* 4: 43–63.

Hall, O. (1951) Sociological Research in the Field of Medicine: Progress and Prospects. *American Sociological Review* 16: 639–44.

Henderson, L. J. (1935) Physician and Patient as a Social System. *New England Journal of Medicine* 212: 819–23.

Heritage, J. and Maynard, D. W. (2006) Problems and Prospects in the Study of Physician-Patient Interaction: 30 Years of Research. *Annual Review of Sociology* 32: 351–74.

Huber, J. (1991) Introduction. In J. Huber (ed.,) *Macro-Micro Linkages in Sociology* (pp. 1–18). Englewood Cliffs, NJ: Sage.

Jensen, C. (2008) Power, Technology and Social Studies of Health Care: An Infrastructural Inversion. *Health Care Analysis* 16: 355–74.

Kendall, E. and Rogers, A. (2007) Extinguishing the Social? State Sponsored Self-care Policy and the Chronic Disease Self-management Programme. *Disability and Society* 22: 129–43.

Langstrup, H. (2008) Making Connections through Online Asthma Monitoring. *Chronic Illness* 4: 118–26.

Latour, B. (2005) *Reassembling the Social: An Introduction to Actor Network Theory.* Oxford: Oxford University Press.

Lehoux, P. (2008) The Duality of Health Technology in Chronic Illness: How Designers Envision Our Future. *Chronic Illness* 4: 85–97.

Mair, F. S., Hiscock, J. and Beaton, S. C. (2008) Understanding Factors That Inhibit Or Promote the Utilization of Telecare in Chronic Lung Disease. *Chronic Illness* 4: 110–7.

May, C. (2007) The Clinical Encounter and the Problem of Context. *Sociology* 41: 29–45.

May, C. (2009) Mundane Medicine, Therapeutic Relationships, and the Clinical Encounter. In B. Pescosolido, J. A. Martin and A. Rogers (eds), *Handbook of the Sociology of Health, Illness, and Healing: A Blueprint for the 21st Century*, New York: Springer.

May, C., Allison, G., Chapple, A., Chew-Graham, C., Dixon, C., Gask, L., Graham, R., Rogers, A. and Roland, M. (2004) Framing the doctor-patient relationship in chronic illness: a comparative study of general practitioners' accounts. *Sociology of Health & Illness* 26: 135–58.

May, C. and Finch, T. (2009) Implementation, Embedding, and Integration: An Outline of Normalization Process Theory. *Sociology* 43: 535–54.

May, C., Finch, T., Mair, F. and Mort, M. (2005) *Towards a Wireless Patient: Chronic Illness, Scarce Care and Technological Innovation in the United Kingdom* 61: 1485–94.

May, C., Rapley, T., Moreira, T., Finch, T. and Heaven, B. (2006) Technogovernance: Evidence, Subjectivity, and the Clinical Encounter in Primary Care Medicine. *Social Science and Medicine* 62: 1022–30.

May, C. R., Rose, M. J. and Johnstone, F. C. (2000) Dealing with Doubt. How Patients Account for Non-specific Chronic Low Back Pain. *Journal of Psychosomatic Research* 49: 223–5.

Melia, K. (1987) *Learning and Working: The Occupational Socialization of Nurses*. London: Tavistock Publications Ltd.

O'Neill, J. (1986) Sociological Nemesis: Parsons and Foucault on the Therapeutic Disciplines. In M. L. Wardell and S. P. Turner (ed.), *Sociological Theory in Transition* (pp. 21–35). London: Allen and Unwin.

Ong, B. N. and Hooper, H. (2006) Comparing Clinical and Lay Accounts of the Diagnosis and Treatment of Back Pain. *Sociology of Health & Illness* 28: 203–22.

Orr, J. (2006) *Panic Diaries: A Genealogy of Panic Disorder*. Durham, NC: Duke University Press.

Parsons, T. (1951) *The Social System*. London: Routledge and Kegan Paul.

Parsons, T. (1965) *Social Structure and Personality*. New York: Free Press.

Parsons, T. (1977) On Building Social System Theory: A Personal History. In T. Parsons (ed.), *Social Systems and the Evolution of Action Theory* (pp. 22–77). New York: Free Press.

Percival, J. and Hanson, J. (2006) Big Brother or Brave New World? Telecare and Its Implications for Older People's Independence and Social Exclusion. *Critical Social Policy* 26: 888–909.

Petersen, A. and Lupton, D. (1996) *The New Public Health: Health and Self in the Age of Risk*. London: Sage.

Pilgrim, D. and Rogers, A. (1993) *A Sociology of Mental Health and Illness*. Buckingham. Philadelphia, PA: Open University Press.

Rapley, T. (2008) Distributed Decision Making: The Anatomy of Decisions-in-Action. *Sociology of Health & Illness* 30: 429–44.

Rogers, A., Kennedy, A., Nelson, E. and Robinson, A. (2005) Uncovering the Limits of Patient-Centeredness: Implementing a Self-management Trial for Chronic Illness. *Qualitative Health Research* 15: 224–39.

Roth, J. (1963) *Timetables*. Indianapolis, IN: Bobbs Merrill.

Salmon, P. (2000) Patients Who Present Physical Symptoms in the Absence of Physical Pathology: A Challenge to Existing Models of Doctor-Patient Interaction. *Patient Education and Counseling* 39: 105–13.

Salmon, P. and Manyande, A. (1996) Good Patients Cope with Their Pain: Postoperative Analgesia and Nurses' Perceptions of Their Patients' Pain. *Pain* 68: 63–8.

Scambler, G. and Britten, N. (2001) System, Lifeworld and Doctor-Patient Interaction: Issues of Trust in a Changing World. In Scambler, G. (ed.) *Habermas, Critical Theory and Health*. London, Blackwell.

Sinclair, S. (1997) *Making Doctors: An Institutional Apprenticeship*. Oxford: Berg.

Timmermans, S. and Haas, S. (2008) Towards a Sociology of Disease. *Sociology of Health & Illness* 30: 659–76.

Twaddle, A. C. (1980) Sickness and the Sickness Career: Some Implications. In L. Elsenberg and A. Kleinman (ed.), *The Relevance of Social Science for Medicine* (pp. 111–34). Dordrecht: Reidel/Kluwer.

Ware, N. C. (1999) Toward a Model of Social Course in Chronic Illness: The Example of Chronic Fatigue Syndrome. *Culture Medicine and Psychiatry* 23: 303–31.

Webster, A. (2007) *Health, Technology and Society: A Sociological Critique*. Basingstoke: Palgrave Macmillan.

Whelan, E. (2007) 'No One Agrees Except for Those of Us Who Have It': Endometriosis Patients as an Epistemological Community. *Sociology of Health & Illness* 29: 957–82.

8
'Chronicity', Proto-Stories and the Doctor-Patient Relationship

Alan Radley

Introduction

The potential for doctors to grasp the patient's story is more than a chronicle of events, as it also provides clues to those 'hidden truths and meanings' that will assist in unravelling the details of the illness (Hurwitz, 2000). In that sense, doctors do not need to be introduced afresh into the narrative sphere, for the simple reason that they are there already; it is just that some have failed to recognize this (Hunter, 1991). They, along with other health professionals, are regularly engaged in what Mattingly (1998) has called 'healing dramas'. This idea follows from the argument that narratives refer not only to past experiences, but also create present experiences for those involved. The doctor's encouragement of a story – and participation as listener – provides the grounds for future action, where that action might be a reasoned line of therapy, or even a conciliatory silence (Kelly and Dickinson, 1997). It also provides a context or perhaps a benchmark against which medical information can be provided in return.

Hunter (1991) describes the physician's task as being threefold: (a) to acknowledge the patient's subjective experience (b) to formulate it as a medical version and then (c) to feed that back to the patient, 'still to understand and affirm the life narrative of which it is a part' (ibid.: 147). These are general tasks for any physician, but are especially required in cases where the chronicity of the condition is such as to include the history of the patient's dealings with the medical system. This is something that is common for many patients, including those diagnosed with Inflammatory Bowel Disease (IBD), who are the focus of this chapter. The chronicity of the doctor-patient relationship, to which May et al. (2004) refer as potentially problematic, is a relevant and potentially important feature of the story whose construction takes place over time and across a number of fields. To take this one step further, the doctor is likely to be party to a narrative that draws upon past treatment meetings and therapies, together with their relative successes and failures.

What is it that encourages or enables physicians to achieve the three tasks of listening, reformulating and feeding back to patients? In the case of patients with IBD – or with IBD-like symptoms – Kelly (1986), reporting his own life experiences, argues that different features of the patient's illness have different trajectories *through time*. This highlights the importance of taking not just a longitudinal look at consultations and patients' histories, but also addressing the temporal potential of storytelling in the conversation. Though rarely acknowledged, this potential is realized in the storytelling potential of the doctor, whose powers to encourage opportunity, rather than constrain understanding, have tended to be overlooked. Medical conceptions are not illegitimate reifications from a lay point of view, even though such knowledge often turns out to be ambiguous and limited. As Bury concluded in his essay on biographical disruption in chronic illness, 'A more careful treatment of the continuity and discontinuity between lay and specialised modes of thought is called for' (1982: 179). This chapter follows this line of argument by examining how doctors create *proto-stories* in order to facilitate continuities between medical and lay thinking about illness.

Seeing a different doctor each visit

One of the most common complaints that patients make about repeat visits to the outpatient clinic is that too often they see a different doctor each time. These consultations require different doctors to become acquainted with the patient's history on each occasion, and in consequence for the doctors to use an interrogative style (Byrne and Long, 1976). Typically, after a brief exchange, the doctor goes on to ask questions about the patient's present symptoms and the effectiveness of the current treatment regime. Throughout the meeting the doctor is guided by the medical notes, to which she adds information on the basis of the patient's answers to her questions. These questions, about symptoms and the effectiveness of treatment, are given meaning in terms of medical knowledge that mediates her view of the patient's illness. Drawing upon the work of Latour (1998), we can say that these mediators form a chain in the transformation of what a patient experiences locally (for example, the appearance of symptoms in her everyday life). This provides any medical professional with a 'view' of the disease and its likely response to changes in treatment. What are made apparent are matters that *the doctor* can apprehend, some of which need to be told to patients if they are to comply. Patients need to be schooled in this way of seeing, but only insofar as this recruits their cooperation in treatment.

Medical assessments of a patient's illness are achieved through such things as regular blood tests and endoscopies, providing numerical data that can be charted and recorded. As Latour (1998) argues, in order to achieve distance from the body one has to have some mediators (technologies) to carry across the reference in such a way as to conserve certain features (for example, measures of properties of the blood). He points out that this act of measurement involves not just information transfer, but information *transformation*. This transformation across the mediation often involves different material forms (for example, paper charts, electronic displays), which enable the pathology of the body to be re-inscribed, plotted, modelled and otherwise rendered meaningful. However, what medicine gains in precision the patient can experience as alienation, because the clarity of vision at which science aims demands that its chosen mediators (measures) 'escape their origin' (ibid.: 424). In this, as in all such cases, the origin is the patient's experience of illness in everyday life, through and on her body, taken as vehicle and object. For that reason, it is not illness at its origin that the doctor wants to take hold of: the answers that the patient gives are only the first step in what will become the measurement of selected variations in her bodily condition. Therefore, while patients can and do attempt to render their subjective experience of illness visible through bodily presentation, it is not this presentation *as such* to which the doctor is attending. Because making sense of illness, *medically speaking*, is a process of transformation across mediators, this has implications for how the doctor attends to what the patient tells her. That is why in such meetings the local features (of everyday pain) that are dramatically re-enacted in the consulting room too often achieve 'neither interactional nor diagnostic significance' (Hindmarsh and Heath, 2003: 64).

Where to go next: The proto-story as a kind of tour

Medico-scientific thinking depends upon a particular version of space-time, one in which the organization of practices surpasses the locality of the patient's lived body, with its associated subjective experience, to create meaning at a distance. This distance is facilitated by medical technologies and associated forms of spatial organization. For example, symptoms are separated out for inspection, the patient's body is examined endoscopically and tests are made upon bodily fluids and parts. The clinic (in the broad sense of the term) is a diversified terrain that answers to medicine's transformation of information through its transfer across forms of mediation. As far as the consulting room is concerned, it is also a place to which information is brought back and put together to make sense of the patient's illness *as disease*.

Only within a certain conception of time and space can such objectified measures (scientific objects) be assembled together for the doctor's consideration. The medico-scientific mode of signifying produces and sustains a space in which the various forms of mediated information define illness distantly, thus enabling their representation in the notes, on the screen. We might call this, for simplicity, an 'objectifying space', activated by the reading of measures and indices that refer away to illness that cannot be seen or felt directly *now*, once transformed. It is, however, a space that enables denotation through measurement, as well as discussion of the validity of those measures. Doctors and nurses can point here and there on the chart, or to this information in the notes. This kind of discussion can be conducted by anybody with the (medical) training to understand the transformations that have been made in the course of information transfer. Latour summarized this argument as follows:

> Tell me what is on the move and what transformations it undergoes and I will tell you what sort of space and what sort of time has been *designed*. Consequently, since each regime of representation defines differently what should be maintained intact through displacements, each regime defines space-time differently. (Latour, 1988: 25, emphasis in original)

What other kind of transformations might take place in the consultation? What other kind of space might there be, aside from that which enables and is supported by distance technologies? Before providing an excerpt from research with IBD patients, it is worth summarizing a case described at length by Mattingly (1994) in her discussion of the healing potential of narrative in medicine.

The case concerned a 20-year-old man, recently recovered from a coma, who was being transferred for the first time to a wheelchair. The occupational therapist responded to his written request to be 'taken for a ride' by turning this into a tour of the hospital, taking in those rooms where he would soon receive treatment, and thus showing him 'his particular version of the hospital'.

> While both gaze toward the mat in the occupational therapy room, she quite literally points to a future story. She sketches, in the barest phrase, what kind of story they are in. (Ibid.: 817)

The tour made in this context refers both to the literal trip around the hospital and to the story – a metaphorical or imagined tour – that the occupational therapist creates about the young man's future treatment. To provide a metaphorical tour is like the answer one might make to a stranger who asks the question, 'Where am I?' when in the vicinity of your home. Realizing that simply to name the place (or give its grid reference) would leave the stranger none the wiser, 'you might go on to tell a story about the place – about your associations with it and the people who have lived and visited there' (Ingold, 2000: 237). In effect *the story of the place* draws upon previous journeys made, some in the company of other people, thus making it into a local space through the narrated linkages that temporalize it. In doing this you might refer to a map, but only as an adjunct to the story, because the position of the place in physically represented space is of secondary concern. A map reference does not answer the question in the terms in which it has been asked.

In the case of the consultation, we might say that *the story enables the tour*, rather than, as in Mattingly's example, the tour enabling the story. And this way of knowing also creates space differently from that which depends upon navigating with a map, a representation of features transferred at the expense of other, local material. We argue that medicine – or the practise of medicine – can also work in this alternative way, 'storying' or *re-presenting* the place in which the patient finds herself.

Unlike the medico-scientific regime, which distributes patients among separate places, each dedicated to specific forms of information transfer, the story cuts across places using narrative forms, thus linking up different kinds of knowledge.

How is this linking achieved? The social theorist Michel de Certeau (1984) identified the *tour* with everyday talk, for example, 'you come into the room through a low door'. This is a way of defining space through journeying, specifying operations of how to enter each room. Like narration, it establishes an itinerary by, in effect, becoming a guide. By comparison, the *map* (for example, 'the girls' room is next to the kitchen') is a way of talking that depends upon common reference to knowledge of an order of places. For de Certeau, to pass from the tour to the map in talking is to pass from everyday culture to scientific knowledge (in Mishler's

(1984) terms, from the 'voice of the lifeworld' to the 'voice of medicine'). Applied to the consultation, this corresponds to the two ways of signifying described above. Proto-stories, as tours, 'go ahead of [patients'] lives in order to open a field for them' (de Certeau, 1984: 125).

Making time: The consultation as an occasion

All people with chronic illnesses are concerned to know about the future – how their disease might be influenced by the various treatments available. This can be summarized by the question, 'Doctor, will I get well?' The medico-scientific framework addresses this question by predicting – for any patient – the effects of treatments and different courses of medical management. Rendering information into a single time-space in effect produces a particular kind of past and future. These are to do with linear time and cause and effect. Medico-scientific thought searches out causes of pathology and strives to produce distinct results. The time it takes to inform patients of this depends upon how it is conveyed, for it can be communicated within that framework – as a prescription – or else within a narrative form of the kind that we saw employed in the tour above.

Patients in the IBD study (Radley, Mayberry and Pearce, 2008) only ever talked of time in the medico-scientific regime in terms of its hurriedness, even, on occasions, when the actual (clock time) length of the consultation was longer than some others. The medical regime points towards locations within a totalizing vision that connects different times and places. For these locations to be seen and their significance appreciated takes 'no time', or only the time required for them to be pre-scribed by the doctor. This is appointment time, filled by the speed of the examination and the length of questioning in the clinic. By comparison, consultations where the doctor had listened to patients, given them the opportunity to be heard and was present to them, were those that they spoke of as ones in which the doctor 'had time' for them. This underlines Latour's point, that different ways of signifying *design* time; they do not lie within a common time frame except as we apply that way of thinking (as when we measure the length of utterances in a conversational exchange).

The focus here is how the doctor's use of proto-stories creates a different sense of time from that of what is 'passing by' in the clinic. This implies a difference between the consultation as a container of events (information) and the consultation as an *occasion*. It is the occasion for a 're-storying' of the patient's illness, in which journeys or tours create a sense of time as they move between and around events in the patient's past and future. The possibilities that follow from taking or not taking this or that medication are not predicted alternatives from a fixed array. These possibilities link up with other, more local matters, that the medico-scientific view excludes.

To illustrate this point, the excerpt below is from the third consultation recorded with a woman in her mid-thirties, with a long history of ulcerative colitis. She had become a mother for the first time six months previously. In the first interview she said that becoming a mother had sharpened the problems surrounding her symptoms (for example, needing to rush to the toilet while changing the baby); these problems threatened her enjoyment of motherhood. In an earlier consultation the consultant suggested she try again a liquid diet (that is, no solid food) and she agreed to this in spite of knowing that, on a previous occasion, she had found this dietary regime too difficult to follow for more than a matter of days. In a subsequent consultation she saw a junior doctor, who didn't provide her with the support she felt she needed at that meeting, and so she curtailed the diet. This raised the problem of what she should do next.

In a third consultation, excerpted below, she is sitting, holding her baby, opposite the consultant. Both are on easy chairs, with no desk between them. They are discussing her treatment with the drug azathioprin.

Patient TF Consultation 3

P   *To be honest I wouldn't want to be on it all those years*

D   *No*

P   *You know I hate taking medication anyway and the quicker I'm off it the better*

D   *Well I'd suggest we perhaps start you on it for a year and then stopped it. How would you feel about that? Or would you rather be on it for a shorter time?*

P   *I don't want to feel like I have done but I don't want to be on it for ever either [begins to cry, quietly] [the doctor waits]*

D   *Right mm why don't we look at it ( ) why don't we plan to look at it in 6 months time I think 6 months is probably – I think stopping it at 3 months would be a bit silly because that's almost like taking a dose of steroids and you know dropping it down takes 3 months to do, if we give it to you for 6 months by then your bowel should be much more normal, we'll have gone out of that sort of post-delivery stage particularly as you're not breast-feeding so if we gave it 6 months and then we talked about when you want to stop it then and if you do then we just stop it*

P   Yeh

D   *You might say having said that well actually I feel great and it felt so terrible when it's bad and I want another 6 months well we can stop it at any time after that you want to stop it we just do it and if you stopped it, you're not pregnant and it all flared up then you've got a message that you need to go on it long-term*

P   *Mm I suppose I'm just at the stage when I'm fed up with it [begins to cry]*

D   *I think that's understandable you've had a pretty rough pregnancy and a pretty rough period just after it as well. There is another approach ( ) which is to think about surgery ( ) what would be your views about surgery? Or do you not think about it at all? ( )*

P   *I know that life's different now, I've got [the baby], I've got a family and things are different, I suppose I'm just really down with it all*

D   *Mm you've had a really rough time I suppose I think we should – today and yesterday were both better days*

P   *Yeh so I*

D   *We need to have been better for a month or 6 weeks before we start thinking about anything else*

P   *Yeh*

And later in the consultation, concerning new treatment options:

D   *Yes but it's just down the road it's not a long way away there are lots of other drugs, there's even this amazing idea of now making these probiotic drinks which have got drugs produced by bacteria which again are specifically directed at bowel problems and that's all just round the corner so I think in the next 2 or 3 years you know the off- the availability of things is going to be hugely different*

P   *Yeh*

D   *So I don't think you should rush into anything. Surgery itself is much much better than it was when we first met, they can do, they can take away the colon through keyhole surgery now but nobody in L. is doing that so we would send you to somewhere else if you wanted to have it done and basically so you end up with 4 scars ( ) they do the bottom bit obviously through the bottom but they can take away the whole colon and you can have a pouch procedure done all through keyhole surgery and the operation, the place that would do that is [hospital] in London and we would send ( ) and so there for people the bottom bit would be sore obviously*

P   *Yeh*

D   *But you're out of hospital for a big operation in under a week*

P   So you wouldn't go to the toilet through the bottom it would be through a bag?

D   *No it would be through your bottom they may suggest a stage they may do a stage I'm not quite certain with the keyhole operation, there may be a stage procedure*

P   Yeh

D   *The lady I met had not had a stage she had a 5 scar procedure so she must have had it done all in one go but a lot of surgeons prefer to do it in 2 stages because they say they want all the stitching to heal up nicely before they make the final join so that it's all wonderful and well sealed but no the idea is that you will pass motions through the bottom and what they do is to take all of the large bowel away and make a new rectum using the small bowel. So they do some pouch surgery where they basically expand the bottom bit of the small bowel into a new rectum*

P   Yes

D   *( ) so you still have the same muscles using the controlling the bowel, you do go more often because you no longer have the colon to remove fluid so you might go 3 or 4 times a day but with no blood no urgency and most people feel a lot better*

At a surface level the excerpt is about future options, and what the patient might do. The doctor's talk is replete with references to future weeks and months, and to years past. These options are not laid out as a prescribed path that the patient should make, but are couched in phrases that underline the possibilities raised, considered and compared. '*Why don't we plan to look at it in 6 months time – I think stopping it at 3 months would be a bit silly...if we give it to you for 6 months by then your bowel should be much more normal, we'll have gone out of that sort of post-delivery stage...and then we talked about when you want to stop it then.*' These are matters considered in the course of what might happen, what might have happened and what the patient would really like to happen. As well as this, there is the issue of what failed to happen in the previous consultation, where support for this patient (TF) continuing a liquid diet was not forthcoming from the junior doctor. She expressed this need for support only in a later interview, after the support failed to appear.

Equally important in this consultation was what this doctor *did not do*, given the practice of medicine as understood by patients in the UK. He did *not* sit at the desk separated from his patient; he did *not* ask her questions that limit the range of local features she can introduce; he did *not* look at and write in the notes in the course of their conversation; he did *not* speak quickly or indicate that he is working with reference to a clinic schedule. These are not mere absences – signifying nothing – but transgressions that communicate a breach in the regime of medical signification. Summed up by several patients as the doctor's 'manner', this breach invites the patient to place her experience alongside those of other women whose stories he tells. These accounts of other patients – pregnant women with colitis – encourage the patient to recognize herself in relation to others, and to voice as yet unspoken concerns. Her situation is no longer exceptional or unknown; she can be *recognized* (Berger and Mohr, 1967: 70).

Rather than pointing away to the woman's disease across a chain of signifiers, the doctor's 'manner' refers back to a complex of mediators (his tone of voice, his posture, his speed of talking, his pauses to allow for silences etc.) that direct her attention *to him* as a vehicle through which these comparisons with other patients can be made. The important point here is that in appearing in this way the doctor *becomes present* to the patient. This is not a matter of 'revealing himself as a person' (his likes and dislikes) but of establishing his presence as the form of mediation to which her local experience can be brought. In order to distinguish this way of signifying from the medico-scientific regime, where inscription dominates, we shall refer to this other way of telling as *medico-presentational*, involving a different physical and discursive presence for both patient and doctor.

By transgressing the medico-scientific way of signifying, the doctor 'draws attention to himself' as the locus for the telling and the receipt of stories about illness. This is reinforced in this excerpt by the doctor's silence in response to the patient crying, and to his quiet and slow response. The effect of this breaching of the dominant regime is to enlarge the range of signifiers that are relevant to the exchange. Pauses, quiet speaking, encouragements of the patient's story, the use of everyday phrases in telling about other patients' experiences, all work to 'stop' the transformation of illness experience that prevents its local shape being unfolded (that is, the patient's story remaining untold). As mentioned above, we heard from several patients that the doctor's 'manner' made a big difference to how 'heard' they felt and how they were able to express concerns. They recognized this in the doctor's style but could not set out explicitly what it was or how it worked.

We suggest that the doctor's 'manner' (using this as a summary expression) legitimates the 'here and now' of the consultation as appropriate for the presentation of local experience. In the case of this patient (TF) this involved the *re-presentation* of her illness experience using the body as a medium of expression. Such presentations – including 're-storyings' – *take time*, which is integral to their mode of fabrication. Therefore, it is not just the time 'of' the story that is important here, but the fact that taking time to tell and to hear it is also important.

In this excerpt, the doctor is creating *proto-stories* about treatment options. He does this in response to the patient, so that whatever is being created here involves a joint collaboration. She says '*You know I hate taking medication anyway*', reminding the doctor not of past consultations only, but also of her preferred orientation to illness. In her crying she shows that her current strategy has come to a halt, and that she might have to take medication or think of something else. In this presentation (in contrast to denoting symptoms) her subjective experience of illness is realized with the body. At this point in the consultation the patient's future is indeed uncertain.

The doctor responds first by an acceptance of her weeping in the consultation. Recognizing her situation, legitimating her distress, he says: '*I think that's understandable you've had a pretty rough pregnancy*'. He places this in context, acknowledging the patient's recent past, and begins in effect a 're-storying' of her situation. This 're-storying' creates a key temporal dimension, and takes up some of the narrative properties that characterize this way of relating. As Mishler (2006) has pointed out, stories are constructed retrospectively, looking back from their endings, so that narrative time works backwards even as it moves forwards. The therapeutic potential of stories involves both the sense of moving towards the future and the sense of having re-ordered, perhaps rescued something from the past. For this patient, motherhood and its demands – which she so wants to meet – create a problem that the doctor, in turn, meets with his story of what opting for surgery might entail for her.

It was clear from interviews with this woman that the idea of surgery was something that she had turned her back on in the past. Now, raised again, the idea of surgery is animated by the proto-story of '*the lady I met*', the patient mentioned by the doctor as someone who had successfully received this surgical procedure. In the biography of TF's illness it was a frontier that she did not wish to approach, let alone cross. The idea of *frontier* is interesting because it is something that can be animated in the story by the actors who breach it. To give simple examples used by de Certeau: coming from the 'other side', as it were, the wolf breaches the forest, and the crocodile parts the river, both being 'mouthpieces of the limit', articulating what was previously inanimate (de Certeau, 1984: 127). Similarly, work is done in this proto-story by 'the lady I met' who successfully transits the space of surgical treatment.

This should not be read as a prescription that TF ought to take this option, but a propositional narrative that some of her hopes (about motherhood) might be realized by *turning a frontier (surgery) into a crossing*. What the doctor offers is not a single authoritative story but a nexus of movements (proto-stories) in which possible treatments lead from one place to another; where past experiences are storied into possible journeys, as well as revivifying what has been achieved or even lost. What mattered in the past might not matter so much now; the future of life as a mother requires a new story on the patient's part, of *how to be a mother with IBD* (Kelly, 1986). By laying down his stories alongside her account of illness, the consultant initiates further exchanges along these lines, legitimating this way of telling as appropriate to the consultation.

How did this patient view this consultation afterwards? She said in the subsequent interview that the doctor *'put me on the right road really'*, and gave her hope, *'it's given me thought for the future and it's [surgery] not so daunting now you know I know that six months of azathioprin and see how we go by then I'm hoping I'll be well enough and come off it ...'*

Not only did she feel she knew how to go forward – to enact the journey that the proto-story outlined – but the fact that the idea of surgery was not so daunting also meant that she was re-figured in relation to past ideas about her illness. She expressed herself as being less fearful, in spite of the actual outcome being unpredictable, and surgical treatment (never wanted, always feared) now being a more probable option.

Discussion

The comparison made in this chapter between medico-scientific and medico-presentational ways of signifying bears a strong resemblance to Roter and Frankel's (1992) overview of the medical dialogue, where quantitative and qualitative approaches were described in navigational terms. The question then arises, are we proposing two distinct ways of communicating between doctor and patient, or do these appear together in the clinic?

The answer to this is that, as *regimes* of signification, the two ways of making sense of illness are exclusive. They are not reducible to doctors' or patients' styles of communication. If one tries to do this – such as in analyses of communication or talk – then both structural and processual ways of contextualizing talk risk being obscured.

The next question must be as to whether these two ways of signifying can appear together in the same consultation. Our analysis suggests that indeed they can. Just as many patients have adopted modern medical ways of thinking, so too have some doctors retained in their practice medico-presentational ways of conducting the consultation (Hunter, 1991; Hurwitz, Greenhalgh and Skultans, 2004). This does not mean that these two ways of signifying are mixed, or become unrecognizable – rather that they can be operated in tandem, so to speak. In none of our interviews did patients ever suggest that they wanted to 'be understood' in preference to gaining medical help. This is perhaps because they did not draw a distinction between the two. To have their story listened to by the doctor and returned informed by medical knowledge was – as we understood it – their precise therapeutic aim.

Rita Charon (2006) has promoted the use of what she calls the 'patient's chart', in which patients write about their own experiences and reflections by family members, a record lying within the official medical notes. This recommendation follows the recognition that, if the doctor has the power to influence the workings of the clinic, then it is to medical professionals that we need to look for change. First, there is the therapeutic potential for listening on the part of the physician, which is an act of consolation, bringing the prospect of generosity as a paradigm for medical treatment (Frank, 2004). Second, there is the therapeutic potential of the stories that doctors tell. We have identified some of these as proto-stories in our analysis, falling short of full-blown narratives that might be told. (There is no intended implication that 'the doctor's story' is a ready-made narrative.) The interweaving of possible ways of moving forward can be both multiple and tentative, even though the 'success stories' of other patients who have successfully passed that way can be a powerful inspiration indeed (Morris, 2005).

Finally, attention is drawn to the benefit of analysing consultations in terms of regimes of signification – embodied, spoken, material, spatial – over analyses that focus upon particular levels or media. This is a way of trying to understand particularities and differences along with mapping the configurations that shape them, and to which they refer (Saukko, 1998). By invoking Latour's (1998) idea of signifying regimes, there follows the possibility of examining the consultation within its institutionalized context and, perhaps more importantly, in terms of the various ways in which doctors and patients make sense of illness and treatment for each other. Making sense occurs in two ways: by transforming information, holding certain features constant (measurement), and also by preserving information through re-shaping it – acting it, picturing it, 're-storying' it. Medicine as science depends upon the first; medicine as *re-presentation* (as 'art') depends upon the second. Deploying the two – and the balance between them – requires sensitivity to the importance of 'chronicity', not just in disease and illness, but in the doctor-patient relationship as well.

Note

This chapter is an edited version of an article:

Radley, A., Mayberry, J. and Pearce, M. (2008) Time, space and opportunity in the outpatient consultation: 'The doctor's story'. *Social Science & Medicine*, 66: 1484–96.

References

Berger, J. and Mohr, J. (1967) *A Fortunate Man: The Story of a Country Doctor.* London: Allen Lane.

Bury, M. (1982) Chronic Illness as Biographical Disruption. *Sociology of Health & Illness* 4: 167–82.

Byrne, P. S. and Long, B. E. L. (1976) *Doctors Talking to Patients.* London: HMSO.

Charon, R. (2006) *Narrative Medicine: Honoring the Stories of Illness.* Oxford: Oxford University Press.

De Certeau, M. (1984) *The Practice of Everyday Life.* Trans. S. F. Rendall. Berkeley: University of California Press.

Frank, A. W. (2004) *The Renewal of Generosity: Illness, Medicine and How to Live.* Chicago, IL: University of Chicago Press.

Hindmarsh, J. and Heath, C. (2003) Transcending the Object in Embodied Interaction. In J. Coupland and R. Gwyn (eds), *Discourse, the Body and Identity* (pp. 43–69). Houndmills: Palgrave Macmillan.

Hunter, K. M. (1991) *Doctors' Stories: The Narrative Structure of Medical Knowledge.* Princeton, NJ: Princeton University Press.

Hurwitz, B. (2000) Narrative and the Practice of Medicine. *Lancet* 356: 2086–9.

Hurwitz, B., Greenhalgh, T. and Skultans, V. (eds) (2004) *Narrative Research in Health and Illness.* Oxford: BMJ Books and Blackwell.

Ingold, T. (2000) *The Perception of the Environment: Essays on Livelihood, Dwelling and Skill.* London: Routledge.

Kelly, M. P. (1986) The Subjective Experience of Chronic Disease: Some Implications for the Management of Ulcerative Colitis, *Journal of Chronic Diseases* 39: 653–66.

Kelly, M. P. and Dickinson, H. (1997) The Narrative Self in Autobiographical Accounts of Illness. *The Sociological Review* 45: 254–78.

Latour, B. (1988) Opening One Eye while Closing the Other... A Note on Some Religious Paintings. In G. Fyfe and J. Law (eds), *Picturing Power: Visual Depiction and Social Relationships.* London: Routledge.

Latour, B. (1998) How to Be Iconophilic in Art, Science and Religion? In C. Jones and P. Galison (eds), *Picturing Science Producing Art* (pp. 418–40). New York: Routledge.

Mattingly, C. (1994) The Concept of Therapeutic 'Employment'. *Social Science & Medicine* 38: 811–22.

Mattingly, C. (1998) *Healing Dramas and Clinical Plots: The Narrative Structure of Experience.* Cambridge: Cambridge University Press.

May, C., Allison, G., Chapple, A., Chew-Graham, C., Dixon, C., Gask, L., Graham, R., Rogers, A. and Roland, M. (2004) Framing the Doctor-Patient Relationship in Chronic Illness: A Comparative Study of General Practitioners' Accounts. *Sociology of Health & Illness* 26: 135–58.

Mishler, E. G. (1984) *The Discourse of Medicine: Dialectics of Medical Interviews.* Norwood, NJ: Ablex.

Mishler, E. G. (2006) Narrative and Identity: The Double Arrow of Time. In A. De Fina, D. Schiffrin and M. Bamberg (eds), *Discourse and Identity* (pp. 30–47). Cambridge: Cambridge University Press.

Morris, D. B. (2005) Success Stories: Narrative, Pain and the Limits of Storylessness. In D. B. Carr, J. D. Loeser and D. B. Morris (eds), *Narrative, Pain and Suffering. Progress in Pain Research and Management Volume 34* (pp. 269–85). Seattle, WA: IASP Press.

Radley, A., Mayberry, J. and Pearce, M. (2008) Time, Space and Opportunity in the Outpatient Consultation: 'The Doctor's Story', *Social Science & Medicine* 66: 1484–96.

Roter, D. and Frankel, R. (1992) Quantitative and Qualitative Approaches to the Evaluation of the Medical Dialogue. *Social Science & Medicine* 34: 1097–103.

Saukko, P. (1998) Poetics of Voice and Maps of Space: Two Trends within Empirical Research in Cultural Studies. *Cultural Studies* 1(2): 259–75.

9
Chronic Illness, Self-management and the Rhetoric of Empowerment
Mike Bury

Introduction

In the history of human experience chronic illness is hardly a new phenomenon. As every school student of ancient Egypt knows, conditions such as iron deficiency, arthritis, tuberculosis and polio were common experiences. Bone samples and DNA taken from exhumed bodies testify to the presence of conditions which give rise to long-standing pain and suffering. It is also clear that throughout human history, and despite the devastating effects of epidemic and pandemic infections, life-threatening conditions could also be chronic in character. Again, tuberculosis is an exemplar here. In the modern era the temporal dimensions of this particular disease gave rise to one of the classic sociological studies in medical sociology (Roth, 1963) as did the uncertainty surrounding polio management (Davis, 1963). As Gerhardt (1990) has pointed out, many conditions that were once acutely life threatening have, under conditions of improved treatment, been transformed into chronic ones. Renal failure, cystic fibrosis, and some forms of cancer and heart disease have taken on this profile. By the end of the twentieth century, Arthur Frank (1995) could talk of the 'remission society' in which many if not most members of advanced countries were either undergoing treatment or in (limited) recovery.

As the burden of infectious disease has lessened (speaking here, again, of advanced societies) so the issues surrounding chronic illness have become more salient – to sufferers, their immediate intimates and the wider society and its health-care systems. These changes have been driven by social process as much as medical and scientific ones. In recent years commentators such as Bunker (2001) have estimated that about a half of the increase in life expectancy over the past 50 years is the result of improving medical interventions and care. At the same time, social conditions such as improved living standards, educational and employment levels have underpinned these improvements and to a great extent have been the foundations for investment in medical research and treatment. Reductions in fertility and the extension of average longevity have led to an ageing society where degenerative and chronic disease predominates. Thus, social and medical processes have developed within a complex dialectic. In turn the dynamics involved have given rise to a restructuring of health care away from medical dominance and towards managed consumerism (Bury and Taylor, 2008; McKinlay and Marceau, 2002).

Against this backcloth, this chapter explores two main developments in chronic disabling illness. The first is the advent of sociological studies in chronic illness. Beginning in the US, but then taken up in the UK, a number of studies have set out a framework for understanding the impact of illness on everyday life and on more formal healthcare provision. The use of terms such as 'biographical disruption' has allowed researchers to explore the everyday realities of living with illness. Developments of and critical commentaries on this work will also be discussed, including those who emphasize the continuity involved in illness experience as well as those drawing attention to wider social determinants. The response of disability activists will also be noted, especially their focus on political rights rather than health-related problems. The second part of the chapter documents the incorporation of some of the main insights of sociological research into mainstream health policy. In this context the self-management of chronic illness (the latter now attracting a new nomenclature as 'long-term conditions') is joined to a much more individualistic and psychologically oriented frame of reference. In this approach an emphasis on empowerment and self-efficacy require a restructuring of patient experience and behaviour. An alignment with the agenda of managed expectations and a reduction in expenditure is also involved. A consideration of the implications of this transformation of chronic illness experience constitutes a third and final section of the chapter.

The rise of sociological research on chronic illness

Providing a starting date for the development of a given line of thought or research will always be arbitrary. In the study of chronic illness, the year 1973 might perhaps act as a convenient entry point. In that year, Anselm Strauss published a paper in *Society* called 'America: In Sickness and in Health (helping the chronically ill)'. Noting the changes in disease pattern discussed above, Strauss went on to quote a national survey from 1964 showing that some 40 per cent of the American population was suffering from a chronic disease and that one in four of these was losing time off work (Strauss, 1973: 33). What was less evident, Strauss argued, was despite all the information 'pouring out' on the subject its social dimensions were largely ignored. 'How', he asked, 'can patients and professionals cope with health-related problems of family disruption, marital stress, role destruction and adjustment, stigmatization and even loss of body mobility?' (ibid.).

Although Straus recognized the importance of health-care professionals for many chronic illness sufferers, they were neither the focal point nor the primary component of living with a chronic illness. For Strauss it was the everyday tasks that patients needed to undertake that were the main concern, and thus the focus of sociological research. These, he averred, were: managing medical crises, managing treatment regimens, controlling symptoms, organizing time, preventing or living with social isolation, adjusting to the disease trajectory, and normalizing interaction and everyday life. In order to do this the sufferer was seen to adopt strategies requiring a given level of organization (of family and friends) and the presence of material resources. A great deal of the daily life of the chronically ill person also involved the employment of 'interactional and social skills in order to make the necessary arrangements' (ibid.).

In a subsequent collection of essays entitled *Chronic Illness and the Quality of Life* (1975), Strauss and Glaser illustrated these issues with empirical studies largely undertaken by students and colleagues following Strauss' general line of argument. Perhaps the most important point to note here is that the management of chronic illness for Strauss was not so much a question of identity or self-management, but the successful or otherwise deployment of interactional and social skills in managing the disease's impact. Whether in cases such as arthritis or emphysema, authors focused on the strategies and tactics which were observed in naturally occurring settings. These might be developed and employed to cover up the visibility of the disease or its effects, or to achieve a socially desirable end such as to interact with friends or family without the disease intruding.

In other words, it was what people *do* in the face of chronic illness (especially in interacting with others) that mattered to Strauss. It should also be noted, in the light of the discussion below, that this focus on what people do was not on what people *should do*. Reinforcing the point,

in subsequent research with Jennifer Corbin, Strauss went on to emphasize the 'work' involved in living with 'chronic illness'. Three lines of
work could be identified: illness work involving symptom management,
together with diagnostic difficulties and crisis prevention; everyday life
work in daily tasks of self-care, child care or paid employment; and
biographical work in reconstructing continuity in the individual's biography (Corbin and Strauss, 1985, 1988). Thus, the chronically ill were
seen to be active agents in their own management tasks, minimizing
the deleterious effects of the illness and maximizing as far as possible
their quality of life.

   The emphasis on biography (as a meeting point between self and
others, between the individual and social context) and the active
responses to illness in Strauss' work was picked up and developed
in subsequent research on chronic illness, especially in the UK. In a
paper published in 1982, Bury coined the term 'biographical disruption', and drew attention to the ways lay people facing the onset of
chronic illness, arthritis in this instance, handled their condition and
their disrupted lives (Bury, 1982, 1991). The assault on the lifeworld
and the sense of continuity of the self (together with life planning), it
was observed, occasioned a reappraisal of both practical and symbolic
universes. The strategic handling of everyday interactions, whether at
home or at work, involved a delicate balancing act in seeking help from
others and yet not overreaching the 'limits of tolerance'. Decisions on
disclosing and disguising (of symptoms or treatments), on explaining
to others the impact of symptoms and on legitimizing a reduction in
role performance were all seen to require active engagement in managing social interaction as well as illness or symptom management. The
delicate mechanisms involved in such processes paid testament to the
influence of variable social structural contexts. A series of other sociological studies were produced at this time, including those focusing on
the family as a particular context in which practical and symbolic problems had to be solved (Anderson and Bury, 1988).

   Various attempts to extend a biographical approach followed. Two
particular studies underlined some of the difficulties involved in specifying or advocating a particular approach to illness self-management.
In one study of 44 HIV-positive gay men and haemophiliac patients in
Paris, Carricaburu and Pierret (1995) pointed out that a 'situation at risk
of illness' obtained when uncertainty about future prospects was acute.
This often involved 'biographical work' of an elaborate kind. Not only
did the body require close management but the distinction between
'felt' and 'enacted' stigma was an ever-present difficulty. The fear of

the consequences of illness had immediate and profound effects on everyday interactions. The haemophiliac respondents in this study had already adopted strategies (again in the workplace or at home) to reduce the effects of the illness. The advent of HIV threatened to overwhelm them, and a withdrawal from social interaction occurred. In contrast, the gay men were seen to be more active, mobilizing resources on a number of fronts.

The relay between the body in illness and the social world is evident here. In a paper written by Kelly and Field (1996), the importance of the 'corporeal dimension' to chronic illness management was underlined. As a number of writers have pointed out, daily life involves an 'assumptive world', hidden from view and from consciousness. Indeed, social life would be impossible if every action and motive were conscious. Much of what we experience of the working of the body falls into this realm. With the onset of illness, especially chronic illness, such assumptions come to the fore. Actions that were once automatic (for example, those involving mobility and dexterity) now require active engagement and planning. Kelly and Field pointed out that those suffering from chronic illness become aware of the requirements of the wider society to be 'culturally competent' and how much this is premised on bodily performances. The performative nature of culture has long been recognized in social anthropology, especially in 'exotic' locales, but the study of chronic illness has brought out its importance in everyday mundane settings. Here, too, the variability in the strategies used to maintain a sense, or appearance of 'competence' was stressed.

The approach to chronic illness emphasizing biographical disruption, biographical work or active responses in self-management has not been without its sociological critics. For example, Simon Williams, in a far-reaching essay (Williams, 2000), has pointed out that the emphasis on disruption and discontinuity in chronic illness can underplay the continuity in biography that may occur in the occurrence of illness. It may also reinforce, he argues, what some disability activists regard as an overemphasis on the 'personal tragedy' approach to disabling illness in which 'medical sociology is said to be complicit' (ibid.: 41). Studies by Pound, Gompertz and Ebrahim (1998) and Faircloth et al. (2004) have argued that for many people facing the onset of chronic illness 'biographical flow' as much as disruption occurs. Age and social context are important here. The older the person is and the more difficult the social circumstances are, the more likely it is that responses will be fashioned in terms of 'yet another problem to be faced' rather than one that radically dislocates an assumptive world.

The emphasis on political rights by disability activists has also sought to highlight the limitations of a focus on disruption, and on the need for artful social interaction. Debate has sallied back and forth between medical sociologists and disability writers (Bury, 1996; Oliver, 1996) concerning the links between chronic illness and disability. In recent years, however, a greater recognition of the limitations of a radical 'social model' of disability has become evident, as disability writers have emphasized the persistent and intrusive nature of bodily impairments and the limits of political or social action in dealing with them. Whatever the results of political campaigning may be, those living with visual impairments or with conditions such as back pain still have to deal with the obdurate character of the body and its impact on everyday life (Barnes and Mercer, 2003; Shakespeare, 2006).

Whilst the debate about the value of the notion of 'biographical disruption' has continued, the main issue at stake in the present discussion is the nature of the responses made by those living with a chronic illness. Whether discontinuity or continuity is emphasized or whether the body or society becomes the focus, the picture presented in much sociological research is of active lay responses to the challenges chronic disabling illness presents. For some commentators, especially those in the US, such responses can lead to a new sense of self, 'transcending the loss' that the illness may involve (Charmaz, 2000) or in fashioning a new narrative of the self that gives a new 'moral necessity' to life (Frank, 1995: 176). But whatever the emphasis, sociological research has highlighted the contextual nature of chronic illness and the day-to-day engagement lay people have with their health-related conditions. As Corbin and Strauss (1988) had pointed out earlier, such 'work' on the part of patients needed to be recognized rather than cut across by formal health services. As will become clear, however, recent official responses and initiatives in the chronic illness area have brought a different agenda to bear on the subject, with far-reaching consequences.

The transformation of chronic illness and self-management

As sociological research on chronic illness continued throughout the 1980s and 1990s, those responsible for developing and delivering health services were becoming increasingly concerned about the demand for health care. The growing results of an ageing population and the transformation of disease patterns in developed countries were seen to create a mutually reinforcing trend. Demographic and epidemiologic transitions were bringing about a perceived need for 'care transition' (Bury and Taylor, 2008). An apparently paradoxical situation obtained. Social research had indicated in a number of studies that the demand for formal care was less than the need for it. In their 'pathways to care' study, Rogers, Hassell and Nicolas (1999), for example, found that people modulated and regulated their use of services. Social networks were seen to play a central role in accessing formal care. Women were seen to regulate their own use of services and play a central role in the use of other family members and dependents: 'lay knowledge about illness and health action is developed over time and "stored up" for use when needed' (ibid.: 122). The picture painted here, in the main, was of careful and judicious actions, based on long-term lay experience and a desire only to use services when necessary.

At the same time service use by an increasingly ageing population was being seen to outstrip supply. The relatively heavy use of primary and secondary care by the elderly (together with the new born and infants) and a growth in the numbers of the (very) old appeared to presage a crisis in care. The demographic 'time bomb' was waiting to explode (Mullan, 2000). The facts on health expenditure and use seemed to speak for themselves. In England Wales for example, in 2002/3 it was reported that 'those aged 85 and over received some £4,147 per head, more than six times the average amount spent on the under 85s' (Social Trends, 2005: 111). In the survey, attendance at outpatient or casualty departments (or emergency room) in a three-month period prior to interview showed a steady rise with age, with some 20 per cent aged 75 or over using services, compared with 10 per cent of those aged 16–24. Moreover, surveys of chronic conditions showed that some 40 per cent of those aged 75 and over reported suffering from a 'limiting long term condition' (Social Trends, 2007: 89). Whilst it is possible to see such figures in a positive light (60 per cent of those aged 75 and over do not report a 'limiting long term condition') for policy-makers alarm bells began ringing.

Taking the experience in England and Wales and the National Health Service (NHS) as an example, a series of initiatives and policy documents dealing with old age and long-term conditions began appearing in the late 1990s and early 2000s. In essence, these marked out a transition in health care from one in which services were provided to (younger) patients suffering from acute conditions to one where quality, choice and 'partnership' with (older) patients would become the watchwords. Though much rhetoric has flowed under the health policy bridge with these developments, their importance to the current understanding of chronic illness should not be underestimated. Two key dimensions of 'long-term condition management' in the NHS can illustrate the issues involved. These two dimensions show how long-term conditions have been brought centre stage in health care and health policy, and have become closely associated with managing expectations and costs in health care. Where they were once neglected, long-term conditions are now in receipt of intense policy interest.

The first dimension concerns 'case management'. In 2004, the Department of Health in England published a document entitled the *NHS Improvement Plan*. At its centre lay the so-called Kaiser Triangle – a model of care borrowed from the Californian HMO, Kaiser Permanente. Three levels of care are identified in this model: professional care for high-risk cases at the top of the triangle; shared care for disease management in the middle; and self-care and self-management for the majority of patients at the bottom. This approach is seen in the *Improvement Plan* as a specific response to the growing demand for health care from those with long-term conditions. The aim of case management, following the Kaiser model, is to provide integrated services that will help people (towards the more severe top end of the triangle) to stay out of acute facilities and rehabilitate them after any unavoidable inpatient episode.

This new initiative was partly based on the work of Chris Ham, who became Director of the Department of Health's Strategy Unit in 2001. In a paper published in the *BMJ* in 2003, Ham and colleagues undertook an analysis and comparison of the care of patients in California and in England. Through the examination of routinely available data, they argued that the integrated and managed care offered by Kaiser could lead to reductions in admission rates and lengths of stay in the NHS where they remained relatively high. The Kaiser staff, Ham et al., argued, were motivated to work within 'an envelope of resources' because they were aware that the overall success of the enterprise, of which they were members and beneficiaries, was dependent on their judicious use (Ham et al., 2003: 1260). In addition, specialists worked closely with other services specified within the Kaiser model, and had no interest in keeping patients in hospital. Finally, the model brought together prevention, diagnosis, treatment and care. This, it was argued, was particularly noticeable in the management of long-term conditions such as heart failure or asthma (ibid.).

Subsequent discussion and debate about case management, and the relevance of the Kaiser model to the NHS has cast considerable doubt on its applicability. Two reports from the National Primary Care Research and Development Centre in Manchester, UK, have examined several aspects of the problem. In the first report, Roland et al. (2006) looked at a cohort of older patients at 'high risk' of admission and readmission to hospital care. They found that if these high-risk patients are tracked over time, their use of services tends to fall towards the mean for their age group as a whole. They argue that this is the result of a number of factors, including deaths amongst the cohort. Importantly, such falls in the rate of utilization might be falsely attributed to interventions such as case management, 'because the admissions would probably decline anyway' (ibid.: 291). In a second study, Gravelle et al. (2007) studied the Evercare model of case management and found no reduction in hospital admissions. Though nurses within the programme reported intervening successfully with long-term condition patients, the lack of impact on admission rates was probably explained by the fact that these nurses were essentially 'case finding'. That is, they were identifying new 'unmet need' rather than preventing known patients from (re) entering the health-care system (ibid.: 33). Despite these critiques of managed care, its place within the DoH's approach to long-term conditions remains important. Dealing with the demand for and the costs of emergency and acute health care from older patients with long-term conditions remains a high priority for the NHS. The association of such patients with heavy demand and cost remains a crucial concern for policy-makers.

The second dimension of long-term condition management relates to the bottom section of the Kaiser Triangle – that concerned with promoting self-care and self-management among the majority of lower-risk patients. This, too, has led to initiatives taken from the US experience, this time from a 'chronic disease selfmanagement (CDSM) programme' in California. Kate Lorig, Professor of Medicine, and Director of the Stanford Patient Education Research Centre, who has a background in nursing and public health, has become well known on the international stage for her promulgation of self-management and the CDSM. The website of the centre describes her fulsomely as 'our leader' (http://patienteducation.stanford.edu/staff.html, accessed 17.11.08. In a paper published in *The Lancet* in 2002, Lorig put forward the idea that patients were not just consumers of health care, but could become producers of it too. Welcoming the national initiative of the Expert Patients Programme (EPP) (just launched in the English NHS) Lorig argued that although patients could be regarded as experts in their long-term conditions and their care, 'patients ought to be provided with the education for this new role' (Lorig, 2002: 814).

In order to achieve this goal, Lorig argued that in contrast to disease-based patient education, self-management programmes 'are aimed at giving patients the knowledge and skills to manage their illness daily' (ibid.). Lorig goes on to quote Corbin and Strauss in this connection. These authors, she claims, 'have identified three self management tasks for patients with chronic diseases: medical management, such as taking medicines and exercising; maintaining and adapting important life roles, such as those of mother or worker; and managing the anger, fear, frustration or depression which come, singly or together, with having an uncertain future' (ibid.). The aim, the article states, is to help people through 'goal setting and mastering new skills' to raise their confidence in managing their condition. In the same vein, health-care professionals are asked to move to a more partnership stance with respect to their patients: 'they must make it clear that they want patients to become expert patients' (ibid.: 815).

It is possible to argue that Lorig misrepresents a key aspect of Strauss' work on chronic illness in her formulations. Corbin and Strauss did not so much 'identify three tasks for patients' as identify those tasks patients were observed to be carrying out. As stated earlier in this chapter, this inversion involves a shift from *is* to *ought*. This is a crucial move, transforming what patients do into what patients should do. The ambiguity involved in this situation is reinforced by the fact that others following Lorig's lead, including the Chief Medical Officer for England, have often started from a position that stresses the 'wisdom and experience' of patients and the fact that 'the expertise of patients could be harnessed to play a part in addressing the challenge of this shifting burden of disease' (Donaldson, 2003: 1279). But if patients are seen to be experts, or as carrying out the kinds of task identified by Corbin and Strauss, why should they need to be educated through a chronic disease self-management programme?

It could be, of course, that *some* patient are 'experts' and some not, but this view has little in common with the sociological research base invoked by Lorig. The idea of judging patients as 'expert' or 'non expert', or 'successful' or 'unsuccessful' in managing their illness is clearly problematic. In fact, research has demonstrated that most people who sign up to join chronic disease self-management programmes such as the EPP are already good 'self managers'. In addition, some may react negatively to 'lay leaders' running courses who present themselves as getting things right (EPP Evaluation Team, 2005; Rogers, Bury and Kennedy, forthcoming). The point to stress in this context is that the process of formulating patient 'expertise' and 'self-management' involves moving the focus away from the contextualized nature of living with a chronic illness to one where specified skills to be acquired by individuals are adumbrated and prescribed. It also marks a shift from a sociological to a psychological approach, in that patient confidence is reformulated in terms of 'self efficacy' (Newbould, Taylor and Bury, 2006). The attraction for policy-makers is that, like case management, self-management and specific courses such as the EPP, when scaled up to involve thousands of patients holds out the apparent promise of reducing demand and containing costs. In this way self-management, like case management, becomes central to care transition (Taylor and Bury, 2007). The implications of this for the future of chronic illness will be considered in the third and final section of this chapter.

Implications for the future

When sociological research began to tackle the issue of chronic illness, it was often stressed that the topic was marginal to the main preoccupations of the health-care system. Most developed countries had been focusing their attention on acute life-threatening illness, and the 'glamorous' world of hospital medicine. Indeed, within medicine, specialisms dealing with chronic conditions among the elderly such as rheumatology, rehabilitation and geriatrics were regarded as low status. Public health (variously termed social medicine, or community medicine) had suffered a similar fate. Throughout the 1970s and 1980s, those working in such fields had recurrent crises in confidence. Sociological research in these areas was often premised on the call for greater recognition of the (health care) needs of the chronically ill, and the 'unending work and care' involved for patients and carers at home (Corbin and Strauss, 1988). The demand for greater support for sufferers and their families rested on the perception that most of the care delivered was by relatives, neighbours and friends. To repeat an earlier point, it was stressed that health services should work with the grain of these informal, care giving structures (Anderson and Bury, 1988). The best sought so to do.

In the early part of the new century, however, a transformation began to occur. From being neglected, chronic illnesses (now, as we have seen, referred to in England at least as 'long-term conditions') moved centre stage. But the construction of the issues involved, in political and policy circles, were couched in terms of the problems they posed to health-care systems rather than the needs of patients and their families. In the present context, it is the putative demand for care and its cost that preoccupy policy-makers, rather than a needs assessment. The results of demographic and epidemiologic transitions have come to haunt health services, with long-term conditions becoming emblematic of the problems they face. In a major review of the future of the English NHS, published in 2002, Derek Wanless predicted that only a 'fully engaged scenario' would deliver value for money. This scenario had at its centre a matching of investment with a greater commitment by patients and the public to look after themselves. Indeed, he saw that in such a scenario 'levels of public engagement with their health are high' (Wanless, 2002: introductory letter). The increases in life expectancy, the arrival of 'baby boomers' into later life, and the changing nature of expectations all figured largely in his thinking.

From this viewpoint, the emphasis on long-term conditions in official circles has come to express some central features of a 'New NHS', one which finds echoes in other developed countries, as we shall see below. An emphasis on quality, choice and high expectations is matched by a demand for greater involvement by the public in their health. By supporting patients (and their carers) with initiatives such as case management and the EPP, policy-makers hope that this will manage down expectations and keep people out of formal care as much as possible. In this way increasing levels of investment can be matched with strenuous efforts of cost control. The emphasis is as much on patients and the public adopting new attitudes towards care as on the earlier call on those in the health services to work with the grain of informal practices. The co-production of health gains renewed emphasis (Cayton, 2006). Such approaches might be summarized in a paraphrase of JFK's famous speech: ask not what your health services can do for you, but what you can do for your health services.

Of course, as this chapter has made plain, the nature of epidemiologic and demographic transitions *do* pose challenges to health-care systems, though it needs emphasizing once again that most care is already carried out by patients and their carers in their homes. Sociological research has demonstrated over and again the presence in everyday life of the kind of 'engagement' now being called for. Observational studies have documented in detail the creative and often artful way in which patients maintain as much quality of life as is possible. This body of work, alongside the extensive experience of clinicians working with patients over the decades, makes some of the calls for 'new' approaches sound hollow. Moreover, there are several features of the emphasis on long-term conditions in official thinking, particularly in relation to prescriptive programmes such as the EPP that give cause for concern for the future. Scepticism about their implications is not confined to the British situation.

In Australia, for example, debates about the value of self-management programmes have begun to emerge in public, despite their enthusiastic endorsement by health chiefs in a number of states. In January 2007, the ABC National Radio held a debate on the topic, first interviewing Lorig and then, on a later occasion, Marta Buszewicz, visiting from University College in London. Norman Swann, the presenter of the programme, introduced the topic thus: 'The biggest health problem facing Australians personally and as taxpayers is not heart disease, or cancer, or arthritis, or depression, or dementia. It's the combination of them which accumulates in each of us in various permutations as we age. It's got the label – chronic disease. Conditions which once we have them won't go away and that we'll have to live with for the rest of our lives' (ABC, 2007). In the interview with Buscewicz, she was asked about her research on arthritis (Buscewicz et al., 2006) and the question of reductions in service use. A number of studies, including those of Lorig and her colleagues, have shown that despite small changes in a range of other indicators, little reduction in demand can be detected. Buscewicz confirmed that in their large trial of arthritis patients no reduction in use was seen. Indeed, service use may actually increase as the result of involvement in chronic disease self-management courses such as the EPP – at least in the short term. In so far as managing down demand is a goal of such interventions, as with case management, there is growing recognition that this is an unlikely outcome.

In more general terms, enthusiasm for prescriptive programmes may outstrip their perceived value by a large margin. Again, in the Australian context, even those who have supported and developed self-management programmes there have argued for caution in expecting too much of them. Richard Osborne, the author of a number of studies of self-management, including collaborative studies with Lorig (Osborne et al., 2007), has warned against high expectations on the part of policy-makers and health service providers of such programmes delivering major benefits. In a recent paper with Joanne Jordan (Jordan and Osborne, 2007) the scale of investment in self-management initiatives in Australia is outlined. Some 250 million Australian dollars are being spent on a 5-year programme on 'preventing and promoting health' with self-management as a core component; $14.8 million for the promotion of effective management and self-management of arthritis and osteoporosis; and $250,000 for new education and training in the area, aimed at general practitioners, nurses and allied workers (ibid.: 84).

Yet, in their paper, Jordan and Osborne go on to note a number of barriers to the effective implementation of such initiatives. For example, they review evidence from the UK and the US and conclude that these programmes have had 'limited reach' in recruiting patients and even less in being supported by health-care professionals. Indeed, they state that Kaiser Permanente in California 'met with resistance from health care professionals because the scope and purpose [of the programmes] were not well understood' (ibid.: 85). They also argue that the nature of the trial data on self-management programmes is severely compromised by the lack of published studies including men and minority ethnic groups. This leads to a lack of generalizability of findings. Their main point, however, is that even if one accepts that such programmes can be effective, at least to some degree, the lack of flexibility in developing them, the reliance on one type of programme such as the CDSMP or EPP, and the low level of integration of them into mainstream health service provision raise the distinct possibility that a great deal of money may be wasted.

Against this backcloth, there must be concern about the growing rhetorical character of policy focusing so enthusiastically on self-management of chronic conditions. If programmes are less effective than supposed (for evidence reviews see Newbould et al., 2006, Newman, Steed and Mulligan, 2004) and are not able to reduce demand for health services, what is their attraction? It may be that the limited cost effectiveness of initiatives such as the EPP (Kennedy et al., 2007) and of case management provide an ongoing allure for policy-makers, offsetting the fear that without them demand for expensive health care might be even higher than it is. In addition, chronic illness is, by definition, largely intractable. No one has a cure for arthritis, Parkinson's or diabetes. Self-management represents one of few options available, alongside routine medical care. Once recognized as such, it is perhaps understandable that enthusiasm outruns realism, and more is asked from initiatives than can possibly be delivered.

At the same time the rhetoric that has accompanied self-management of long-term conditions can be seen to accomplish other social and political tasks. The most obvious of these concerns is New Labour's emphasis on choice. In so far as health systems (whether socialized, as with the NHS, or not) bring to the fore the idea of patient as consumer, then new discursive accompaniments are needed. 'Informed choice', 'personalisation' of services, and 'working together' are all emphasized in recent policy statements on the subject (DoH, 2004). The language of choice and consumerism on its own has clear limitations in the health-care context. None of us can 'consume' health care in the way, for example, we consume electrical goods. We cannot take back medical treatment or surgery to the 'producer' and ask for a refund or replacement. In the instance of Cayton's 'flat pack patient' (Cayton, 2006) the idea of the 'joint production of health' alongside notions of empowerment and self-efficacy convey a sense that the patient can benefit in psychological terms from the new approach to health care. His or her demand for health services is not simply being managed down or restricted in this view. Something positive is being put in its place. Thus additional terms such as 'shared care', 'shared decision-making', 'partnership', the 'active patient' or the 'autonomous patient' – all in wide circulation in health policy circles – are meant to impart a feeling of engagement in health care and a move away from expectations of services simply being provided by professional practitioners.

This also provides a clue to the other side of the rhetorical coin. If the patient is being enjoined to become more active, at the centre of a 'patient-led NHS' (DoH, 2005) this suggest that professionals, and in particular doctors, are less central than they once were. Patient autonomy is stressed rather than professional autonomy. Much of the emphasis on self-management and a more active role for patients can be seen as part of a long-term managerial battle to control the resources in health care that were once under the near complete control of the medical profession. The 'concordat' between state and the medical profession (Salter, 2004) is being transformed through rhetoric bound initiatives, emphasizing patient activation and patient 'expertise'. The prescriptive nature of the rhetorical calls on the patient to be more active, along the prescribed lines of self-management courses, is matched by increasing protocols and bureaucracy in health-care provision. The rhetoric under discussion oils the wheels of a joint and new enterprise – the coming together of the active patient as a rational, psychologically robust and judicious consumer with the evidence-based practitioner employing standardized and carefully costed treatment modalities. Thus, the rhetoric of self-management forms part – an important part – of a wider project: the transformation of health care into a managed and controlled system of production and consumption.

It is no wonder, given the ideological weight that the rhetoric of self-management and the active patient is asked to carry, that a great deal of enthusiasm and pressure are evident among those carrying through the process. Some of this comes from policy-makers and some from patients themselves. Many of the websites and publications emanating from self-management activities use language that employs 'new age' and quasi-religious rhetoric. Testimonials from those who have been involved in self-management courses speak of 'life changing' or 'transformative' experiences, and are used to bolster claims made by policy-makers. Some patients speak of being on a 'mission' to make progress with their health. One participant in the EPP put it in these words:

> I remember one day a friend reading my tarot cards and telling me I was in this black tunnel with no light, and that one day I was going to go through that light and it would all be a life-changing experience. I was very sceptical but how right he was because shortly after in the local paper was an article all about this Expert Patients Programme. I made enquiries and in September 2003 I was a participant. (Quoted in Rogers et al. forthcoming)

For enthusiasts, such language may appear attractive and support-ive. But the peer pressure within such programmes (one of the key techniques through which participants' targets are made and met on courses such as these) can be less than positive. It needs also to be remembered that many of the research evaluations of such programmes are from trials in which there is a considerable drop-out rate – and this from an initial recruitment base of those willing to participate in the first place. As with other areas such as joint decision-making, or partnership in care, self-management may have attractions to some sections of the population but not others, espe-cially the 'older old'.

The main point to be made here is that psychologically oriented pro-grammes of self-management have come together with long-term con-dition management to produce a heady mixture of rhetorically couched policies and initiatives. Where once the 'new age' rhetoric of personal growth, autonomy, empowerment and the like were used by social movements to challenge state-controlled bureaucratic structures and systems, today they have become part and parcel of state activity itself. The employment of such rhetoric may be seen by some as an attempt to incorporate the chronically ill patient's 'lifeworld' into official think-ing. Rather, it may be seen more appropriately as an avoidance of the realities of living with chronic illness, in all its complexities and within all its daily contingencies. It may also disguise the very real need for good quality health care for those with moderate and severe illnesses. Under these conditions, the sociological imperative of bringing to the fore the nature of everyday experience of illness, as found in naturally occurring community settings, remains an ongoing necessity for both research and rational debate.

References

ABC (2007) *The Health Report* ABC National Radio, 29 January.

Anderson, R. and Bury, M. (eds) (1988) *Living with Chronic Illness: The Experiences of Patients and Their Families*. London: Unwin Hyman.

Barnes, C. and Mercer, G. (2003) *Disability*. Cambridge: Polity Press.

Bunker, J. (2001) *Medicine Matters After All: Measuring the Benefits of Medical Care, a Healthy Lifestyle and a Just Social Environment*. London: The Nuffield Trust.

Bury, M. (1982) Chronic Illness as Biographical Disruption. *Sociology of Health and Illness* 4(2): 167–82.

Bury, M. (1991) The Sociology of Chronic Illness: A Review of Research and Prospects. *Sociology of Health and Illness* 13(4): 451–68.

Bury, M. (1996) Defining and Researching Disability: Challenges and Responses. In C. Barnes and G. Mercer (eds), *Exploring the Divide: Illness and Disability*. Leeds: The Disability Press.

Bury, M. and Taylor, D. (2008) Towards a Theory of Care Transition: From Medical Dominance to Managed Consumerism. *Social Theory and Health* 6: 210–19.

Buszewicz, M., Rait, G. et al. (2006) Self Management of Arthritis in Primary Care: Randomised Controlled Trial, *British Medical Journal* 33: 879.

Carricaburu, D. and Pierret, J. (1995) From Biographical Disruption to Biographical Reinforcement: The Case of HIV-Positive Men. *Sociology of Health and Illness* 17(1): 66–88.

Cayton, H. (2006) The Flat-Pack Patient?: Creating Health Together. *Patient Education and Counselling* 62: 288–90

Charmaz, K. (2000) Experiencing Chronic Illness. In G. L. Albrecht, R. Fitzpatrick and S. C. Scrimshaw (eds), *The Handbook of Social Studies in Health and Medicine*. London: Sage.

Corbin, J. and Strauss, A. L. (1985) Managing Chronic Illness at Home: Three Lines of Work. *Qualitative Sociology* 8: 224–47.

Corbin, J. and Strauss, A. (1988) *Unending Work and Care: Managing Chronic Illness at Home*. San Francisco, CA: Jossey Bass.

Davis, F. (1963) *Passage through Crisis: Polio Victims and Their Families*. Indianapolis, IN: Bobbs-Merrill.

Department of Health (DoH) (2004) *The NHS Improvement Plan: Putting People at the Heart of Public Services*. London: Department of Health.

Department of Health (DoH) (2005) *Creating a Patient-Led NHS: Delivering the NHS Improvement Plan*. London: Department of Health.

Donaldson, L. (2003) Expert Patients Usher in a New Era of Opportunity for the NHS. *British Medical Journal* 326: 1279–80.

EPP evaluation team (2005) *Process Evaluation of the EPP – Report II*. University of Manchester: National Primary Care Research and Development Centre.

Faircloth, C. A., Boylstein, C., Rittman, M., Young, M. E. and Gubrium, J. (2004) Sudden Illness and Biographical Flow in Narratives of Stroke Recovery. *Sociology of Health and Illness* 26(2): 242–61.

Frank, A. (1995) *The Wounded Storyteller: Body, Illness and Ethics*. Chicago, IL: University of Chicago Press.

Gerhardt, U. (1990) Introductory Essay: Qualitative Research in Chronic Illness: The Issue and the Story. *Social Science and Medicine* 30: 1149–59.

Gravelle, H., Dusheiko, M. et al. (2007) Impact of Case Management (Evercare) on Frail Elderly Patients: Controlled Before and After Analysis of Quantitative Outcome Data. *British Medical Journal* 334: 31.

Ham, C., York, N., Sutch, S. et al. (2003) Hospital Bed Utilisation in the NHS, Kaiser Permanente and the US Medicare Programme: Analysis of Routine Data. *British Medical Journal* 327: 1257–60.

Jordan, J. E. and Osborne, R. H. (2007) Chronic Disease Self-management Education Programs: Challenges Ahead. *Medical Journal of Australia* 186(2): 84–7.

Kelly, M. and Field, D. (1996) Medical Sociology, Chronic Illness and the Body. *Sociology of Health and Illness* 18(2): 241–57.

Kennedy, A., Reeves, D., Bower, P., Lee, V., Middleton, E., Richardson, G., Gardner, C., Gately, C. and Rogers, A. (2007) The Effectiveness and Cost Effectiveness of a National Lay-led Self Care Support Programme for Patients with Long-term Conditions: A Pragmatic Randomised Controlled Trial. *Journal of Epidemiol and Community Health* 61(3): 254–61.

Lorig K. (2002) Partnerships between Expert Patient and Physicians. *Lancet* 359: 814–5.

McKinlay, J. and Marceau, L. D. (2002) The End of the Golden Age of Doctoring. *International Journal of Health Services* 32: 379–416.

Mullean, P. (2000) *The Imaginary Timebomb: Why an Ageing Population Is not a Social Problem.* London: I.B. Tauris.

Newbould, J., Taylor, D. and Bury, M. (2006) Lay-led Self-management in Chronic Illness: A Review of the Evidence. *Chronic Illness* 2: 249–61.

Newman, S., Steed, L. and Mulligan, K. (2004) Self-management Interventions for Chronic Illness. *Lancet* 364: 1523–37.

Oliver, M. (1996) Defining Impairment and Disability: Issues at Stake. In C. Barnes and G. Mercer (eds), *Exploring the Divide: Illness and Disability.* Leeds: The Disability Press.

Osborne, R., Wilson, T., Lorig, K. R. and McColl, G. J. (2007) Does Self-management Lead to Sustainable Health Benefits in People with Arthritis? A 2-year Transition Study on 452 Australians. *The Journal of Rheumatology* 34: 1112–7.

Pound, P., Gompertz, P. and Ebrahim, S. (1998) Illness in the Context of Older Age: The Case of Stroke. *Sociology of Health and Illness* 20(4): 489–506.

Rogers, A., Hassell, K. and Nicolas, G. (1999) *Demanding Patients? Analysing the Use of Primary Care.* Buckingham: Open University Press.

Rogers, A., Bury, M. and Kennedy, A. (2009) Rationality, Religiosity and Rhetoric in Health Care: The Case of the Expert Patients Programme. *International Journal of Health Service* 39(4): 725–47.

Roland, M., Dusheiko, M., Gravelle, H. et al. (2006) Follow Up of People Aged 65 and Over with a History of Emergency Admissions: Analysis of Routine Admission Data. *British Medical Journal* 330: 289–92.

Roth, J. A. (1963) *Timetables: Structuring the Passage of Time in Hospital Treatment and Other Careers.* Indianapolis, IN: Bobbs-Merrill.

Salter, B. (2004) *The New Politics of Medicine.* Palgrave: London.

Shakespeare, T. (2006) *Disability Rights and Wrongs.* London: Routledge.

Strauss, A. (1973) America: In Sickness and in Health. *Society* 19: 33–9.
Strauss, A. (1975) *Chronic Illness and the Quality of Life.* St Louis: Mosby.
Taylor, D. and Bury, M. (2007) Chronic Illness, Expert Patients and Care Transition. *Sociology of Health and Illness* 29: 27–45.
Wanless, D. (2002) *Securing Our Future Health: Taking a Long Term View.* London H M Treasury.
Williams, S. J. (2000) Chronic Illness as Biographical Disruption or Biographical Disruption as Chronic Illness? Reflections on a Core Concept. *Sociology of Health and Illness* 22(1): 40–67.

10
Understanding Incapacity

Gareth H. Williams

> The production of 'human waste', or more correctly wasted humans ... is an inescapable side-effect of *order-building* (each order casts some parts of the extant population as 'out of place', 'unfit' or 'undesirable') and of *economic progress* (that cannot proceed without degrading and devaluing the previously effective modes of 'making a living' and therefore cannot but deprive their practitioners of their livelihood).
>
> Bauman, 2004: 5

Introduction

The term 'incapacity' is generally used in relation to work and benefits and is typically defined as something like the inability to work associated with sickness or disability (Waddell and Aylward, 2005). Understood in this way the rate of incapacity benefit (IB) claims is both a health indicator and an economic indicator; an 'objective' correlate of those experiences of poor health reported in censuses and surveys and a significant contributor to levels of 'economic inactivity', 'worklessness' or 'joblessness'. These two 'discourses of incapacity' have tended to operate largely independently: the one focusing on the changing nature of labour markets and the problem of 'hidden unemployment'; the other using incapacity as an indicator of ill-health or disability and inequalities in health.

It might seem anachronistic to be discussing incapacity when IB has recently been abolished or, strictly speaking, closed to new claimants, by the Welfare Reform Act of 2007 (see Department of Social Security, 1998; Department for Work and Pensions, 2006, 2008a and 2008b; Freud, 2007; and Black, 2008 for an understanding of the origins, significance and implications of the policies and legislation). However, many of the arguments informing the policy debate over incapacity, work and the future of welfare reflect long-standing pre-occupations within the social sciences. As I write, much of the debate on incapacity and welfare has been given further impetus by the great 'credit crunch' of 2008 and its accelerating effects on the closure of businesses and the consequent rise in the rates of redundancy and unemployment (Hutton, 2008).

The purpose of this chapter is to put some of the current debate over incapacity into a broader context. A great deal of the current discussion is focused in a rather narrow and instrumental way on the problem of non-work and eligibility for benefit. I will argue that the debate over incapacity and its geographical distribution provides an important lens through which to view the relationship between health, work and work-lessness, and the ways in which governments and citizens perceive and respond to the 'spectre of uselessness' in 'the new capitalism' (Sennett, 2006). In conclusion, I will comment on the possibilities for more imaginative civil and political solutions to the problem of incapacity.

Incapacity as a social problem

Waddell and Aylward's (2005) definition of incapacity seems, *prima facie*, unexceptionable. However, definitions in this field are notoriously contentious, and need to be seen in a dynamic historical context (Barnes and Mercer, 2005; Stiker, 1999; Stone, 1985). In the past 20 years or so in the UK the problem of some citizens being incapable of work has been addressed, in turn, by way of 'Invalidity Benefit' (IVB), 'Incapacity Benefit', which replaced Sickness Benefit and Invalidity Benefit in 1995, and most recently 'Employment and Support Allowance' (ESA) which in 2008 replaced IB (and Income Support paid on incapacity grounds) for new claimants.

These policy developments represent the most recent ideological twists and turns in a lengthy tale of 'order-building', in Bauman's sense, going back at least to the English Poor Laws of the early nineteenth century, which attempted to control and reconstruct the traditional needs-based system of begging and vagrancy in the context of rapid population growth and movement (Stone, 1985). Modern welfare states all, in one way or another, 'regulate the poor' (Piven and Cloward, 1971). One key element of this process of regulation has been the development of disability categories to separate those injuries, impairments and illnesses which had to be tolerated as part of normal everyday working life from those which allowed access to disability categories. Entry into these categories provided distinctive entitlements in the form of social aid and exemptions from certain obligations of citizenship, such as the duty to work (Stone, 1985).

Disability in this sense is what Stone calls a form of 'political privilege' which emerges as a complex function of socio-economic development and the State's response to it through changing systems of work and welfare. Medical authority has been central to these developments, for two reasons. First, through its role in the development of 'rehabilitation', medicine has undertaken on behalf of the State 'the task of voiding disparities into its norm' (Stiker, 1999: 136), reintegrating people with 'abnormalities' into some kind of 'normality'. And second because, as Stone puts it, 'Medical certification of disability has become one of the major paths to public aid in the modern welfare state' (1985: 3). Disability benefits (or 'disability insurance' in the language of American public policy) represent a major investment in supporting those for whom access to and retention of work as a means of subsistence and success is disrupted, whether by the impairments themselves or the societal reaction to them in stigma, discrimination and prejudice. Because of the cost to government and taxpayers of these benefits and the underlying complexity of assessing 'fitness for work', incapacity payments are the subject of enduring political anxiety which feeds periodic crises of legitimacy (Williams, 1991).

Whether chronic illness and disability are seen in medical or social terms, they limit access to employment opportunities and become a major cause of poverty and social exclusion. Bambra and Smith (2009) argue that since 1945 the UK's response to this (and those of many other States) has involved a gradual evolution from welfare to workfare: from a system that takes the form of a 'safety net' providing unconditional, non-means tested benefits for those who fall out of the labour market for health reasons; to one which can be seen as a 'trampoline', providing people with benefits, but only on condition that they undertake some form of work or other activity that makes them 'work-ready' to bounce back into the labour market should opportunities arise. The replacement of IB by ESA, Bambra and Smith argue, represents a major step towards a full-blown workfare state.

It is certainly the case, at the time of writing, that most of the discussion of incapacity is framed by New Labour's 'activation policies' (Walker and Wiseman, 2003); encouraging movement from 'inactive benefits' into work or work-readiness, and making that movement worthwhile in financial terms: work for those who can, security for those who cannot, as the UK government put it in an early glimmer of its vision for the future of the welfare state (Department of Social Security, 1998). Hence the move from IB to ESA is not just a change of name, but an important indicator of the shift in understanding of the relationships between illness and fitness for work that has emerged under New Labour; a shift which puts at the heart of the reform programme the notion that even, or perhaps especially, in times of illness work is good for individuals and their families (Department for Work and Pensions, 2009). The extent to which it is actually worthwhile in financial terms is contested (Child Poverty Action Group, 2008).

What is the changing nature of the problem to which ESA is the most recent purported policy solution? There seem to be three key aspects. First, the number of people on invalidity and then incapacity benefits more than trebled from 1979 to the point at which IB was supplanted by ESA. The most regularly quoted figure is 2.7 million people of working age in the UK now claiming some kind of benefit because they are incapable of work for health reasons, and total spending on benefits for disabled people in 2004 was in excess of £19 billion (Faggio, 2005). Although the flow onto IB has stabilized over the past ten years and, to a lesser extent, off flow has increased (Brown et al., 2007), almost 8 per cent of the population of working age remain in receipt of IBs, the duration of time on IB has increased, and there is evidence that duration is strongly linked to the reduced likelihood of a return to work, and the likely causes of this are many and complex. Second, the forms of illness responsible for incapacity claims have changed in recent years. Whereas in the past back problems and other musculoskeletal disorders were the main certificated reasons for incapacity, psychological and behavioural disorders now account for more IB claims than musculoskeletal disorders: by 2003, 44 per cent of IB recipients were diagnosed as having some kind of mental health problem (Henderson et al., 2005). This has given rise to renewed questioning about the most appropriate response to such incapacity. Third, during a historical period of economic growth and low unemployment, rates of incapacity claims are markedly unequally distributed across social classes, regions and deprivation quintiles (Norman and Bambra, 2007). High levels of IB claims can be found most markedly in a number of Britain's post-industrial regions: areas dominated in the past by coal mining, steel production, dock work, shipbuilding and a range of other manufacturing industries. South Wales (particularly, the 'Heads of the Valleys'), north-east England, Glasgow and Merseyside have particularly high rates (see Table 10.1).

Table 10.1   Incapacity claimant rate, top 20 GB districts, August 2006

		% of working age
1.	Merthyr Tydfil	18.9
2.	Easington	18.8
3.	Blaenau Gwent	17.9
4.	Neath Port Talbot	16.3
5.	Rhondda Cynon Taff	15.8
6.	Caerphilly	15.5
7.	Glasgow	15.2
8.	Knowsley	14.2
9.	Barrow in Furness	13.6
10.	Liverpool	13.5
11.	Inverclyde	13.5
12.	Bridgend	13.4
13.	Hartlepool	13.3
14.	Blackpool	13.1
15.	Carmarthenshire	13.0
16.	Barnsley	12.8
17	Wear Valley	12.8
18.	North Lanarkshire	12.7
19.	Burnley	12.7
20.	Sedgefield	12.7

Note: Figures refer to incapacity benefit, NI credits for incapacity and severe disablement allowance.

Sources: DWP, ONS.

From the 1930s to the 1980s 'unemployment' was the measure of labour market disadvantage in poorer parts of the UK economy. However, as Beatty, Fothergill and colleagues have demonstrated in a series of detailed reports, IB claimants have come to dominate populations of workless, most dramatically in post-industrial regions (Beatty et al., 1997, 2002, 2007, 2009; Fothergill, 2008). Those 2.7 million non-employed people claiming IB constitute more than three times the number of claimant unemployed and more than double the number of lone parents claiming Income Support.

Taking south Wales as an example, the five Heads of the Valleys local authorities (Blaenau Gwent, Caerphilly, Merthyr Tydfil, Neath Port Talbot and Rhondda Cynon Taff) have a total of 65,000 IB claimants, accounting for 16 per cent of all adults aged between 16 and state pension age. These Valleys districts occupy five of the six top slots for incapacity claims (out of more than 400 districts) across the whole of Great Britain, with Merthyr Tydfil, alongside Easington in north-east

England, having the highest incapacity claimant rate of all – at approximately 19 per cent, or almost 1 in 5 of all adults of working age. As Fothergill has argued:

It is no exaggeration to say that Incapacity Benefit lies at the heart of the current labour market problem in the Valleys, and in much of the rest of older industrial Britain as well. Reliance on IB is by far and away the most common form of benefit dependency among working-age men and women and one of the principal forms of social exclusion. (Fothergill, 2008: 5–6)

As shown in this analysis, the huge increase in the numbers of men and, increasingly, women claiming IB represents the single most important way in which local labour markets have adjusted to the enormous loss of jobs from older industries during the 1980s and early 1990s, leading commentators like Fothergill and others to see incapacity as representing less a burden of illness, and more a form of 'hidden unemployment'.

Illness and incapacity

Alongside the arguments of Fothergill and others about incapacity as hidden unemployment, there are separate bodies of evidence about patterns of subjectively defined poor health of different kinds. In the 2001 Census, there are three key measures of poor health: 'general health', 'limiting long-term illness' and 'permanently sick or disabled'. At the last Census, the proportion of adults aged 45–64 who have a limiting long-standing illness in Wales, the north-east region of England and Northern Ireland is almost double that in south-east England (as shown in Table 10.2).

If you look at districts within these regions, those with the lowest rates are uniformly in south-east England, while of the worst ten, five are in south Wales, two are in Northern Ireland, one is in the west of Scotland (the city of Glasgow), one in north-west England, and one – the worst of all – is in north-east England. Prevalence of limiting long-term illness (LLTI) is particularly high in former coalfield areas everywhere, higher than inner London areas and rivalled only by old port and industrial areas (Joshi et al., 2001). In Merthyr Tydfil in south Wales and Easington in north-east England, 30 per cent or more of the population report some kind of LLTI. Reports of LLTI are more likely amongst people with heart disease, respiratory illness, mental illness, back pain or arthritis (National Assembly for Wales, 2003).

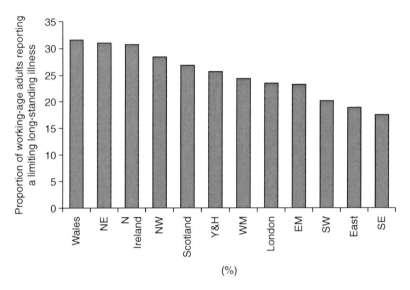

Table 10.2 Comparison of the proportion of adults aged 45 to 64 with long-standing illness in different regions

To take Wales as an example again, these very high rates of LLTI are repeated for other measures with 15 per cent or more of the populations of Merthyr Tydfil, Blaenau Gwent, Neath Port Talbot, Rhondda Cynon Taff and Caerphilly reporting their general health as 'not good' (Not Good Health [NGH]), and the same areas getting higher scores (worse health) on measures of functioning relating to health status. In the *Communities First*[1] area of Gurnos in Merthyr Tydfil almost 60 per cent of households have one or more persons with a LLTI, compared with 42.4 per cent in Wales as a whole; and 21.6 per cent of the population describe themselves as 'not being in good health' compared with 12.5 per cent in Wales (Welsh Assembly Government, 2006). The same six Welsh local authority districts mentioned above rank in the top ten for self-reports of general health not being good and for the percentages of those of working age who are unable to work and claiming benefit for permanent sickness or disability.

These spatial characteristics are interesting because, as Bartley and others have pointed out, LLTI is more concentrated geographically than mortality, suggesting that these subjective measures are encapsulating something that cannot be fully explained in narrowly biomedical (or, indeed, narrowly benefit) terms. There may be characteristics of the people or the places which make subjective experiences of illnesses that limit daily activities more prevalent in some regions and localities than others. It cannot, of course, be simply assumed that LLTI and incapacity are two ways of measuring different severities of the same thing at the population level. Incapacity rates have increased in spite of overall improvements in health (Beatty, Fothergill and Platts-Fowler, 2009); there are some populations with high levels of LLTI, but low rates of incapacity (Salway et al., 2007), and although almost all claimants report health problems or disabilities only a quarter say they 'can't do any work'. Nonetheless, one of the very few detailed empirical examinations has found that

Very strong positive relationships exist between IB and the Census-derived LLTI, NGH and PSD measures, the strongest being for the latter. IB has a more modest relationship with mortality but a strong relationship with unemployment. (Norman and Bambra, 2007: 338)

On this basis they suggest that while IB indicates something important about employment opportunities and labour markets, it also says something about varying levels of population health; and that while people claiming IB may be part of the 'hidden unemployed', many likely also have legitimate long-term health conditions. As Gleave et al. put it:

The perception of oneself as having a limiting illness ... may be a combination of the effect of underlying ill-health and the availability or non-availability of central social roles such as employment as the 'breadwinner'. So the heavy concentration of LLTI in certain areas may be explainable in terms of the shifting availability of such roles to men who are also at high risk of disease. (1998: 21)

The relationship between non-employment and ill health, therefore, is certainly complex, providing evidence of intricate patterns of cause and effect in more than one direction, and unlikely to be amenable to simple political solutions.

Making sense of incapacity

Although Talcott Parsons has had diminishing importance within general sociology since the 1970s, within medical sociology Parsons' concept of the sick role has been (and to some extent still is) used as a theoretical basis for making sense of illness. In an important reprise on Parsons' discussion of the sick role, Simon Williams (1995) reminds us that one of the major criticisms of Parsons' work is that it has limited applicability to chronic illness or other long-term disturbances of functioning. However, as Williams notes, this is something of an oversimplification, because Parsons was clearly concerned with the potentially dysfunctional ramifications of illness for the social system, and the importance of encouraging active participation in society:

> Illness is a state of disturbance in the 'normal' functioning of the total human individual, including both the states of the organism as a biological system and of his personal and social adjustments. It is thus partly biological and partly socially defined. Participation in the social system is always potentially relevant to the state of illness, to its etiology and to the conditions of successful therapy, as well as other things. (1951: 431)

In the light of the theoretically unplugged conceptualizations of incapacity found in most of the policy literature, it is helpful to find in Parsons a forceful reminder of the need to take a holistic perspective on the interrelationship between health, activity and the social system. Participation in the social system is implicated in both the aetiology of the problem (whatever that problem may be) and its alleviation. While many forms of physical and mental illness have social origins, Parsons is insistent that that 'feelings of helplessness' and the 'need for help' are not fictions, but are in fact 'very real': 'Suffering, helplessness, disablement and risk of death, or sometimes its certainty', Parsons tells us, 'constitute fundamental disturbances of the expectations by which we live' (1951: 443). These experiences, Parsons goes on to argue, cannot be accepted by a person without difficult emotional and social adjustments 'unless the patient happens to find *positive satisfactions* in them, in which case there is also a social problem' (443). The problem of illness becomes a social problem when the sick role is regarded not as a temporary role to enable recovery but as an opportunity to escape permanently or at least for longer periods from the demands of everyday life, work and general participation in society. Within Parsons' theory, therefore, the sick role is not only a legitimate social role for those who are unwell, but it also forms a mechanism of social control, embedded in the social system, which channels the experience of illness and prevents such dangerous possibilities as the development of a deviant subculture of the sick.

Gerhardt (1979, 1989) has argued that two distinct models of illness can be discerned within the Parsonian paradigm. The structural 'incapacity model' focuses on illness as a breakdown of role capacity brought about by various social and biological stresses and strains, with the sick role providing a temporary basis for the return to full role capacity. The psychodynamic 'deviancy model', in contrast, views illness as 'motivated deviance' caused by repressed dependency needs and requiring a more intensive approach to treatment and therapy in order to encourage a move from dependence (including, we assume, 'benefit dependency') to independence through various psychodynamic mechanisms. Although early medical sociology had more to say about illness than it did about health, the ideal of health, as Simon Williams (1995) indicates, was at the heart of much of what Parsons had to say, and is strongly connected to his overall functionalist analysis of social systems. Health is the '... state of optimum capacity of an individual for the effective performance of the roles and tasks for which he has been socialized. It is thus defined with reference to the individual's participation in the social system' (1964: 274), and this participation is relative to and differentiated by the person's roles within the social system. Although, as Simon Williams notes, health is defined as capacity for rather than commitment to role performance – what you can do as opposed to what you want to do – the dividing line between these is neither simple nor stable.

The rates of LLTI indicate, in Parsonian terms, long-term disturbances in the relationship between individuals and social systems, which will typically exhibit mixtures of mental and somatic symptoms. These long-term disturbances have both biological and social aspects – requiring us to see them in relation to personal and social adjustments as well as diagnoses of illness or injury. Incapacity benefit embodies an extension of the rights and obligations of the sick role into the rules of medico-legal bureaucracies for the allocation of benefit. The welfare system now being developed under New Labour is different from its predecessors in a number of ways, and the role of medical experts seems to be less about assessing the eligibility for benefit of people who are ill or disabled, and more about assessing their fitness to work in spite of long-term health problems. While some of this change may come from improvements in general health, medical assessment, treatment and rehabilitation, and the role of the disability movement in arguing the 'right to work' of disabled people, it is also closely related to the shift in the welfare paradigm to which I referred earlier.

Policies for the development of the Welfare State and for the distribution of different kinds of benefits have always emphasized 'active welfare' to some degree. Indeed, as modern politicians are keen to point out, the great man himself, William Beveridge, was to some extent an activist; and concern about preventing benefit becoming 'habituated' lies at the very root of the creation of the Welfare State. Although the Beveridge Report, published in 1942, was a response to the impact of the economic slump and the structural unemployment of the 1920s and 1930s, Beveridge was also sensitive to motivations to deviance. In his celebrated report he argued:

> Most men who have once gained the habit of work would rather work – in ways to which they are used – than be idle ... But getting work ... may involve a change of habits, doing something that is unfamiliar or leaving one's friends or making a painful effort of some other kind. The danger of providing benefits which are both adequate in amount and indefinite in duration, is that men as creatures who adapt themselves to circumstances, may settle down to them. (Beveridge, 1942: 57–8)

There is a feeling for the social context as well as a sense of trust in '*most men*', and this seems to inform an understanding of people preferring to work '*in ways to which they are used*'. We can see a similar roundedness of view in Parsons' emphasis on health being about the '*capacity of an individual for the effective performance of the roles and tasks for which he has been socialized*' Notwithstanding their gender-blindness, these are human frames of reference of a kind which seem to be missing from the latest government welfare reforms. As one government advisor puts it:

> The Government has made a commitment to rights and responsibilities a central feature of policy. In return for more support in obtaining employment it would seem appropriate for the state to expect more work-related activity from those on benefit. (Freud, 2007: 8)

Although Freud quotes Beveridge approvingly, there is an altogether harder edge to this stage of order-building, and in the most recent chapter of a grimly relentless 'change agenda', we read that the reform process: '... introduces a regime of benefit sanctions for non-attendance at job centres' (http://services.parliament.uk/bills/2008–09/welfarereform.html).

During the social security reforms of the 1980s and early 1990s increasing restrictions were placed on cash benefits, including the 'all work test' in 1994 (Bambra and Smith, 2009), which emphasized the extent to which people were unable to work at all, not just in their chosen occupation or profession. In the most recent legislation introducing the ESA, the 'Work Capability Assessment' is used 'to determine whether the claimant is placed in the work related activity group or the support group' – that is whether they get a higher or lower rate of benefit. The thrust of the new welfare benefits is that any work is better than no work, regardless of a person's experience or context, and nearly everyone can and should do some kind of work, no matter how demeaning that work may be, how poorly it is remunerated or how destabilizing the 'return to work' would be for other activities which play an important role in the local societies of which people are part. This brutalist approach to the re-designing the machinery of the Welfare State[2] reflects an inability or unwillingness to acknowledge what Parsons clearly understood: the reality of suffering and helplessness as fundamental disturbances of the expectations by which we live. Although Parsons' functionalism limits the critical capacity of his analysis, he does point us towards a view of behaviour as a social phenomenon which needs to be seen in a wider context, to which I now turn.

'Economic progress' and the process of degradation

Much of the policy discussion about incapacity takes place as if the phenomena were a problem of individual motivation for rehabilitation along an otherwise clear pathway from welfare to work. For all the talk of 'personalized conditionality and support' related to 'circumstances' (Gregg, 2008), any awareness of the wider historical and social context of incapacity seems limited, or knowingly curtailed. As has been indicated, rates of both LLTI and incapacity show intense spatial inequalities whether examined in relation to the boundaries of a local authority, an electoral ward, or some smaller geographical area (Norman and Bambra, 2007); and the areas with high rates of LLTI and incapacity are those which have undergone long-term de-industrialization since the 1930s, accelerating during the 1980s and early 1990s to a point of 'economic shock', the consequences of which people continue to live with (Alliance, 2007a,b).

The emotional, visceral impact of the 'economic shock' on the people who went through it is powerfully expressed in the following extract. The author, Robert Cornwall, spent his working life in south Wales, in the fields of employment, life-long learning and regeneration. Here he is recalling a day in his life as the Employment Service Area Manager responsible for the Gwent and Glamorgan Valleys:

> The closure of the Oakdale Colliery in 1992 provided an unforget-
> table insight into its effects on the state of mind of the 750 men
> employed there. The colliery had been adjudged a loss-making
> pit and there was speculation that one coal face would be aban-
> doned with the loss of a third of the workforce. Union representa-
> tives were called to a meeting with management one Thursday and
> [they] arranged a mass meeting of the workforce the next morning
> to inform them of the outcome. At 4.00 pm on the Thursday [I] was
> informed, in confidence, by the National Coal Board that a deci-
> sion had been made to close the [entire] colliery forthwith and [I]
> requested a team of Job Centre staff to attend the colliery the next
> morning to deal with any queries concerning benefits. On enter-
> ing the colliery at 9.00 am the next morning [I] was greeted by the
> sight of hundreds of men wandering around the pit-head in a state
> of shock. All were carrying a single, black plastic bin-bag containing
> the contents of their lockers. Having attended the meeting expect-
> ing to be told that some of them would be losing their jobs they
> were dumfounded to learn that the colliery had actually closed.
> They had already worked their last shift and they needed to empty
> their lockers and leave the site as soon as possible. No-one was even
> allowed down the pit to collect their tools from their last shift for
> fear of sabotage. Perhaps we should not be too surprised that many
> of these men who had given the best years of their lives to the coal
> industry never worked again [and joined] the rapidly growing ranks
> of the economically inactive. (Cornwall, 2007: 5)

The colliers at Oakdale were indeed only a small fraction of the rapidly growing ranks of the economically inactive. As Beatty et al. (2002)
have shown, during the period between the early 1980s and the closure
of Oakdale in 1992, over 160,000 jobs were lost from the coal industry. The reason that official unemployment amongst these redundant
men rose by only 500 during the same period was a consequence of
the redundant workers being re-routed onto invalidity benefit (later to
become IB).

The power of the extract from Cornwall's PhD thesis lies in the way
in which it infuses a simple, factual narrative of events with a strong
sense of *verstehen* or subjective understanding: it manages to illuminate
the meaning of action from the actor's point of view and the context in
which it takes place. The loss of meaning, orientation and respect, and

the looming hardship, are palpable. The simple empirical point is that men made redundant in an area where employment has been dominated by an industry now in decline are more likely to become economically inactive. However, Cornwall is also communicating something else: that the historical relationship of these men to their work and the manner in which that relationship was broken were also partly responsible for subsequent economic inactivity and, by extension, long-term health problems and incapacity.

In a classic work of sociological interpretation, Peter Marris wrote about slum clearance as a kind of bereavement. His words seem to come from a gentler and more hopeful time. He asked:

> What makes slum clearance a kind of bereavement? [...] If we can understand a change of home, like bereavement, as a potential disruption of the meaning of life, we may be able to see more clearly who will suffer grief, and what might help them to retrieve a sense of purpose. (Marris, 1974: 44)

The impact of the loss of employment in coal and the manner in which it was handled had a large but geographically variable impact on the people who lost their jobs and on the wider networks, communities, societies and economies in which they lived. In research undertaken comparing the impact of colliery closure in different coalfields, Bennet and her colleagues make a number of important points, nicely encapsulated in the following interpretation which subtly combines the ideas of Durkheim and Marx and echoes Marris's analysis of slum clearance:

> [In South Wales] this was not just a case of localised economic decline but rather one of cultural crisis. The collapse of coalmining undermined a range of mechanisms of social regulation that were grounded in the politics of the workplace and the trades unions, but spread more widely into local society and politics. There was an acute sense of loss in places in which coalmines closed after decades of existence. This was typically accompanied by a period of grieving as people in these places tried to come to terms with the manifold implications of the precipitate ending of the economic *raison d'être* of their place. (2000: 12)

In 1992, amongst those colliers at Oakdale, rendered surplus to requirements at the fag-end of the British coal industry, there were both moral and financial benefits to being unable to work rather than unwilling to work or simply out of work. And in the coal industry there was of course a long history of people being unfit for work for all kinds of reasons: '... silicotics, arthritics, ripped flesh, smashed bones and damaged souls' as the Rhondda coal miner-turned-novelist Ron Berry (1998: 41) so searingly expresses in his posthumous autobiography. Although it cost the exchequer a little more, it was otherwise what we might refer to nowadays, rather irritatingly, as a win-win-win situation: redundant workers could describe themselves as unable to work because of illness or impairment and gain access to higher rates of benefit; the government was able to redefine them as unfit for work and point to declining rates of unemployment; and doctors working in primary care could feel some satisfaction in the positive role they were playing by acting as a portal to medical benefits. Whether this active use of sickness benefits was primarily part of a cunning plan by Margaret Thatcher to move people off unemployment benefit for political reasons, or an outbreak of benevolent social engineering by primary care physicians was and still is a matter of debate (Bartholomew, 2006; Faggio, 2005; Wynn Davies, Blackhurst and Waterhouse, 1993).

From 'labour aristocracy' to 'lumpenproletariat'[3]: The spectre of uselessness in global capitalism

Although the example of the closure of Oakdale took place well into the Thatcherite period, Britain's post-industrial regions have been in decline ever since the Second World War, if not before. While replacement employment in these areas emerged with growth in steel production and other manufacturing during the 1950s and 1960s the situation now is that '... almost all the post-war investments have disappeared or are a shadow of their former selves' (Winckler, 2008: 8). In south Wales there has been a precipitous decline of employment in steel, notably the closure of the Corus steelworks in Ebbw Vale, the major town in Blaenau Gwent, along with the loss of other major long-term employers such as Hoover in Merthyr Tydfil, whose labour force declined from 7000 at its peak to 600 at the end of 2007, and is now closed. It is clearly not the case, therefore, that the same individuals who were so bruised by the loss of jobs in mining, shipbuilding, dock work and steel production are the ones who are still fuelling the high incapacity rate in post-industrial regions. As Beatty et al. (2009) point out, a high proportion of incapacity claimants are over the age of 50 and while some are former colliers, many of these people are now moving on to state pensions, their place '... being taken by a cohort of largely poorly-qualified workers with health problems or disabilities – including nearly as many women as men' (5).

Global economic restructuring and government policies have transformed many previously high-skilled, well-organized 'labour aristocracies' into the disillusioned and disrespected communities of the 'lumpenproletariat' or the 'underclass'. Incapacity is an institutionalized response to the loss of work, initially at a time of high unemployment, encouraged by the State and implemented by the health system. In a counter-individualistic move, however, I have argued that the loss of work was not only a loss of individual jobs and incomes, but also a loss of meaning and identity in whole regions and their communities. The political economy of change has wide personal and emotional ramifications: the emphasis on flexibility rather than the virtuous continuity of a particular skill or trade and the 'spectre of uselessness' which haunts this historical experience (Sennett, 2006); the personal loss and community disruption to which this has given rise; the movement of people on and off different kinds of benefit over time under shifting welfare regimes; the victim-blaming of those on IB and the individualistic psychological explanations of economic inactivity that are deployed to justify further movements towards workfare.

Against this background 'the most radical reform of the welfare state for generations' (http://www.dwp.gov.uk/welfarereform/) seems less well directed than we are encouraged to believe. It manages to de-historicize the analysis of the causes of incapacity, individualize the solutions and then generalize these to whole communities. While the determination of IB claims focused, however crudely, on the level of someone's 'unfitness' for work – a disability assessment – the new ESA, which went 'live' in October 2008, places much stronger emphasis on 'ability to work', connected to Pathways to Work or another employment and support initiative. Whereas participation in employability programmes is currently voluntary for historic claimants of IB, new claimants seeking ESA will find a two-tier system in which everyone is entitled to a basic benefit, paid at the same rate as Job Seeker's Allowance. This benefit is paid during the first 13 weeks while the claimant undergoes a 'Work Capability Assessment', part of which involves an interview with '... a healthcare professional who has been approved by the Department for Work and Pensions [and] may recommend that you attend a medical assessment. We may also ask you to take part in a Work Focused Health Related Assessment'. The medical assessment involves an interview and 'sometimes a physical examination', if the approved health-care professional feels one is needed. The assessment is likely to be different from what you would expect from your 'own doctor' (see the sections on employment and support allowance at www.jobcentreplus.gov.uk for the source of these quotations).

The outcome of this latest stage in the Welfare State's creation of order from the motley queue of claimants for incapacity-related benefit is the allocation of successful claimants to one or other of two groups: the 'Work Related Activity Group' or the 'Support Group'. The latter will be judged to have an illness or disability which has a severe effect on the claimant's ability to work, and will receive a top-up to the basic benefit. The former will undergo work-focused interviews with a personal adviser to help locate 'suitable work', and if you were to refuse to take part in the interview, 'it may affect your benefit' (www.jobcentreplus.gov.uk).

The historic significance of this is that 'The introduction of the two tiered employment support allowance means that for the first time in the UK conditionality applies to the receipt of sickness related benefits, creating a group of "deserving poor" (those with severe illness or disability) and a group of "undeserving poor" (those considered sick but able to work)' (Bambra, 2008: 517). We can assume that the latter includes many of those vilified by political pundits and opinion-formers as malingerers, fakers and benefit cheats; those latter-day denizens of the lumpen-communities, the 'chavs': '... the dangerous class, the social scum, that passively rotting mass thrown off by the lowest layers of the old society', as Marx and Engels so graciously described them (1967: 92). While the policies are described by departments of government as policies to empower and support the inclusion of disabled people previously excluded from the labour market and its benefits (Department of Work and Pensions, 2006) – which no one could really be against – the reality is that such policies create and sustain a low pay, no pay cycle populated by a flexible and powerless pool of reserve labour for whom any access to benefit is driven by their preparedness to respond positively to job opportunities (Byrne, 2005).

But what exactly are these opportunities that people on benefit in Ebbw Vale, Glasgow or Newcastle are failing to grasp? Areas like Blaenau Gwent and south Tyneside have the lowest levels of job density outside London, with roughly one job vacancy available for every four people unemployed (Winckler, 2008) – and that is before taking account of those on IB. Moreover, and bearing in mind the work history of these areas, many of the job vacancies are for sales and customer service jobs, low paid and insecure (Beck, 2000) forms of non-standard or flexible work (Beck, 2000; Scott, 2004) – with some paid on a 'commission only' basis (Winckler, 2008):

> Job insecurity is no longer a mere temporary break in an otherwise predictable work-life pattern but rather a structural feature of the new labor market [... and ...] whereas the institutional structure of the postwar labor market privileged *security* as a means of tapping the most productivity from workers, the flexibility regime gives primacy to *insecurity* in this context. (Scott, 2004: 143, 148)

The implications for those on IB for a long period, as well as for those becoming ill or disabled more recently, are that they are expected to exchange the stability and social security of life on IB for the precariousness and insecurity of life in a highly deregulated job market, with little, if any, improvement in economic well-being – once everything (including transport and childcare costs, for example) is taken into account. There is good evidence that workers in flexible employment share many of the same labour market characteristics as those who are out of work, and that the new type of work arrangements are as damaging to health as being out of work (Benach and Muntaner, 2007). If a large number of those people who do not automatically qualify for the higher rate of ESA are people with long-term, possibly fluctuating and unpredictable mental or physical health problems, subjective 'job insecurity' and objective precariousness and powerlessness in employment are unlikely to be beneficial in either economic or health terms (Benach et al., 2002; Quinlan and Bohle, 2009). Even the kindest, most supportive and empathetic support system on the demand side will be stymied by the harsh realities of low pay and precarious employment on the supply side.[4] Welfare to work has to be placed in the context of wider processes of regeneration (Winckler, 2008).

Those post-industrial communities with social conditions of the kind I have used in illustration here are the product of the globalization of the world economy and its impact on regional and local markets and communities; but the inequalities these massive structural changes have introduced are transformed through the order-building frameworks of public policy into manifestations of individual failure (Barnes and Mercer, 2005; Beck, 2000). In contrast to the nineteenth-century picture of the honest, hard-working and potentially useful 'old poor', the '... common labourer, who gets his own bread and eats it vulgarly but creditably with his own pocket-knife' (Eliot, 2008 [1859]), now '... for the first time in human history, the poor, so to speak, have lost their social uses':

> The new poor are fully and truly useless and redundant, and thus become burdensome 'others' who have outstayed their welcome. (Bauman, 1997: 5)

Not that the new poor are entirely new, of course, as you see if you take a longer view. During the Middle Ages in Europe, there was concern that '... these disabled and sick, real or simulated, these blind men ... constituted, in certain town quarters, virtual worlds unto themselves, cohesive communities with their own laws and language, their own leaders' (quoted in Stiker, 1999: 67): it would be difficult to think up a more vivid historical example of Parsons' concern about the potentially dysfunctional consequences of unregulated illness, and current political anxiety about communities with high rates of incapacity claims. More recent characterizations of 'the underclass' or the 'New Poor', which developed into a hysterical peak in the 1980s and 1990s but seem to be on the rise again, would probably include people on IB as 'the passive poor', and the passive poor have no place in the relentlessly and breathlessly active New Jerusalem of New Labour.

It is certainly the case that people who are on IB for long periods '... lose confidence and often get depressed. Also, they tended to have specific skills related to the factories or the mines that weren't useful anywhere else' (Cornwall quoted in Seager, 2007). In this sense, as Wilson (1997) showed of the Chicago ghettoes, there is an interaction between structure and agency or between economic opportunities and social attitudes. However, in order to understand the full implications of this we need to recognize that not only have employment opportunities been limited, but the nature of work, in the broadest sense, has also changed. Welfare to work is a panacea neither for the economy nor for the quality of life. The emphasis on getting people into work for their own good is stripped of any notion of what work means, and what forms of work do to people: many of the areas with high incapacity rates have histories of highly skilled jobs, relatively well paid, with strong social cohesion between workers, robust trade unions and employment security. However, catering, cleaning and caring are not similar to these, not because they are unimportant forms of work, but because of their low pay, insecurity and limited opportunities for worker association and solidarity (Toynbee, 2007). In this context, incapacity can be partly understood as a way of preserving respect, a sense of belonging and attachment and a basic income against the degradations of new forms of work.

Conclusion

Chronic illness and disability create the need for all kinds of work – illness work, emotional work and biographical work – many of which may be disregarded because they do not easily lend themselves to the production of goods and services for consumption through a market (Barnes and Mercer, 2005; Corbin and Strauss, 1988). The collapse of the market and the rise in new unemployment alongside existing worklessness provides an opportunity for us to reconsider what is socially necessary work (Gorz, 1999), and how this can be built and supported through a creative interplay of welfare and employment which makes use of 'lay knowledge' (Williams and Popay, 2001), 'civic intelligence' (Elliott and Williams, 2003) or what Gorz calls 'vernacular skills', supported rather than supplanted by professionals and experts of different kinds. This could more honestly empower an approach to work based on 'a model of civil labour' that exhibits, sometimes in fragile form, a bottom up democratic spirit in sustaining community priorities (Beck, 2000; and see Cropper et al., 2007 for powerful examples of this in the health inequalities field).

Until very recently we might have concurred with Bourdieu (1998):

> Everywhere we hear it said, all day long – and this is what gives the dominant discourse its strength – that there is nothing to put forward in opposition to the neo-liberal view, that it has succeeded in presenting itself as self-evident, that there is no alternative. (29)

Whatever emerges from the dust of economic recession, and current constitutional developments in the UK, there is an increasing, percolating feeling that this is no longer the case. History has not ended and there are, in fact, different ideological positions that can be taken and different forms of political practice and protest to be developed, locally and globally (Beck, 2005). Perhaps we can now begin to put forward what Bourdieu championed as an 'economics of happiness' (1998: 40) – and, who knows, a sociology of love! – which will enable us to consider the profits and losses of incapacity and precarious employment in the round of everyday social life. There is certainly an increasingly strong evidence-based moral critique of inequality and inequity (Commission on the Social Determinants of Health, 2008; Wilkinson and Pickett, 2009), and an aesthetics of disgust at the sight of government driving a discreditable underclass off IB into low-wage employment at the same time as the stench of corruption and greed rises from the corridors of élite economic and political institutions. Whether these feelings and arguments can inform a genuinely progressive movement of protest and opposition remains to be seen.

And what is the place of the social sciences in all this? There seem to me to be three key things to be getting on with. First, government in the UK endlessly reiterates a commitment to evidence-based policy. Tired as this might sound, we cannot afford the luxury of cynicism or demoralization; and it is important to point out and criticize the extent to which policy in relation to work and incapacity is underpowered in its relationship to good research evidence (Bambra and Smith, 2009). Evidence of 'what matters' and 'what works' needs to be reviewed and new studies need to be undertaken – with a full appreciation of the complexity of the relationships involved (Williams et al., 2007). Part of the complexity – and this is the second social science role – is the wider questioning of the impact of different kinds of work and non-work on health. I have referred here to some of the research on job insecurity and precarious employment; and the health benefits and risks of work for those with long-term health problems need to be examined, both epidemiologically and through qualitative studies of social experience. Finally, studies of whatever genre and method should recognize the need for new approaches to the study of social experience. In view of the resistance which, I have suggested, incapacity to some extent embodies, we need to create, as Bourdieu (1998: 56) suggested: '... a structure for collective research, interdisciplinary and international, bringing together social scientists, activists and representatives of activists' and, I would say, community members, in 'places of discussion and research', where social scientists are not 'fellow-travellers', 'apparatchiks', 'experts', 'anti-expert experts' or 'prophets' but rather public sociologists (Burawoy, 2005), resisting ideological closure and contributing their knowledge and skills to civic and political discussion and social change.

Notes

1. This is the Welsh Assembly Government's community regeneration programme focusing on the most deprived areas in Wales.
2. For those who are unfamiliar with the detailed processes now in place for claiming health benefits it is worth taking the time to look at the story so far of 'the most radical reform of the welfare state for generations' (http://www.dwp.gov.uk/welfarereform/).
3. The theme of 'from labour aristocracy to lumpenproletariat' was first suggested to me by my colleague, Huw Beynon.
4. In Wales, for example, schemes like JobMatch (Welsh Assembly Government, 2008) can be seen as an attempt to create sustainable and supportive welfare-to-work processes against considerable supply-side odds.

References

Alliance (2007a) *Deprivation in the Former Coalfield Communities of Wales.* Barnsley: The Alliance.

Alliance (2007b) *The Other Half of Britain: Problems and Issues in the Traditional Industrial Areas of England, Scotland and Wales.* Barnsley: The Alliance.

Bambra, C. (2008) Incapacity Benefit Reform and the Politics of Ill-health. *British Medical Journal* 337: 517.

Bambra, C. and Smith, K. (2009, in press) No Longer Deserving? Sickness Benefit Reform and the Politics of (Ill) Health. *Critical Public Health.*

Barnes, C. and Mercer, G. (2005) Disability, Work and Welfare: Challenging the Social Exclusion of Disabled People. *Work, Employment and Society* 19: 527–45.

Bartholomew, J. (2006) *The Welfare State We're In.* London: Politicos.

Bauman, Z. (1997) No Way Back to Bliss: How to Cope with the Restless Chaos of Modernity. *Times Literary Supplement,* 24 January.

Bauman, Z. (2004) *Wasted Lives: Modernity and Its Outcasts.* Cambridge: Polity.

Beatty, C., Fothergill, S. and Platts-Fowler, D. (2009) *Incapacity Benefit in Wales.* Barnsley: The Alliance.

Beatty, C., Fothergill, S., Gore, T. and Herrington, A. (1997) *The Real Level of Unemployment.* Centre for Regional, Social and Economic Research: Sheffield Hallam University.

Beatty, C., Fothergill, S., Gore, T. and Green, A. (2002) *The Real Level of Unemployment 2002,* Centre for Regional Social and Economic Research.

Beatty, C., Fothergill, S., Gore, T. and Powell, R. (2007) *The Real Level of Unemployment, 2007,* Centre for Regional Social and Economic Research: Sheffield Hallam University.

Beck, U. (2000) *The Brave New World of Work.* Cambridge: Polity Press.

Beck, U. (2005) *Power in the Global Age.* Cambridge Polity Press.

Benach, J. and Muntaner, C. (2007) Precarious Employment and Health: Developing a Research Agenda. *Journal of Epidemiology and Community Health* 61: 276–7.

Benach, J., Amable, M., Muntaner, C. and Benavides, F. G. (2002) The Consequences of Flexible Work for Health: Are We Looking at the Right Place. *Journal of Epidemiology and Community Health.* 56: 405–6.

Bennet, K., Beynon, H. and Hudson, R. (2000) *Coalfields Regeneration: Coping with the Consequences of Industrial Decline.* York: Rowntree.

Berry, R. (1998) *History Is What You Live.* Llandysul: Gomer.

Beveridge, W. (1942) *Social Insurance and Allied Services* (the Beveridge Report), Cmd 6404, HMSO, London.

Black, C. (2008) *Working for a Healthier Tomorrow* (Dame Carol Black's Review of the Health of Britain's Working Age Population), London: TSO.

Bourdieu, P. (1998) *Acts of Resistance: Against the New Myths of our Time.* Cambridge: Polity.

Brown, J., Hanlon, P., Webster, D., Turok, I., Arnott, J. and Macdonald, E. (2007) *Turning the Tap Off! Incapacity Benefit in Glasgow and Scotland: Trends over the Past Five Years.* Glasgow Centre for Population Health Research. http://www.hwlresearchgroup.org/media/IB_FullReport_27July.pdf.

Burawoy, M. (2005) 2004 American Sociological Association Presidential Address: For Public Sociology. *British Journal of Sociology* 56: 259–94.

Byrne, D. (2005) *Social Exclusion.* Milton Keynes: Open University Press.

Child Poverty Action Group (2008) Employment and Support Allowance (ESA) Rates: A Comparison with Income Support (IS) and Incapacity Benefit (IB). www.cpag.org.uk/esa.

Commission on the Social Determinants of Health (2008) *Closing the Gap in a Generation: Health Equity through Action on the Social Determinants of Health* (Chair: Sir Michael Marmot), Geneva: WHO.

Corbin, J. and Strauss, A. (1988) *Unending Work and Care: Managing Chronic Illness at Home.* San Francisco, CA: Jossey-Bass Publishers.

Cornwall, R. (2007) *Learning, Soft Skills and Community Regeneration,* PhD thesis, School of Social Sciences, Cardiff University.

Cropper, S., Porter, A., Williams, G., Carlisle, S., Moore, R., O'Neill, M., Roberts, C. and Snooks, H. (eds) (2007) *Community Health and Well-Being: Action Research on Health Inequalities.* Bristol: Policy Press.

Department of Social Security (1998) *New Ambitions for Our Country: A New Contract for Welfare.* London: The Stationery Office.

Department for Work and Pensions (2006) *A New Deal for Welfare: Empowering People to Work: A Consultation Report.* Norwich: HMSO.

Department for Work and Pensions (2008a) *No One Written Off: Reforming Welfare to Reward Responsibility.* Norwich: TSO.

Department for Work and Pensions (2008b) *Raising Expectations and Increasing Support: Reforming Welfare for the Future.* Norwich: TSO.

Department for Work and Pensions (2009) Welfare Reform. http://www.dwp.gov.uk/welfarereform/.

Eliot, G. (2008) [1859] *Adam Bede.* Harmondsworth: Penguin.

Elliott, E. and Williams, G. (2003) Developing a Civic Intelligence: Local Involvement in Health Impact Assessment. *Environmental Impact Assessment Review* 24: 231–43.

Faggio, G. (2005) *Incapacity Benefit Reform: Tackling the Rise in Labour Market Inactivity* (Policy Analysis), Centre for Economic Performance, London School of Economics and Political Science. http://cep.lse.ac.uk/pubs/download/pa005.pdf.

Fothergill, S. (2008) The Most Intractable Development Region in the UK. In J. Osmond (ed.), *Futures for the Heads of the Valleys.* Cardiff: Institute of Welsh Affairs.

Freud, D. (2007) *Reducing Dependency, Increasing Opportunity: Options of the Future of Welfare to Work.* London: DWP.

Gerhardt, U. (1979) The Parsonian Paradigm and the Identity of Medical Sociology. *Sociological Review* 27: 235–51.

Gerhardt, U. (1989) *Ideas about Illness: An Intellectual and Political History of Medical Sociology.* London: Macmillan.

Gleave, S., Bartley, M. and Wiggins, R. D. (1998) *Limiting Long Term Illness: A Question of Where You Live or Who You Are? A Multi-Level Analysis of the 1971–1991 ONS Longitudinal Study. LS working paper 77.* Social Statistics Research Unit, City University, London.

Gorz, A. (1999) *Reclaiming Work: Beyond the Wage-Based Society.* Cambridge: Polity Press.

Gregg, P. (2008) *Realising Potential: A Vision for Personalized Conditionality and Support, an Independent Report to the Department of Work and Pensions.* London: DWP.

Henderson, M., Glozier, N. and Holland Elliott, K. (2005) Long Term Sickness Absence Is Caused by Common Conditions and Needs Managing. *British Medical Journal* 330: 802–3.

Hutton, W. (2008) Smoke Clears to Reveal Monster of Rising Unemployment. *The Observer* (Comment), 19 October, p. 29.

Joshi, H., Wiggins, R., Bartley, M., Mitchell, R., Gleave, S. and Lynch, K. (2001) Putting Health Inequalities on the Map: Does Where You Live Matter, and Why? In H. Graham (ed.), *Understanding Health Inequalities* (pp. 143–55). Buckingham: Open University Press.

Marris, P. (1974) *Loss and Change.* London: Routledge and Kegan Paul.

Marx, K. and Engels, F. (1967) *The Communist Manifesto.* Harmondsworth: Penguin.

National Assembly for Wales (2003) *A Statistical Focus on Disability and Long-Term Illness in Wales.* Cardiff: National Assembly for Wales (Statistical Directorate).

Norman, P. and Bambra, C. (2007) Incapacity or Unemployment? The Utility of an Administrative Data Source as an Updatable Indicator of Population Health. *Population, Space and Place* 13: 333–52.

Parsons, T. (1951) *The Social System.* London: Routledge and Kegan Paul.

Piven, F. and Cloward, R. (1971) *Regulating the Poor: The Functions of Public Welfare.* New York: Vintage Books.

Quinlan, M. and Bohle, P. (2009) Overstretched and Unreciprocated Commitment: Reviewing Research on the Occupational Health and Safety Effects of Downsizing and Job Insecurity. *International Journal of Health Services* 39: 1–44.

Salway, S., Platt, L., Chowbey, P., Harriss, K. and Bayliss, E. (2007) *Long-term Ill-health, Poverty and Ethnicity: A Mixed Methods Investigation into the Experiences of Living with a Chronic Health Condition in the UK.* Bristol: The Policy Press.

Scott, H. (2004) Reconceptualizing the Nature and Health Consequences of Work-related Insecurity for the New Economy: The Decline of Workers' Power in the Flexibility Regime. *International Journal of Health Services* 34: 143–53.

Seager, A. (2007) High Unemployment: Merthyr Tydfil. *The Guardian*, 13 March (quoting Robert Cornwall, 2007).

Sennett, R. (2006) *The Culture of the New Capitalism.* New Haven: Yale University Press.

Stiker, H-J. (1999) *A History of Disability.* Trans. W. Sayers, Ann Arbor, MI: The University of Michigan Press.

Stone, D. (1985) *The Disabled State.* London: Macmillan.

Toynbee, P. (2007) McJobs Are Giving Britain a Reputation as Europe's Offshore Banana Republic. *The Guardian*, 25 May.

Waddell, G. and Aylward, M. (2005) *The Scientific and Conceptual Basis of Incapacity Benefits.* London: TSO.

Walker, R. and Wiseman, M. (2003) Making Welfare Work: UK Activation Policies under New Labour. *International Social Security Review* 56: 3–29.

Welsh Assembly Government (2006) *Communities First: a 2001 Baseline.* Cardiff: Welsh Assembly Government (Statistical Policy Unit).

Welsh Assembly Government (2008) *Jobs Strategy to Aid Regeneration of Heads of the Valleys* (Press Release, 15 May), Cardiff: WAG.

Wilkinson, R. and Pickett, K. (2009) *The Spirit Level: Why More Equal Societies Almost Always Do Better.* Harmondsworth: Allen Lane, Penguin.

Williams, G. (1991) Disablement and the Ideological Crisis in Health Care. *Social Science and Medicine* 32: 517–24.

Williams, G. and Popay, J. (2001) Lay Health Knowledge and the Concept of the Lifeworld. In G. Scambler (ed.), *Habermas, Critical Theory and Health.* London: Routledge.

Williams, G., Cropper, S., Porter, A. and Snooks, H. (2007) Beyond the Experimenting Society. In S. Cropper, A. Porter, G. Williams, S. Carlisle, R. Moore, M. O' Neill, C. Roberts and H. Snooks (eds), *Community Health and Well-Being: Action Research on Health Inequalities.* Bristol: Policy.

Williams, S. (1995) Parsons Revisited: From the Sick Role to...? *Health* 9: 123–44.

Wilson, W. J. (1997) *When Work Disappears: The World of the New Urban Poor.* New York: Vintage Books.

Winckler, V. (2008) *Rethinking Regeneration: The Heads of the Valleys.* Tredegar: The Bevan Foundation.

Wynn Davies, P., Blackhurst, C. and Waterhouse, R. (1993) Analysis Shows 420,000 May be Excluded: Ministers Firm over Invalidity Benefit Cuts. *The Independent*, 16 June.

11
The Biopolitics of Chronic Illness: Biology, Power and Personhood
Simon J. Williams

Introduction

This chapter starts from a simple yet for some perhaps provocative premise, namely, that the sociology of chronic illness would benefit not simply from a more avowedly political but a more explicitly biopolitical form of analysis and engagement.

This argument rests on two key premises. First, that we are seeing important developments and transformations in bioscience, biomedicine and biotechnology today which themselves are embedded in and expressive of broader social, political and economic transformations and changes in the global age and neoliberal era. Second, that these developments and transformations in turn are serving to, or at the very least have the potential to, reconfigure the nature and experience of chronic illness in contemporary society, including fundamental issues pertaining to authority and expertise, patienthood and personhood, citizenship and identity, rights, risks and responsibilities, and other collective forms of activism and engagement.

My thinking in this respect is influenced by the recent work of writers such as Turner (2004) on the need for a 'new' medical sociology, Fuller (2006) on the new biological 'challenge' to the social sciences and the wealth of work now occurring on biosocieties and biopolitics, particularly the contribution of writers such as Rabinow (1996) and Rose (2007) on biosociality and the politics of life itself. My approach, as this suggests, is based on recognition of the value, if not a reconciliation or rapprochement, of different theoretical perspectives and different levels of analysis in the service of a full and proper engagement with the complexities of contemporary biopolitics in the global age.

The chapter is divided into two main parts. First, as further grounding for these claims and premises, I provide a necessarily brief sketch
of the current state of play in the sociology of chronic illness and of
various deployments of the term 'biopolitics' to date, including my own
particular take on these issues. Second, the remainder of the chapter
focuses on what I take to be some of the key biopolitical issues and agendas
for the sociology of chronic illness to engage with both now and in the
years ahead. The chapter concludes with some further thoughts and
reflections on these matters, including future agendas in this changing
and challenging field of enquiry.

From biographical disruption to biopolitics?

Important work has been conducted in the sociology of chronic illness
over the past 30 or so years, particularly around the meaning and experience of chronic illness and its management in everyday life away from
formal health-care facilities. Early, largely sterile sociological debates on
whether chronic illness fitted the Parsonian sick role, in this respect,
gave way to a growing body of theoretically informed empirical sociological work on chronic illness from the mid-1970s onwards, including
Glaser and Strauss' (1975) groundbreaking book *Chronic Illness and the
Quality of Life*, and work in the British tradition on the biographically
disruptive nature of chronic illness (Bury, 1982), the importance of illness narratives (Frank, 1995; Kleinman, 1988; Williams, 1984), assaults
on selfhood (Charmaz, 1987) and the stigmatizing consequences of
chronic illness (Scambler, 1989). Studies of many different chronic illness conditions have followed in this vein including work on diabetes
(Kellehear, 1998), multiple sclerosis (Robinson, 1994), colitis (Kelly,
1992) and chronic respiratory illness (Williams, 1993). Important work
has also charted different styles of adjustment in chronic illness (Radley,
1989), and has sought to further delineate responses to chronic illness
in terms of *coping, strategy* and *style* (Bury, 1991).

   Much of this work has been heavily indebted to symbolic interactionist traditions of research, hence the focus on the *meaning* and *experience*
of chronic illness and its implications for selfhood and social interaction.
This work in turn has been joined by phenomenological explorations
of the body in chronic illness, including the vicissitudes of embodiment across the chronic illness trajectory (Williams, 1996) and other
attempts to incorporate a more explicit biological or material dimension into the analysis of chronic illness and its implications for selfhood and identity (Kelly and Field, 1996; see also Williams, 2000).This

sociological research has in turn occurred in the context of other more explicit political analyses of chronic illness and disability, both past and present, including the work of Zola (1989, 1991) and Williams (2000) on the politics of chronic illness, Kelleher's (2006, 2004) Habermasian inspired analyses of self-help groups and social movements as a 'challenge' to medicine, and Taylor and Bury's (2007) more recent work on the expert patient programme (see also this volume).

This, to be sure, is an important and impressive body of work. At one and the same, however, the sociology of chronic illness has, somewhat strangely (i) maintained an almost exclusive focus on physical illness rather than the chronic, long-term implications of mental health problems; (ii) proved a problematic terrain or field of enquiry in relation to the disability movement which, in adopting and advocating its favoured social model, has accused medical sociologists (unfairly in my view) of complicity with a medical model through a 'personal tragedy' approach to chronic illness and disability (Oliver, 1990). Whilst these rather 'hostile' challenges from disability theorists have now, thankfully, given way to more recent 'reconciliatory' or 'bridge-building' exercises (Barnes and Mercer, 1996) – including more considered or tempered perspectives by disability theorists themselves (Shakespeare, 2007, 2003; Thomas, 2007) – they signal precisely the sorts of issues I want to flag here, namely, the need for more explicitly political forms of analysis which in this particular case are biopolitical through and through.

So what exactly does biopolitics or the biopolitical mean? A variety of definitions and deployments may be discerned here, from Aristotle's distinctions between *Zöe* and *Bios* through to other more recent deployments in the work of writers such as Agamben (1998) on 'bare life', Hardt and Negri (2000) on 'empire'. Perhaps the most obvious and well-known reference, however, concerns Foucault's (1991, 1979) deliberations on biopower and biopolitics: terms he deployed to capture or convey the way in which life itself, during the course of seventeenth- and eighteenth-century European history, became the focus of various strategies of political calculation and governance – a 'vital' politics concerned with administration of life in the name of individual and collective health and well-being. Biopolitics, in this respect, ties the management of populations and their characteristics to the governance of bodies and conduct. In the hands of Foucauldian inspired writers such as Rose, therefore, it is deployed as a perspective which brings into view

> ... strategies involving contestations over the ways in which human
> vitality, morbidity, mortality should be problematized, over the

desirable level and form of interventions required, over the know-ledge, regimes of authority, and practices of intervention that are desirable, legitimate, efficacious. (2007: 54)

This very field of political investments, moreover, as we shall see, has itself undergone significant change during the course of the twentieth century and early twenty-first century given important developments in the biosciences, biomedicine and biotechnology themselves.

Clearly, as this suggests, the notion of biopolitics has strongly Foucauldian connotations. One does not, however, have to be an avowed or fully paid up Foucauldian, a point I am at pains to stress and elaborate below, in order to appreciate that (i) life itself, including chronic illness and disability, has become increasingly politicized; (ii) the very nature and character of this contemporary politicization of life is intimately and inextricably bound up with transformations in bio-medicine, bioscience and biotechnology; and (iii) these transformation and development themselves are deeply embedded in and expressive of broader transformations in the social, political and economic orders of advanced neoliberal societies in the global age or era, including new modes of governance based on 'enterprising selves' (Maasen and Sutter, 2007; Rose, 2007, 1990). What is needed, indeed, as we shall see below, is the deployment of different theoretical perspectives and different levels of analysis in order to capture these trends and transformations in contemporary biopolitics.

What then of these trends and transformations and what implica-tions do they have for the biopolitics of chronic illness? It is to these issues that we now turn.

Mapping biopolitics: Trends and transformations

Vulnerability and Suffering   The world of chronic illness, as Bury (1982) articulated long ago, thrusts upon us profound existential questions of vulnerability, suffering and finitude which, in the normal course of day-to-day life, remain only distant possibilities or the plight of others. Much of the work in the sociology of chronic illness, as already noted, has been taken up with the exploration and elaboration of these issues (that is, the experience of illness), paying particular attention to its bio-graphically disruptive nature and consequences, the role narrative in symbolically repairing these ruptures between body, self and society, and the management of chronic illness in everyday life away from for-mal health-care facilities. This has also included more explicit attention to the biological or material dimensions of chronic illness and their implications for selfhood and suffering. The links between these issues and broader political questions of vulnerability, suffering and human rights, however, have proved neglected topics within the sociology of chronic illness to date.

Turner's (2004) recent work, however, provides one more or less promising way forward in addressing these issues in a sociologically robust fashion. The argument here rests on the simple fact that we are, by virtue of our embodiment, biologically frail, vulnerable creatures – we age, experience varying levels of health, illness and disability across the life course and sooner or later die. These material embodied facts in turn provide the ontological grounds for a universal theory of human rights based on notions of human vulnerability and the precariousness of social institutions. This is a position, moreover, which goes beyond a strong constructionist stance on these matters without necessarily rejecting constructionism altogether. Our vulnerability, in this respect, is itself variable but 'all humans, by virtue of their common humanity, are vulnerable' (Turner, 2004: 70). Protecting human rights derives from this vulnerability and social precariousness, based in part on the fact that we see in the plight of other human beings our own vulnerability reflected back at us and the potential for misery and suffering contained therein – an anticipation, in other words, of our own dependence, vulnerability and frailty (ibid.: 188).

This argument regarding the ontological basis of human frailty in turn hinges on the distinction between pain and suffering: the latter a culturally variable or relative matter related to notions of selfhood and a loss of dignity and respect, the former a fundamental (neurologically based) experience of all organic life which is *'not entirely subject to or captured by its cultural context'* (ibid.: 189). Pain, in other words, is *never solely or simply a 'culturally mediated matter'* (see also Bendelow and Williams, 1995; Kleinman, Das and Lock, 1997 and Wilkinson 2005 for important anthropological and sociological work on pain and suffering). There are important connections here, as Turner himself notes, to Zola's (1991, 1989) attempt to defend moral universalism against cultural relativism in relation to the politics of disability and impairment; a stance which, in 'bringing bodies back in' and arguing for 'universal policies' rather than 'special needs', recognizes that the *entire population* is, in an important sense, 'at risk' in terms of chronic illness and disability (Turner, 2004).

Turner's stance, then, provides a more or less robust set of ontological arguments or foundations for a theory of human rights which are grounded in our biological frailty, embodied vulnerability and the precariousness of social institutions. This, to repeat, is not a position which rejects constructionism outright, except perhaps strong constructionism. Rather it simply recognizes the limits of constructionism and attempts to go beyond them in an attempt to find a universal basis for the articulation and elaboration of human rights. It also provides a more or less useful foundation for a broader set of sociological theorizations about the links or connections between changes in the global economy, in social capital, in citizenship and in health and illness. Disease, from this perspective, is always mediated or filtered through the protective network or social capital and citizenship which mitigate both biological vulnerability and social inequality (that is, citizenship as social glue and capital as social solidarity in the face of vulnerability). Social structure, global change and individual experience, therefore, are inextricably connected at the embodied level through changes in social capital, social order and citizenship which in turn have real material-corporeal consequences and implications for the health and illness of the individual. To comprehend these complex processes and relations between global processes and individual experience, Turner concludes, we need a 'new' medical sociology: a reiteration, in effect, of Mills' (1959) sociological advice to connect personal troubles (that is, experience of illness) to the broader canvass, which in this case pertains to the political economy of modern societies and the process of globalization. The private narrative of illness, in other words, from this perspective, not only tells of 'fortitude in the face of human frailty, vulnerability and finitude', but also indexes issues of 'wealth, power, status, inequality and injustice' which necessitate and demand a robust articulation and defence of human rights (Turner, 2004: 313).

Perhaps most importantly for our purposes and for the analysis that follows, this is an approach which, as Turner himself acknowledges and advocates, is based on a recognition and reconciliation of different theoretical perspectives and levels of analysis ranging from individual experience, the social organization of chronic illness and disability in terms of socio-cultural categories, the macro or societal level of welfare provision, and the politics of disability. The management of chronic illness and disability in this respect may profitably be regarded (in Foucauldian terms) as a form of 'governmentality' and an exercise of normative control over the bodies of individuals and populations (cf. Rose, 1990), but we also need to explore (in phenomenological terms) individual experiences of misfortune, frailty, disease, disability, finitude and their bodily or embodied basis. Foucauldian and phenomenological perspectives, in this way, may not simply be profitably reconciled, but connected up to broader socio-economic and socio-political transformations and changes in the global economy and neoliberal era.

There are, to be sure, dangers here in glossing over important ontological and epistemological differences between these perspectives. Turner's own emphasis on vulnerability, moreover, is potentially open to criticism in terms of other more positive approaches to human rights based on human capabilities and human flourishing (Nussbaum, 2000; Sen, 1999). Nonetheless, this is an approach I wish to defend in the face of these (potential) criticisms, precisely because (i) it allows us theoretical room for manoeuvre at many different levels of analysis, and (ii) issues of frailty, vulnerability and the body are critical to agendas in medical sociology, particularly in relation to chronic illness and disability. Biomedicine, in this respect, alongside other forms of welfare provision, can itself be seen as an institutional expression of and response to the biological frailties and vulnerabilities of the human body, albeit one which itself is morphing or mutating in significant ways.

Biomedicine: Continuity and Change Despite the fact that much of the day-to-day reality of coping with or managing chronic illness goes on in everyday life, behind closed doors, away from formal health-care facilities, the lives of those with chronic illness are still, nonetheless, intimately bound up with medicine or biomedicine. By definition, of course, chronic illness continues to pose challenges to biomedicine, exposing its limits and weaknesses. The reality of much treatment, moreover, despite significant advances in biomedicine in recent decades, continues to be pretty much the same; variants on well entrenched themes of care and rehabilitation which at best slow progression and alleviate symptoms, and at worst cause as many problems as they allegedly solve – cf. Jobling's (1988) apposite notion of the 'Sisyphus syndrome', playing on Greek mythology, to capture trials and tribulation of the medical regimen (that is, considerable effort with little or no reward).

Biomedicine nonetheless is currently undergoing a more or less profound series of transformations in its knowledge base if not its modes of intervention. Whilst most people indeed, as Rose (2007) rightly notes, continue to think or imagine their bodies at the 'molar' level of limbs, organs, tissues, blood, and so on (that is, the body of clinical medicine which took shape during the course of the nineteenth century), this 'clinical gaze', Rose contends, has been supplemented if not supplanted by a new 'gaze' which envisages life at the molecular level of DNA, including the molecular basis of disease and treatment (that is, new molecularly crafted chemicals). Whilst many diagnoses and treatments, in this respect, continue to be conducted in molar terms of pathologies of organs, tissues and systems, this 'molecular turn' nonetheless remains significant, not least because it

> ... strips tissues, proteins, molecules and drugs of their specific affinities – to a disease, to an organ, to an individual, to species – and enables them to be regarded ... as manipulable and transferable elements or units, which can be delocalized – moved from place to place, from organism to organism, from disease to disease, from person to person; thereby conferring a new form of mobility on life, or more properly elements of life, itself. (Rose, 2007: 14–15)

These developments in turn are part and parcel of a reconfigured set of possibilities which themselves are reworking, if not taking us beyond, the existing poles of health and illness, normality and abnormality, treatment and enhancement. This includes contemporary concerns and technologies pertaining to *'genetic susceptibility'* and other new or promised technologies concerned to improve or *'enhance'* us in various ways. On the one hand, these technologies serve to 'bring potential futures into the present' rendering them quantifiable through the calculus of risk in order to 'optimise' life chances. On the other hand, they carry with them the potential to widen the net of (potential) pathology still further, thereby rendering many, if not all, of us, 'pre-symptomatically ill' or 'pre-patients' (ibid.: 19–20).

It is in this context, for example, that various 'genetic markers' or 'susceptibility genes' or 'single nucleotide polymorphisms' (SNPs) for conditions such as cystic fibrosis, breast cancer, schizophrenia, bipolar disorder are being identified in the 'post-genomic' era. It is also in this context that fierce battles have been waged within the disability rights movement over reproductive genetic technologies such as Pre Genetic Diagnosis (PGD) in which various conditions and disabilities are screened 'for' if not screened 'out', which it is claimed, amounts to nothing short of eugenics by policy outcome if not policy intent (Shakespeare, 2003). Considerable concern, at one and the same time, is currently being expressed around the possibilities and prospects of a new era of so-called cognitive enhancement agents – drugs, that is, whose uses extend far beyond the clinic given their ability to boost alertness and concentration, memory and performance on a range of cognitive tasks – including concerns about their long-term safety implications, the social and ethical implications of these drugs in terms of issues such as equality, freedom, choice and competition, and the extent to which their use should be regulated (Academy of Medical Sciences, 2008; British Medical Association, 2007; Department of Trade and Industry, 2005).

Again, to repeat, these developments may seem far removed from the everyday if not mundane realities of chronic illness. They are nonetheless, as already suggested, far from insignificant in terms of the problems and possibilities they pose for us all, both now and in the future, in sickness and in health. They also, of course, generate new hopes, fears and expectations for the future, around which scientists, doctors, patients (or proto-patients for that matter) and the public in general mobilize, often in alliance with one another. This includes the advent of new drugs for the treatment of conditions such as Alzheimer's and cancers of various kinds – which patient groups, often encouraged or supported by pharmaceutical companies, then lobby bodies such as the National Institute for Health and Clinical Excellent (NICE) to fund on the NHS – and the considerable hype and hope surrounding stem cell therapies in the age of regenerative medicine. It also extends to developments such as pharmacogenetics and pharmacogenomics (PGX) which, according to some at least, promise to usher us in a new era of so-called personalized medicine based on genetic tests which match us up to bespoke medicines with few side-effects or adverse reactions (see, for example, Hedgecoe, 2004).

Identity, selfhood and citizenship   These developments in turn, it is claimed, are opening up the prospect or possibilities of new forms of identity, selfhood, sociality and citizenship. The more biomedical knowledge and biomedical interventions permeate or penetrate the realms of everyday life – as they undeniably and inescapably do in cases of chronic illness – the greater the potential for thinking about ourselves, including our bodies, our identities and indeed our rights and responsibilities as citizens, in biologically mediated or biosocial ways.

People with diabetes, for example, may come to think of their bodies, if not themselves, in highly biomedicalized ways, including the monitoring of insulin levels and the avoidance or prevention of hypoglycaemic episodes or incidents. Similarly, developments in neuroscience, including clinical applications such as psychopharmacology, carry within them the potential to reconfigure notions of selfhood and identity in various 'neurochemical' ways (Rose, 2007). Ritalin, SSRIs and other new drugs currently in development which, as noted above, promise to 'cognitively enhance' us in various ways are all cases in point. These new drugs, as Rose (2007: 211) rightly notes, are not so much concerned with psychiatric coercion or the chemical cosh, as a means of 'coping' or 'taking control' of one's life and one's conduct, if not 'improving' oneself or getting in touch with the 'real', 'true' or 'authentic' self – a distinctly neurochemical form of self-realization in effect (cf. Kramer, 1993). Conceived more broadly, these psychiatric and psychopharmaceutical technologies are part and parcel of processes and practices in which we are all obliged, beyond any notion of patienthood or protopatienthood, to 'monitor and evaluate our moods, emotion and cognition according to ever finer, more continuous process of self-scrutiny' (Rose, 2007: 223).

Rose, to be sure, is also careful here to stress that these new 'biosocial' or 'neurochemical' ways of relating to and understanding ourselves have not so much displaced or replaced all others, but instead are 'layered onto other older senses of the self, and invoked in particular settings and encounters with significant consequences' (2007: 222). To date nonetheless they remain, in large part, more or less fruitful theoretical speculations in need of further empirical investigation and specification: issues which medical sociology is well placed to address.

Another more or less promising new concept to think with here concerns the notion of 'biological citizenship' to denote the reconfigured rights, duties and expectations of individuals in relation to matters of life, health and illness, and their reorganized relations to biomedical authorities, the state and to themselves in term of their corporeal being and bodily existence. We see this term deployed to good effect, for example, in Petryna's (2002) fascinating and compelling study of 'biological citizens' after Chernobyl, a work which movingly documents the mobilization of citizens in Ukraine around this biological catastrophe and the demands for recognition and compensation on account of their 'biologically damaged' bodies. Petryna in this respect guides us through

> ...some of the contested spaces and politics of population management in the Chernobyl aftermath, highlighting the patterns by which science has become a key resource in the management of risk and in democratic polity building, and showing how Ukrainians employ knowledge of biological injury as a means of negotiating public accountability, political power, and further state protections in the form of financial compensation and medical care. (2002: 7)

This citizenship, however, may take many different forms in contemporary neoliberal society, including active mobilization and involvement on the part of patient support groups and related social movements which take as their problematic a biological cause or concern. Novas's (2006) study of patient organizations and the political economy of hope, for example, illustrates these issues well. Patient organizations, he shows, drawing on two illuminating case studies – the Pseudoxanthoma Elasticum (PXE) international and political activism associated with Canavan disease in the US – provide key sites where practices of identity formation and socio-political action take place and intersect. They also play an increasingly important role in biomedical research itself, fuelled and fashioned through the hope of helping facilitate the process by which cures or therapies are developed in accordance with their collectively shared goals or ideals: a process which Novas characterizes as a 'political economy of hope'. The direct involvement of patient groups in biomedical research, in this respect, is 'a product of, and adds novel dimensions to, neoliberal inducements for individuals, families and communities to take responsibility for the management and provision of their own health' (2006: 290). Patient groups moreover, in doing so, help transform 'the ways in which the vital life processes of organisms are known and visualized – blood, tissue, DNA are increasingly visualized at the molecular level and known in such a way as to make them open to transformation into potentially useful therapies or products' (ibid.: 290).

There are obvious links here to existing work in medical sociology and the sociology of chronic illness on self-help groups (Kellehear, Gabe and Williams, 2006), social movements in health (Brown et al., 2004) and to other health consumer groups (Allsop, Jones and Baggott, 2004; Jones, 2008). Cast in this more biopolitical light, however, notions such as biological citizenship and other forms of biosociality (see, for example, Gibbon and Novas, 2008) add important new insights and dimensions to the picture here. They also, of course, raise important related questions concerning the contested nature of authority, expertise and ethics in contemporary society.

Expertise and ethics   Here we arrive at what is, perhaps, one of the prime ways in which a Foucauldian perspective on biopolitics cashes out, namely, in relation to issues of governmentality or the governing of conduct. We are currently in the midst, so it is argued, of new ways of governing human conduct which are bound up with the rise of multiple forms of authority and expertise related to the 'management' of various aspects of 'somatic existence' (Rose, 2007: 6) – a phalanx which includes scientists, doctors specializing in various branches of medicine and a growing number of counsellors who advise, guide, care and support for individuals and families in sickness and in health. Recent years have also, of course, witnessed the meteoric rise of 'bioethics' (and most recently of all, neuroethics) as yet another new branch of expertise which has secured a solid institutional niche for itself in adjudicating, evaluating and legitimating all aspects of bioscience, biomedicine and biotechnology from the bench to the bedside.

The very notion of 'expertise', at one and the same time, has been opened up, contested, debated, democratized in recent years. We see this, for example, very clearly through debates over the nature and status of 'lay' worlds in the contemporary era, not simply within medical sociology (Prior, 2003; Shaw, 2004) but in wider policy and public arenas. These debates themselves, in part, are fuelled through the potentially 'democratizing' power of the internet and the challenges it poses to medicine and other professionalized bodies of knowledge, power, authority and expertise (see, for example, Hardy, 1999, and for other more cautious or considered accounts, Nettleton, Burrows and O'Malley, 2005; Henwood et al., 2003 and Kellehear, Gabe and Williams, 2006).

Perhaps the most immediate or obvious point of reference here, for our purposes, is the advent of the so-called expert patient programme: an American import based on the notion of a partnership of expertise between health-care professionals and patients in the management of chronic disease (see, for example, Taylor and Bury, 2007 and Bury this volume). On the one hand, this may be viewed in a positive light given years of campaigning if not outright championing, on the part of medical sociologists, about the need for a more equal partnership between patients and professionals if not, to quote the title of an influential book, a 'meeting between experts' (Tuckett, Bolton and Williams, 1985). On the other hand, it raises a series of critical sociological questions concerning not simply the 'efficacy' of the programme and the criteria by which it is judged or evaluated, or the 'interests' served through the rolling out of these initiatives, but the extent to which it exacerbates rather than mitigates social inequalities, including the creation of invidious templates of 'successful' illness management against which patients are clinically and socially judged (see again Taylor and Bury, 2007 and Bury this volume). From a Foucauldian perspective, moreover, what this amounts to is the development of a further micro system of social regulation or governmentality that involves normative control over the bodies of those in whose name such programmes are devised and constructed; a further instance, in other words, of 'therapies of freedom', based on 'willing selves', which 'govern the soul' all the more effectively for precisely this reason in the neoliberal era (Maasen and Sutter, 2007; Rose, 1990). Ethics, as such, becomes increasingly focused on and grounded in the fleshy, material-corporeal body: a 'somatic ethics' (Rose, 2007), in effect, in a 'somatic society' (Turner, 1993, 2004).

Bioliberalism and biovalue Here we arrive at a fifth, and for the purposes of this chapter final, set of issues concerning the placing of contemporary biopolitics in the broader economic and political orders of advanced capitalist societies in the global age. In many ways, indeed, it would not be too much of an exaggeration to suggest that biomedicine, bioscience and biotechnology have become key sources of commercial and economic value in the neoliberal era. Fuller (2006), for example, argues precisely along these lines, claiming that we have moved into a new era of 'bioliberalism' as the dominant ideology of our time, conceived as the 'natural outcome' of neoliberalism whereby the biomedical industries have become the 'ascendant mode of production' and where decisions concerning the design, commercialization and termination of life are taken with minimal state intervention. Waldby (2000), too, directs our attention more specifically to the way in which life itself has become a political source of value, one which may yield returns in term of new knowledge, improved health and or sustainable growth and development.

A new economic space, as this suggests, has opened up which quite literally 'capitalizes on life itself': a new 'bioeconomy' and a new form of capital 'biocapital', as Rose (2007) puts it, based on these 'economies of vitality'. This, for example, is clearly evident in relation to the pharmaceutical industry, given its complex, if not controversial, links to science and technology on the one hand, and commercial shareholder values on the other. Life itself, in this respect, has been rendered amenable to new economic relations (that is, the subsumption of our biology to forms of capital that even Marx himself could not have envisaged) as vitality is

... decomposed into a series of distinct and discrete objects – that can be isolated, delimited, stored, accumulated, mobilized, and exchanged, accorded a discrete value, traded across time, space, species, contexts, enterprises – in the service of many discrete objectives. In the process, a novel geopolitical field has taken shape, and biopolitics has become inextricably intertwined with bioeconomics. (2007: 7)

It may be somewhat speculative or fanciful here, following Rose, to rework these issues, in classical Weberian terms, through recourse to some sort of 'elective affinity' between this new spirit of 'biocapital' on the one hand, and a new 'somatic ethics' on the other. What is clear and indisputable nonetheless is that commercial value is now being attached to vital life processes themselves and that this value now operates and circulates within a global geopolitical field of prospects, possibilities and shareholder values.

The biopolitics of chronic illness, in this respect, must contend amongst other things with (i) the willing or voluntary donation of biological resources by patients and the public for scientific purposes, both public and commercial, in advanced neoliberal democracies; (ii) the political economy of 'hope' invested in new drugs and treatments for chronic or life-threatening conditions; (iii) the power and interests of the pharmaceutical industry in drugs for the treatment of chronic illness in affluent societies – including what some have dubbed its 'disease-mongering' tactics (Moynihan, 2002; Moynihan and Henry, 2006; Moynihan, Health and Henry, 2002) – vis-à-vis the limited investment in drugs to tackle the global health problems of those in poorer parts of the world today; and (iv) the black market in organ trafficking across the globe, whereby those in the poorer parts of the world sell their organs to the rich in order to feed their families – what Schepper-Hughes (2001) has appositely termed a kind of 'auto-cannibalism' based on the 'politics of the belly'.

These biopolitical matters in turn cast a long shadow over the rather 'inward' or 'insular' focus of much sociological work on chronic illness to date. They also, of course, return us full circle to some of the arguments articulated above about relations between the body, identity, selfhood, citizenship and rights in the global age, this time albeit through a recognition that life is now implicated or imbricated in the logic of capital relations which opens it up to interventions of many different kinds, and which call into question the very integrity or inviolability of the body itself. The stakes are high; they implicate us all.

Concluding comments

Let me take this opportunity in this concluding section to further reflect on some of the key issues this chapter has addressed, with particular reference to future research agendas.

The key argument on which this chapter rests, it will be recalled, is that the sociology of chronic illness, which has characteristically focused on biographical issues to do with the meaning and experience of chronic illness and related issues of narrative reconstruction and so forth, would benefit from a more explicit linking of these themes and issues to biopolitical agendas in the global age. This, as we have seen, includes key biopolitical questions and issues concerning (i) vulnerability, suffering and human rights (ii) changing configurations and constellations of biomedical thought and practice (iii) newly emerging (biosocial) forms of identity, selfhood, sociality and citizenship (iv) changing configurations of power, authority, expertise and ethics, and (v) the advent or emergence of a new era of biocapital, bioliberalism and biovalue.

This is an approach, I have stressed, which demands and necessitates a variety of theoretical perspectives, given the many different levels of analysis it involves and entails – from the meaning and experience of chronic illness, through shifting configurations of biomedical power/ knowledge and the governance of bodies, to the broader macro economic and geopolitical context within which biomedicine, bioscience and biotechnology now operate as 'ascendant' modes of production in the global age. It cannot, therefore, to repeat, be read as any simple or straightforward Foucauldian or neo-Foucauldian rendition of these issues, however pertinent such analyses and their accompanying concepts may be. Elaborating on this latter point, we may say that whilst neo-Foucauldian analyses are powerful and wide ranging – taking in everything from these new 'molecularized thought styles of biomedicine' to the birth of this new 'economics of vitality' – they nonetheless have their limits when it comes to studying the meaning and experience of illness, or any attempts to ground human rights in 'universal' features of the human body: a problem captured, in part, by Rose's confession that 'my analysis concerns not what human beings are, but what they think they are: the kinds of human beings they take themselves to be' (2007: 25). This in turn is compounded by another characteristic feature of Foucauldian scholarship, namely, the absence of any normative stance in relation to the issues under investigation. Moreover, the analysis of the global nature and dynamics of these issues, including the advent of the bioeconomy and biovalue, again take us far beyond any simple or straightforward Foucauldian or neo-Foucauldian rendition of these matters. Concepts such as biopolitics, biosociality, biological citizenship, biocapital and biovalue, in this respect, may be good to think with, and may facilitate new agendas in the sociology of chronic illness and beyond, but there is merit in doing so, to repeat, from multiple perspectives or viewpoints which does not necessarily commit us to a full-blown Foucauldian or neo-Foucauldian form of analysis. In all these ways then, we need to keep our theoretical options open when it comes to the multiple, mobile, mutating landscapes of biopolitics in the twenty-first century.

A return to Turner's call for a 'new' medical sociology is also instructive at this point; a call, it will be remembered, which lays 'greater emphasis on economics, politics, rights and citizenship in order to provide a more comprehensive and sophisticated understanding of health and illness in the contemporary world' (2004: 271). To the extent that the lines of analysis developed in this chapter take us in a more explicitly biopolitical direction involving precisely these sorts of issues, then this appears to chime or fit well with Turner's call for a 'new' medical sociology. To the extent, however, that it draws in large part on existing perspectives, then it may best be regarded as the application or deployment of different approaches to a newly emerging issue (that is, the growing politicization of life itself in the global age of biological 'control'). This is a politics, as we have seen, which implicates us all as living beings, in sickness and in health. When life itself, moreover, is conceptualized at the molecular, when it is studied, sampled, frozen, banked, mobilized, traded, recombined in this way (Rose, 2007), then what is at stake in contemporary biopolitics is the very integrity of the body itself.

It is also worth spelling out perhaps, at this point, the relationship between the issues discussed in this chapter and the notion, contained in the title of this book, of 'assaults' on the lifeworld. Certainly, as the earlier discussion of vulnerability and suffering suggests, chronic illness can be construed as an assault on the lifeworld. Yet, as I have also argued elsewhere (Williams, 2001, 2003), the notion of chronic illness as biographical disruption may miss, mask or minimize the ways in which chronic illness may not simply be a biographically anticipated or expected life course event (that is, an expected part of the embodied biographical life course) but a biographically reaffirming or reinforcing experience – see also Pound, Gompertz and Ebrahim (1998), Carricaburu and Pierret (1995) and Fairclough et al. (2004) for further empirical support for these contentions. It is also clear, as we have seen, that whilst the permeation or penetration of biological, biomedical or biosocial ways of knowing and understanding ourselves and acting in the world may, in Habermasian terms, amount to nothing short of a 'colonization' of the lifeworld, they nonetheless form the basis for new ways of thinking and acting both individually and collectively, including new forms of biopolitical activism, entitlement and mobilization. Viewed in this light, then, it may not so much be a case of 'assaults' on the lifeworld as shifting 'assemblages' or configurations of problems, prospects and possibilities which coalesce or crystallize around various biopolitical axes, forms of praxis and modes of identification. What future research agendas, then, does this signal or suggest? There is certainly, I suggest, a need for more empirical work in this area which engages more fully with the theoretical and empirical utility of the concepts and issues raised in this chapter concerning the biopolitics of chronic illness. The degree, for example, to which people are indeed coming to both think of themselves and act in these new or novel bio-social ways is an open empirical question which warrants further investigation, in chronic illness as elsewhere. This includes related issues to do with collective action through patient groups and organizations and other forms of political activism and mobilization tied to new forms of biological citizenship and biosociality. Further work is also required, in this vein, concerning the political economy of hope and expectations in terms of the multiple interests and investments at stake in the field of chronic illness. This, moreover, includes an approach to chronic illness which combines the analysis of both mental and physical conditions. The relays between these issues and broader trends and transformations in the bioeconomy and global order, I suggest, provide a key frontier for future work in the sociology of chronic illness and disability.

In these and other ways then, to conclude, a variety of more or less promising new agendas suggest themselves for future work in the sociology of chronic illness in particular and medical sociology in general: biopolitical matters, in short, which lie at the heart of contemporary forms of power and personhood in the twenty-first century.

References

Academy of Medical Sciences (2008) *Brain Science, Addictions and Drugs*. London: AMS.

Agamben, G. (1998) *Homo Sacer: Sovereignty and the Bare Life*. Stanford, CA: Stanford University Press.

Allsop, J., Jones, K. and Baggott, R. (2004) Health Consumer Groups in the UK – a New Social Movement? *Sociology of Health & Illness* 26(6): 737–56.

Barnes, C. and Mercer, G. (eds) (1996) *Exploring the Divide: Illness and Disability*. Leeds: The Disability Press.

Bendelow, G. and Williams, S. (1995) Transcending the Dualisms: Towards a Sociology of Pain. *Sociology of Health & Illness* 17(2): 139–65.

British Medical Association (2007) *Boosting Your Brain Power: Ethical Aspects of Cognitive Enhancements*. London: BMA.

Brown, P., Zavestoski, S., McCormick, S., Mayer, B., Morello-Frosch, R. and Altman, R. (2004) Embodied Health Movements: New Approaches to Social Movements in Health. *Sociology of Health and Illness* 26: 50–80.

Bury, M. (1982) Chronic Illness as Biographical Disruption. *Sociology of Health & Illness* 4(2): 167–82.

Bury, M. (1991) The Sociology of Chronic Illness: A Review of Research and Prospects. *Sociology of Health and Illness* 13(4): 451–68.

Carricaburu, D. and Pierret, J. (1995) From Biographical Disruption to Biographical Reinforcement. *Sociology of Health & Illness* 17(1): 65–8.

Charmaz, K. (1987) Struggling for a Self: Identity Levels of the Chronically Ill. *Research in the Sociology of Health Care* 6: 283–321.

Department of Trade and Industry (Office of Science and Technology) (2005) *Drugs Futures 2025.* London: DTI.

Fairclough, C. A., Boylstein, C., Rittman, M., Young, M. E. and Gubrium, J. (2004) Sudden Illness and Biographical Flow in Narratives of Stroke Recovery. *Sociology of Health & Illness* 26(2): 242–61.

Foucault, M. (1991) The Politics of Health in the Eighteenth Century. In P. Rabinow (ed.), *The Foucault Reader.* London: Penguin.

Foucault, M. (1979) *The History of Sexuality, Volume 1.* London: Allen Lane.

Frank, A. W. (1995) *The Wounded Storyteller: Body, Illness and Ethics.* Chicago, IL: University of Chicago Press.

Fuller, S. (2006) *The New Sociological Imagination.* London: Sage.

Gibbon, S. and Novas, C. (eds) (2008) *Biosocialities, Genetics and the Social Sciences.* London: Routledge.

Glaser, B. and Strauss, A. L. (1975) *Chronic Illness and the Quality of Life.* St Louis: Mosby.

Hardt, M. and Negri, A. (2000) *Empire.* Cambridge, MA: Harvard University Press.

Hardy, M. (1999) Doctor in the House: The Internet as a Source of Lay Knowledge and the Challenge to Expertise. *Sociology of Health & Illness* 21(6): 820–35.

Hedgecoe, A. (2004) *The Politics of Personalised Medicine.* Cambridge: Cambridge University Press.

Henwood, F., Wyatt, S., Hart, A. and Smith, J. (2003) 'Ignorance Is Bliss Sometimes': Constraints on the Emergence of the 'Informed Patient' in the Changing Landscapes of Health Information. *Sociology of Health & Illness* 25(6): 589–607.

Jobling, R. (1988) The Experience of Psoriasis under Treatment. In R. Anderson and M. Bury (eds), *Living with Chronic Illness.* London: Unwin Hyman.

Jones, K. (2008) In Whose Interests? Relationships between Health Consumer Groups and the Pharmaceutical Industry in the UK. *Sociology of Health & Illness* 30(6): 929–43.

Kelleher, D. (1998) *Diabetes.* London: Routledge.

Kelleher, D. (2004) Self Help Groups and Their Relationship to Medicine. In D. Kelleher, J. Gabe and G. Williams (eds), *Challenging Medicine.* 2nd Edition, London: Routledge.

Kelleher, D. (2006) New Social Movements in the Health Domain. In G. Scambler (ed.), *Habermas, Critical Theory and Health.* London: Routledge.

Kelleher, D., Gabe, J. and Williams, G. H. (eds) (2006) *Challenging Medicine,* 2nd Edition, London: Routledge.

Kelly, M. (1992) *Colitis.* London: Routledge.

Kelly, M. and Field, D. (1996) Medical Sociology, Chronic Illness and the Body. *Sociology of Health & Illness* 18(2): 241–57.

Kleinman, A. (1988) *The Illness Narratives: Suffering, Healing and the Human Condition.* New York: Basic Books.

Kleinman, A., Das, V. and Lock, M. (eds) (1997) *Social Suffering*. California: University of California Press.

Kramer, P. (1993) *Listening to Prozac*. London: Penguin.

Maasen, S. and Sutter, B. (2007) *On Willing Selves: Neoliberal Politics and the Challenge of the Neuroscience*. Basingstoke: Palgrave Macmillan.

Mills, C. W. (1959) *The Sociological Imagination*. Oxford: Oxford University Press.

Moynihan, R. (2002) Disease-Mongering: How Doctors, Drug Companies, and Insurers Are Making You Feel Sick. *British Medical Journal* 324(13 April): 923.

Moynihan, R. and Henry, D. (2006) The Fight against Disease Mongering: Generating Knowledge for Action. *Public Library of Science – Medicine* 3(4) (April), e 191.

Moynihan, R., Health, I. and Henry, D. (2002) Selling Sickness: The Pharmaceutical Industry and Disease Mongering. *British Medical Journal* 324(13 April): 886–91.

Nettleton, S., Burrows, R. and O'Malley, L. (2005) The Mundane Realities of Everyday Lay Use of the Internet for Health. *Sociology of Health & Illness* 27(7): 972–92.

Novas, C. (2006) The Political Economy of Hope: Patients' Organisations, Science and Biovalue. *BioSocieties* 1(3): 289–305.

Nussbaum, M. C. (2000) *Women and Human Development: The Capabilities Approach*. Cambridge: Cambridge University Press.

Oliver, M. (1990) *The Politics of Disablement*. London: Macmillan.

Petryna, A. (2002) *Life Exposed: Biological Citizens after Chernobyl*. Princeton, NJ: Princeton University Press.

Pound, P., Gompertz P. and Ebrahim, S. (1998) Illness in the Context of Old Age: The Case of Stroke. *Sociology of Health & Illness* 20(4): 489–506.

Prior, L. (2003) Beliefs, Knowledge and Expertise. *Sociology of Health and Illness*. 25(Silver Anniversary Issue): 41–57.

Rabinow, P. (1996) *The Anthropology of Reason*. Princeton, NJ: Princeton University Press.

Radley, A. (1989) Style, Discourse and Constraint in Adjusting to Chronic Illness. *Sociology of Health & Illness* 11(3): 230–52.

Robinson, I. (1994) *Multiple Sclerosis*. London: Routledge.

Rose, N. (1990) *Governing the Soul: The Shaping of the Private Self*. London: Routledge.

Rose, N. (2007) *The Politics of Life Itself: Biomedicine, Power and Subjectivity in the Twenty-First Century*. Princeton, NJ: Princeton University Press.

Scambler, G. (1989) *Epilepsy*. London: Routledge.

Scheper-Hughes, N. (2001) Commodity Fetishism in Organs Trafficking. *Body & Society* 7(2–3): 31–62.

Sen, A. (1999) *Development as Freedom*. Oxford: Oxford University Press.

Shakespeare, T. (2003) Rights, Risks and Responsibilities: New Genetics and Disabled People. In S. J. Williams, L. Birke and G. A. Bendelow (eds), *Debating Biology*. London: Routledge.

Shakespeare, T. (2007) *Disability Rights and Wrongs*. London: Routledge.

Shaw, I. (2004) How Lay Are Lay Beliefs. *Health* 6(3): 287–99.

Taylor, D. and Bury, M. (2007) Chronic Illness, Expert Patients and the Care Transition. *Sociology of Health & Illness* 29(1): 27–45.

Thomas, C. (2007) *Sociologies of Disability and Illness: Contested Ideas in Disability Studies and Medical Sociology*. Basingstoke: Palgrave Macmillan.

Tuckett, D., Bolton, M. and Williams, A. (1985) *Meeting between Experts*. London: Tavistock.

Turner, B. S. (1993) *Regulating Bodies: Essays in Medical Sociology*. London: Routledge.

Turner, B. S. (2004) *The New Medical Sociology*. New York/London: W.W. Norton & Co.

Waldby, C. (2000) *The Visible Human Project: Infomatic Bodies and Posthuman Medicine*. London: Routledge.

Wilkinson, I. (2005) *Suffering: A Sociological Introduction*. Cambridge: Polity Press.

Williams, G. H. (1996) Representing Disability: Some Questions of Phenomenology and Politics. In C. Barnes and G. Mercer (eds), *Exploring the Divide: Illness and Disability*. Leeds: The Disability Press.

Williams, G. H. (1984) The Genesis of Chronic Illness: Narrative Reconstruction. *Sociology of Health & Illness* 6(2): 175–200.

Williams, S. J. (1993) *Chronic Respiratory Illness*. London: Routledge.

Williams, S. J. (1996) The Vicissitudes of Embodiment across the Chronic Illness Trajectory. *Body and Society* 2(2): 23-47.

Williams, S. J. (2000) Chronic Illness as Biographical Disruption or Biographical Disruption as Chronic Illness? Reflections on a Core Concept. *Sociology of Health & Illness* 22(1): 40–67.

Williams, S. J. 2003. *Medicine and the Body*. London: Sage.

Zola, I. K. (1989) Toward the Necessary of Universalizing of Disability Policy. *Milbank Quarterly* 67: 401–8.

Zola, I. K. (1991) Bringing Our Bodies and Ourselves Back In: Reflections on Past, Present and Future 'Medical Sociology'. *Journal of Health and Social Behavior* 32(March): 1–16.

Index

Abberley, P., 42, 61
ABC National Radio, 173
Afentouli, P., 5, 106
Aldenkamp, A., 108
alert assistant, 21
Archer, M., 111
Armstrong, D., 141
Asbring, P., 17
Aspis, S., 60
assaults on the life world, 78–83
  biological, theorizing, 83–9
  meaning of, 8
Asylums, 13
auto-cannibalism, 218
awareness
  bodily, 17, 23, 70, 73
  of discourses, 3
  and grounded theory, 15
  and normalization, 24
  reflexive, in field, 88, 91–2
  and uncertainty, 16
Awareness of Dying, 13
Aylward, M., 181

Bambra, C., 182, 196
Barnes, C., 42, 47, 57
Barton, L., 42
Basics of Qualitative Research, 11
Batten disease, 5, 78
  and assault, 78–83
  biological assault on lifeworld,
    theorizing, 83–9
  cultural capital, 94, 95
  economic capital, 99–102
  field, defining, 89–91
  force configuration in, within
    field, 86
  habitus and reflexivity, 91–3
  review of literature, 80–3
  social capital, 95–9
  symbolic capital, 94
  types, 79

Batten Disease Family Association
  (BDFA), 80, 89
Bauman, Z., 88, 180
Baxter, C., 82
Beatty, C., 192, 194
Beresford, P., 60
Berry, R., 194
Beveridge Report, 190
Bhaskar, R., 110
biocapital, 217, 218
bioeconomy, 217
bioethics, 216
biographical continuity, 18, 21
biographical disruption, 2, 15, 18, 40,
  65, 123, 162, 164
biographical flow, 165
biographical reinforcement, 15
biographical work, 164, 165
bioliberalism and biovalue, 217–18
biological citizenship, 214–15
biological mechanisms, 121, 122
  see also epilepsy, impact on
    individual
biomedicine, continuity and change,
  211–13
biopolitics, 205
bioliberalism and biovalue, 217–18
biomedicine, 211–13
  expertise and ethics, 215–17
  identity, selfhood and citizenship,
    213–15
  mapping, 208
  meaning and significance, 207–8
  vulnerability and suffering, 208–11
biopower, 40
biosociality, 205, 213, 214, 215
body
  awareness of, 17, 23, 70, 73
  Foucauldian perspective, 210
  and human vulnerability and
    suffering, 209
  in illness, and social world, 165

body – *continued*
  mainstream sociological writing
    on, 47
  as medium of expression, 155–6
  as real entity, 112
  and self, 20
Bourdieu, P., 5, 84, 86, 125, 199, 200
Brackenbury, H. B., 130
British Disability Studies, 72
Brown, S., 82, 83
Buetow, S.142
Bunker, J., 161
Bury, M., 2, 6, 63, 65, 147, 161,
  207, 208
Butler, J., 62

capital
  accrual of, and families, 86
  cultural, 85, 94, 101
  economic, 85
  loss of, 88
  negotiation around, 93
  physical, 86, 93–4
  social, 85, 95–9
  symbolic, 85–6, 94, 101
capitalism and oppression, 61
Carricaburu, D., 164, 220
Case, S., 83
categorization and labelling
  systems, 3
causal history, 111, 113
Charmaz, K., 2, 4, 8, 40, 65, 134
Charon, R., 158
Chicago School roots of grounded
  theory, 13–14
chronic disease self management
  (CDSM) programme, 169
chronic illness, 161
  corporeal dimension, 165
  and disability, 166
  rhetoric, of self-management,
    174–5, 176
  sociological research, 162–6, 171–2
  transformation, and self
    management, 166–71, 173
  see also individual entries
Chronic Illness and the Quality of Life,
  13, 19, 21, 163, 206
Clarke, A., 9

clinical encounter, 129
  cognitive participation, 137–8
  coherence and, 136
  collective action, 138–40
  forming and framing of, 133–5
  participants in, 134
  reflexive monitoring, 140–1
  sickness, embedding work of, 135–
  special character of, 130–33
clinical gaze, 6, 211
cognitive enhancement agents,
  212–13, 214
cognitive participation, 135, 137–8
coherence and sickness, 136
collective action, 135, 138–40
communal appraisal and reflexive
  monitoring, 141
Communities First programme, 186
conflict theorists, 40
constructionism and human
  rights, 210
contextual integration, 140
convergence hypothesis, 142
Cooper, J., 81
coping, social aspects of, 123
co-production process of health and
  health-care, 135
Corbin, J. M., 11, 21, 22, 134, 166, 170
Corker, M., 42
Cornwall, R., 191
Cornwell, J., 134
corporate ecology, 135
couples in concert, managing
  symptoms, 21–2
Creaven, S., 81
critical realism, 57, 110, 113, 124
Crow, L., 59
cultural capital, 85, 94, 101
cultural templates, 87–8

Davis, F., 13, 16
de Certeau, M., 150
deconstructionism, 43–4
  and disability studies, 44
diagnosis, 116, 122
  approach to, 16–17
  doubt of, 17
  reflexivity and, 92–3
  significance of, 15–16

Dieppe, P., 18
disability activism and scholarship,
    in North America, 40–1
disability benefits, 182
Disability Discrimination Act (DDA),
    45, 49
disability pride, 64
disability studies, 41
    cancer, living with, 48–51
    contemporary understanding of, 42
    and chronic illness, 166
    and deconstructionism, 44
    and disablism, 42, 46
    impairment effects, 47
    materialist perspectives on, 43
    medical certification, 182
    and political privilege, 182
    post-structurlaism, 43
    psycho-emotional dimensions of
        disablism, 46
    social model, 41–42
    sociology of, and chronic illness,
        44–51
    see also medical sociology
disabled people's lives, complexity
    of, 57
    and impaired, dynamic nature of,
        67–72
    materialist disability studies,
        58–64
    see also social model of disability
Disabled People's Movement
    (DPM), 41
disablism, 42, 46
    and impairment effects, 47
    material and psycho-emotional, in
        cancer survivor lives, 49–51
    meaning of, 37
discrimination and impairment,
    60, 64
discursive othering, 82
doctor–patient relationship and
    chronicity and inflammatory
    bowel disease, 146
    consultation as occasion, 151–7
    medical assessment and mediation,
        147–8
    medico-presentational
        thinking, 155

medico-scientific thinking, 148–9,
    150, 151
proto-stories, 148–51, 156–7
re-presentation, of illness
    experience, 155–6, 158
Dolan, L., 83
Donovan, J., 18
Dowling, M., 83
Drummond, N., 18

Ebrahim, S., 18, 165, 220
economic capital, 85, 99–102
    and informal social capital, 96
    institutionalized, 100
    personal, 100
economic inactivity, 192–3
    case of Oakdale Colliery, 192
elective affinity, 218
emancipatory research
    paradigm, 61
embodied doubt, 17
Employment and Support Allowance
    (ESA), 191, 195–6
    transition from Incapacity Benefit,
        182–3
epilepsy, impact on individual, 106
    aetiology, 108
    critical turning point, 119
    diagnosis and reactions, 116
    discrimination and stigma, 118
    effects of, 108–9
    exploratory data, 114–21
    first seizure and reactions of friends
        and families, 116–17
    genetics, 107–8
    ictal/peri-ictal effects and
        inter-ictal effects, difference
        between, 109
    medical state, 115–16
    patients' perception and impact,
        120
    public understanding and support,
        118–19
    realist framework, 110–14
    social research mechanism to study
        ERQOL, 121–4
    timing and context, 117
    work and education, 117–18
epilepsy habitus, 5, 125

epilepsy-related quality of life
(ERQOL), 109, 114
social research mechanism to
study, 121–4
Evercare model, of case
management, 169
everyday life work, 164
existential uncertainty, 16
expertise and ethics, 215–17
expert patients
programme, 169, 176, 216
by proxy, 86, 95

Fagerhaugh S., 29n7
Faircloth, C. A., 165, 220
felt stigma, 40
feminists, on sex/gender distinction,
61, 62
field
capital types and, 85–6
and clinical encounter, 135
defining, 84, 89–91
force configuration in Batten
disease within, 86
legitimation of place within,
89–90
non-doxic, 88, 92
reflexive awareness in, 88, 91–2
see also capital; habitus
Field D., 165
Finkelstein, V., 41, 62
Foote-Ardah, C., 24
Foucauldian perspective and
biopolitics, 210, 215, 216–17
Foucault, M., 39, 40, 207, 208
Frank, A., 48, 161
Frankel, R., 157
Freidson, E., 2
French, S., 59
Friedin, B., 21
frontier and proto-story, 156–7
Fuller, S., 205, 217

gender relations and oppression, 61
generative mechanisms
and open systems, 110
operation of, 114
genetic susceptibility, 212
Gerhardt, U., 133, 161, 189

Giddens, A., 86
Glaser, B. G., 10, 11, 12, 13, 15, 16,
29n8, 163, 206
Gleave, S., 187
Goffman, E., 13, 39
Gompertz, P., 18, 165, 220
governmentality, 210, 215
Graham, R., 135
Gravelle, H., 169
grounded theory, 8
ambiguities in classifying and
using, 10–13
awareness and uncertainty, 16
Chicago School roots of, 13–14
contributions to illness experience
study, 14–15
diagnosis, significance of, 15–16, 17
illness meaning, 15–16, 18, 19
illness with life, managing, 19–22
illness, disclosing, 25–6
interview methods and, 12–13
normalization process, 22–5
on self and identity, 9, 15
sick role, challenging of, 14
theory construction and, 12

Haas, S., 133
habitus, 86–88
reflexivity and, 88, 91–3
unthinking exercise of, 92
see also field; self
Ham, C., 168
Hardt, M., 207
Hassell, K., 167
healing dramas, 146
health, definition of, 189
Henderson, L. J., 130
Hendriks, M., 108
hidden distress model of epilepsy,
45–6, 125
Higginson, I., 83
Hinojosa, R., 18, 21, 26
homo sacer, 47
Hood, J., 29n6
Hopkins, A., 3, 108, 128
Hughes, B., 46
Humean empiricism, 110
Hunt, P., 41
Hunter, K. M., 146

identity
  redirection, 18
  and selfhood and citizenship,
    213–15
illness as deviance, 40
illness meaning, 15–16, 18
  and embodied experience, 19
illness narrative, 65
illness work, 164
impairment
  and discrimination, 60
  dynamic nature of disability and,
    67–72
  frustration and, 71
  hierarchy of, 103
  intensity of, 103
  preference for different solutions
    with similar, 63
  social model's neglect of, 59
impairment effects, 3, 49
  cancer and, 48, 50
  legitimacy and social model and, 47
  meaning of, 37
incapacity, 6, 180
  active participation in society, 188
  Beveridge Report, 190
  economic progress and degradation
    process, 191–4
  as hidden unemployment, 184–5
  and illness, 185–7
  illness models, 189
  limiting long-term illness (LLTI)
    rates, 189
  sick role, 188
  as social problem, 181–5
  uselessness in global capitalism,
    194–8
  Work Capability Assessment, 191
individual appraisal and reflexive
    monitoring, 141
inflammatory bowel disease *see*
    doctor–patient relationship and
    chronicity and inflammatory
    bowel disease
informal carers, 83
interactional workability, 138
interactionist theory, 40
International Classification of
    Functioning (ICF), 52n7

on disability, 65–7
  limitations of, 67
International Classification of
    Impairments, Disability and
    Handicap (ICIDH), 52n7
International Education Conference
    on Batten Disease, 81

Jobling, R., 211
Johnson, J., 20
Johnston, L., 81

Kaiser Triangle model, 168, 169
Kelleher, D., 6, 7, 22, 24, 207
Kelly, M., 165
Kelly, M. P., 147
Kings College London Ethics
    Committee, 89
Kleinman, A., 65, 123
knowledge, acquired, 92

Labbe, E. E., 80
Last Liberation Movement, disability
    rights struggle as, 64
Latour, B., 147, 148, 158
legitimacy, 182, 208
  for capital, 86
  of consultation, 155, 157
  and deviance, 137
  of distress, 156
  and expert judgement, 14
  and impairment effects, 47
  of long-term health conditions, 187
  of moral status, 16
  of physical symptoms, 17
  of place within field, 89–90
  of professionals, 94–5
  and sick role, 2, 133, 188
  and social model, 47
Lehoux, P., 141
Liberation Network of People with
    Disabilities, 59
limiting long-term illness (LLTI),
    185–7
  rates of, 189
Lorig, K., 169, 170
loss of self, 2, 40, 123
Luker, K. A., 16
Lysosomal Storage Disorders, 78

materialist perspectives
  on disability and disablism, 43
  on social model of disability, 58–64
Mattingly, C., 146, 149, 150
May, C., 5, 129, 146
mechanisms and structures, 113–14
medical certification, of disability, 182
medical sociology, 38–41, 52n4
  conflict theorists and post-structuralists, 40
  formative structural functionalism and, 39
  see also biopolitics; disability studies
medico-presentational thinking, 155
medico-scientific thinking, 148–9, 150, 151
metaphorical tour, 150
Meyer, G. A., 21
micro process, link to macro conditions, 17–18
Mills, C. W., 210
Mishler, E. G., 156
Mole, S. E., 81
Moore, D. L., 19
moral judgements, 26
moral necessity to life and self, 166
Morris, J., 42, 59
mothers, as alert assistants, 21
motivated deviance, illness as, 189
Murray, P., 82

narrative reconstruction, 2–3, 123
narrative research, 65
Närvänen, A.-L., 17
National Health Service (NHS), 4, 167, 168
National Institute for Clinical Excellence (NICE), 4
National Institute for Health and Clinical Excellent (NICE), 213
National Primary Care Research and Development Centre, 168–9
naturalistic fallacy, 111
Negri, A., 207
Nettleton, S., 17
neuronal ceroid lipofuscinoses *see* Batten disease
neutrality, affective, 131

New England Journal of Medicine, 130
Newton, P., 5, 77
NHS Improvement Plan, 168
Nicolas, G., 167
non-employment and ill-health, relationship between, 187
Nordic relational concept, 65
normality, 71, 182
  challenging of, 90–1
normalization, 22–5
  and clinical encounter, 134
  diabetes and, 24
  forms, 24
  from structural standpoint, 23
  types, 23–4
Novas, C., 215

objectifying space, 149
object nature and causal powers, 113
objects of enquiry and reality, 110, 111
Office of Disability Issues (ODI), 45
Oliver, M., 3, 41, 57, 61, 63
ontological basis, of human frailty, 209–10
open systems and generative mechanisms, 110
oppression paradigm, 3
  see also social oppression
order-building, 180, 181, 190

parent–professionals partnership, 82–3
Parsonian paradigm, 131
  models of illness, 189
Parsons, T., 2, 14, 38, 131, 133
participation, in social system, 188
Passage through Crisis, 13
patient's chart, 158
personalized medicine, 213
Petryna, A., 214
Peyrot, M., 22, 25
physical capital, 86, 93–4
Pierret, J., 15, 164, 220
Pinder, R., 29n7
political economy of hope, 215
political privilege, disability as, 182
positivism, 110
post-structuralism, 40, 43
  and sex/gender distinction, 62
Pound, P., 18, 26, 165, 220

Pre Genetic Diagnosis (PGD), 212
proto-stories, 148–51
    frontier and, 156–7
psychodynamic deviancy model, 189
psycho-emotional dimensions of
    disablism, 46
psychological mechanisms, 121, 122
    see also epilepsy, impact on
    individual

quality of life, with restricted growth,
    67, 69–70
Quint, J. C., 16

Rabinow, P., 205
Radley, A., 5, 146
reconfiguration and reflexive
    monitoring, 141
Reeve, D., 47
reflexivity
    and awareness, 88, 91–2, 93
    and diagnosis, 92–3
    and habitus, 88, 91–3
    and monitoring, 135, 140–1
    need for capital, 93 *see also* capital
Reframing Stigma, 45
Reif, L., 20
relational integration, 139
remission society, 48, 161
re-presentation, of illness experience,
    155–6, 158
re-storyings, 156
rhetoric of self-management,
    174–5, 176
Rier, D., 26
Rogers, A., 167
Roland, M., 169
Rose, N., 205, 211, 212, 214, 217, 219
Roter, D., 157
Roth, J., 13, 16
Roulstone, A., 42

Salander, P., 24
Sanders, C., 18, 26
Scambler, G., 1, 3, 5, 40, 45, 46,
    106, 121
Scambler, S., 1, 5, 45, 77
Schepper-Hughes, N., 218
Schoenberg, N. E., 16, 26, 27

SeeAbility, 80
Selai, C., 5, 106
self
    assault on, 26
    and body, 20
    and citizenship, 213–15
    and identity, 9, 15, 213–15
    loss of, 2, 40, 123
    and moral necessity to life, 166
    reconstruction of, 18
    see also habitus; normalization
self-management *see* chronic illnes
sex/gender distinction, feminists on,
    61, 62
Shakespeare, T., 5, 46, 57, 78
sickness work, 5
sick role, 14
    and social problem, 188
signification, 5–6
    regimens, 157
    see also doctor–patient relationship
    and inflammatory bowel disease
Sisyphus syndrome, 211
skill-set workability, 139–40
slum clearance, as bereavement, 193
Smith, K., 182
social capital, 85, 95–9
    formal, 97–8
    gaining of, 97
    informal, 96
social care system, 81, 95, 98, 100
social changes, 4, 64
social conditions, 47, 162, 197
social construction, 2, 122, 137
social context, 15, 122, 130, 136, 164,
    165, 190
social deviance paradigm, 5, 38–9,
    40, 41, 48
social mechanisms, 121, 123
    see also epilepsy, impact on
    individual
social model of disability, 3, 41–2,
    45, 57
    barrier-free utopia, 62–4
    better models, building, 64–7
    impairment and disability,
        distinction between, 62
    and legitimacy, 47
    neglect of impairment, 59–60

social model of disability – *continued*
  and oppression, 60–1
  origins of, 65
  weakness, 59–64
social networks, 139, 167
social oppression, 37, 41
  contemporary understanding
    of, 42
  disability endorsement as, 59
social policy, of France, 15
social structures and human action,
    18, 111, 112, 210
social world and body in illness, 165
Society, 162
*Sociologies of Disability and Illness
  Contested Ideas in Disability
  Studies and Medical Sociology*,
    38, 44
sociology of disablism and
  impairment *see* impairment
  effects
somatic ethics, 217, 218
somatic existence, 216, 217
somatic society, 217
Somerville, C., 16
Spiegle, J. A., 82
static impairments, 59
Stigma, 13
Stockl, A., 16, 17
Stone, D., 182
Strauss, A. L., 10, 11, 13, 15, 16, 20,
    21, 22, 29n7, 134, 162, 163, 166,
    170, 206
structural functionalist analysis of
  medicine in society, 2
structural incapacity model, 189
structures and objects, 113
surveillance medicine, 141
symbolic capital, 85–6, 94, 101
symbolic interactionism, 13
symptoms, 17–18, 79
  hiding of, 23, 24
  managing of, 14, 21–2, 164
  normalizing and, 22, 23–5
  onset, 89
  physical, 17, 70
  prognosis and, 20
  reading, learning of, 21
  suffering, for years, 16

undiagnosed, 17
visibility, 19, 21
systematization, 141

taken-for-granted, 24
  and body, 20
  diagnosis of epilepsy, 122
  and practices of actors, 86–7
  and response, 23
  and world, loss of, 8, 9
Taylor, D., 207
technogovernance, 139
Temkin, O., 122
temporality, 15, 18
The Discovery of Grounded Theory,
    10–11
The Lancet, 169
The Politics of Disablement, 41
therapeutic potential *see* proto-stories
The Social System, 38, 130
Thomas, C., 5, 37, 46, 52nn2,3, 58, 60
Time for Dying, 13
Timetables, 13
Timmermans, S., 21, 133
transformation, of information, 148
Tremain, S., 62
Turner, B. S., 39, 205, 209, 210, 220
Twaddle, A. C., 135

Uncertainty, 19, 91, 95, 108
  and awareness, 16
  definitions, fading of, 18
  and doubt, 17
  existential, 16
  of patient's future, 156, 164, 170
Union of the Physically Impaired
    Against Segregation (UPIAS),
    52n6, 58–9
utopia, barrier-free, 62–64

van den Pol, R. A., 82
vitality, economies of, 217–18, 219
vulnerability and suffering, 208–11
  Foucauldian thoughts on, 210–11

Waddell, G., 181
Waldby, C., 217
Walmsley, J., 42
Watson, N., 5, 46, 57

Welfare Reform Act (2007), 180
Wiener, C., 23
Williams, C., 21
Williams, G., 2, 6, 65, 180
Williams, S., 6, 59, 112, 165, 188, 189
Williams, S. J., 85, 205, 207
Wilson K., 16
Wilson W. J., 198
wireless patient, 141

Work Capability Assessment,
    191, 195
Work Focused Health Related
    Assessment, 195

Young, B., 25
Young, I. M., 42

Zola, I. K., 40, 41, 65, 207, 209